What's Wrong with Rights?

What's Wrong with Rights?

Social Movements, Law and Liberal Imaginations

Radha D'Souza

First published 2018 by Pluto Press
345 Archway Road, London N6 5AA

www.plutobooks.com

British Library Cataloguing in Publication Data
A catalogue record for this book is available from the British Library

ISBN   978 0 7453 3540 7   Hardback
ISBN   978 0 7453 3541 4   Paperback
ISBN   978 1 7837 1726 2   PDF eBook
ISBN   978 1 7837 1728 6   Kindle eBook
ISBN   978 1 7837 1727 9   EPUB eBook

This book is printed on paper suitable for recycling and made from fully
managed and sustained forest sources. Logging, pulping and manufacturing
processes are expected to conform to the environmental standards of the
country of origin.

Typeset by Stanford DTP Services, Northampton, England

Simultaneously printed in the United Kingdom and United States of America

In memory of Uday Mahale
Comrade, friend, fellow traveller …

Contents

Acknowledgements

This book has been a long time in the making and many people have contributed to the development of the arguments in it. Over the years many activists around the world have invited me to speak at public events on a wide range of themes: conditions of workers, peasants, indigenous peoples, women, environment, multilateral trade agreements, civil liberties and much else. The events were attended by people who were deeply concerned about the future. At those meetings and outside, people contributed generously to the debates, raised questions and engaged with the arguments in this book. This book has grown from those dialogues and conversations with people committed to a better world. Their engagement encouraged me to write this book. I wish to take this opportunity to thank all of them wherever they may be.

Thanks to Renée Vellvé of GRAIN, a non-profit organisation working with Third World farmers on community-controlled biodiversity-based food systems, for inviting me to the panel discussion which was published in *Seedling* (October 2007) under the same title: *What's Wrong With Rights?* The reservations of farmers and rural activists from Africa and Asia on the panel about rights, people whose voices are seldom heard in mainstream academic discourses, gave me the confidence to pursue my own project on rights. Thanks to Reza Banakar for inviting me to contribute to his edited volume on rights even though I am not labelled as a human rights scholar within the academia. It forced me to go beyond speaking to activists and put pen to paper, or rather fingers on keyboard, to think about rights more theoretically and induct my critique into academic scholarship. Thanks to Brewster Kneen who has, over the years, been an unwavering 'cheer leader' for the project. Aziz Choudry organised public and academic events and provided me with valuable opportunities to engage with his students.

Anyone who writes anything knows the importance of a sympathetic but critical reader. Nicola Perugini gave his time very generously and painstakingly went through a rough and ready first draft of the manuscript line by line, paragraph by paragraph and provided valuable comments. I have benefitted a great deal from his feedback. I am indebted to him for his labours and his generosity. The shortcomings in the book are of course my own.

David Shulman in Pluto was very patient, kind and understanding about the many interruptions in the writing of this book. Thank you David. Thanks to the Pluto team for seeing the publication to fruition. This book was not possible without the support of the library staff at the University of Westminster. I want to say a special thanks to the Interloan Document Delivery team in the library. Every time I needed something, and it was always urgent and frantic, I filled out the online IDD form and bingo, like magic the article, or book chapter or book turned up in my inbox or pick-up shelf at work faster than I had expected.

Knowledge is a social phenomenon. In writing something that is copyrighted as my own, I stand on the shoulders of intellectual giants: scholars, thinkers, philosophers, poets who have shaped my mind and my thoughts in ways that go beyond academic conventions for source citations that property rights to knowledge requires. My ongoing debts to all those predecessors who have inspired me to follow in their footsteps.

Amma, Bharti, Kunal, Jaya, Ajeet can I thank you enough? Uday, how I wish you were here to read my book.

Abbreviations

AFTA	ASEAN Free Trade Area
APEC	Asia Pacific Economic Cooperation
BIT	Bilateral Investment Treaties
CCPC	Commission on Crime Prevention and Control
CSCE	Conference on Security and Cooperation in Europe
CSO	Civil Society Organisations
CVR	Corporate Voluntary Rescue
DCN	Debt Crisis Network
ECOSOC	Economic and Social Council
ESG	Emergency Stabilization Fund
EU	European Union
FCN	Friendship, Commerce and Navigation treaties
G7	Group of Seven
GGP	Good Governance Programme
ICC	International Criminal Court
ICCPR	International Covenant on Civil and Political Rights
ICESCR	International Covenant on Economic, Social and Cultural Rights
ICJ	International Court of Justice
ICSID	International Center for Settlement of Investment Disputes
IEO	International Economic Organisation
IEM	International Election Monitoring
IHRLG	International Human Rights Law Group
ILC	International Land Coalition
IMF	International Monetary Fund
INGO	International Non-Governmental Organisation
IO	International Organisation
LPG	Liberalisation-Privatisation-Globalisation
MDG	Millennium Development Goals
MIGA	Multilateral Investment Guarantee Agreement
NAFTA	North American Free Trade Agreement
NATO	North Atlantic Treaty Organization

NCI	National-Competitive-Industrial
NED	National Endowment for Democracy
NGO	Non-Governmental Organisation
NIE	New Institutional Economics
NIEO	New International Economic Order
NSM	New Social Movements
OAS	Organization of American States
OPEC	Organization of the Oil Producing Countries
OSM	Old Social Movements
Post-WC	Post-Washington Consensus
RoL	Rule of Law
SAP	Structural Adjustment Programme
SDG	Sustainable Development Goals
TAN	Transnational Advocacy Networks
TMF	Transnational Monopoly Finance
TNC	Transnational Corporations
TTIP	Transatlantic Trade and Investment Partnership
UDHR	Universal Declaration of Human Rights
UK	United Kingdom
UN	United Nations
UNCTAD	United National Conference on Trade and Development
UNDP	United Nations Development Programme
UNGA	United Nations General Assembly
UNICEF	United Nations International Children's Fund
UNOHCHR	United Nations Office of the High Commissioner for Human Rights
UNSC	United Nations Security Council
US	United States
USAID	United States Agency for International Development
VDPA	Vienna Declaration and Programme of Action
WB	World Bank
WC	Washington Consensus
WSF	World Social Forum
WTO	World Trade Organization
WWI	World War I
WWII	World War II

Preface

The ideas in this book have germinated over many decades during the course of my involvement with social movements as a social justice activist in India, New Zealand, Asia, the UK, and internationally, as a constitutional lawyer in India involved in labour, civil rights and public interest cases and later as an academic in New Zealand and in the UK. Rights were very much at the centre of debates within social movements, in the court-rooms and within the academia and continue to dominate all three arenas. The arguments in each of these constituencies – social movements, legal practice and academic scholarship – were of very different types however. The three distinct types of practices that I engaged in revealed, at least to me, radically different assumptions about rights that the three constituencies made about what rights were, their histories, their role and purpose and the interrelationships between rights in social philosophy, in political theories and practices, and in legal doctrine and practice.

In the 1990s I was drawn into international issues, first during the campaign against Harkin's Bill, the Child Labour Deterrence Bill proposed by US Democratic Senator Tom Harkin. The Bill prohibited importation into the US, products made by child labour, an issue with serious consequences for millions of poor Indian families whose children worked in the carpet industry, an important export item. I found myself arguing against rights introduced, supposedly, to protect Indian children as an activist while at the same time defending children's constitutional rights in the courts. I was drawn into regional campaigns against the impacts of International Monetary Fund (IMF)-led Structural Adjustment Programmes in the Asia-Pacific region and later to campaigns against linking labour standards to international trade agreements proposed by the World Trade Organization (WTO). Both issues had devastating consequences for well-established constitutional rights: collective bargaining rights of workers, land rights of peasants, and rights of indigenous peoples in the Indian constitution. Many precedent setting litigation flooded the Indian courts against the impacts of IMF's structural adjustment policies and WTO agreements on people's lives and livelihoods such as closure of industries and job losses, flexible hiring and firing policies and job insecurity, expansion of casual and contract work, evictions from shanty-towns, rehabilitation and resettlement of people displaced by development projects funded by the World Bank (WB), violations of civil liberties by state authorities, strikes and protests and so on. I was involved in some of those court cases.

Those cases highlighted the fact that even one of the most articulate and egalitarian liberal constitutions in the world, such as India's, could do little to stop, even mitigate, the impacts of the international agreements that the government had signed up to. The government's justification that the international agreements were necessary in the national interest and for the nation's economic security could not be called into question in the courts. What do we make of the constitutional guarantees if they are unable to protect the most vulnerable sections of society from international forces? What do we make of representational politics if it allows governments to sign international agreements that displace people, destroy the environment and livelihoods and constrain national courts? What do we make of an economy when economic policies turn upside down the very notion of a nation? It seemed to me the macroeconomic changes underway presented a fait accompli to lawyers, academics, activists and regional and municipal-level decision-makers. What we, the lawyers, academics et al. at the micro level were doing was to adapt and adjust to the macroeconomic changes over which we had little or no control, democratic or otherwise. All this drew me more and more into public international law, international anti-globalisation movements and critical globalisation academic literature where rights reappeared in an international avatar. These international experiences added an additional dimension to the already confounding nature of rights. With globalisation, new types of social movements burst onto the scene. These new social movements brought with them what I call the 'rights resurgence' not seen in the Third World even during the anti-colonial movements. Courts became an important, often the most important, site of struggle for these new social movements. Even when activists remained sceptical about rights, law and courts outside the court-rooms in the political domain, litigation became an important political strategy.

I believed, rather naively in retrospect, that joining the academe would help me to step back from two very emotive and contradictory types of practices that dominated my life – legal practice and social movements – and allow me the intellectual and social space to resolve what had become an existential conflict. I was wrong. Academic scholarship on rights complicated things even more. The assumptions about rights in social philosophy, in political theory and in legal theory confounded the tensions rather than resolved them. We continued to quote and cite European Enlightenment thinkers in our works. Their writings no longer made sense to me, a member of the 'educated classes' that British colonists claimed was their single biggest achievement in the colony they proudly claimed was the 'jewel in the Crown'. There was the ever present problem of making connections between the academic debates and the real world out there, which for me was the Third World, with which I was required to engage as a social justice activist, lawyer and academic and as an individual with home, family and friends.

In this book I confront the contradictions between the apparent and real – between the normative ideals suggested by rights and the institutional realities ramified by rights. This book is *not* about rights as such. The critique of rights in this book is about how social movements understand and engage with the concept of rights, and how their understandings and engagements ramify certain types of practices for social transformation to bring about a just world. In the broadest possible sense, a just world is one that is able to reproduce the conditions needed to sustain life. Social justice movements seek to change something about the way things are. Social movements oppose the injustices in our world, locate it within wider social structures of capitalism and imperialism but give away with one hand what they wrest with the other. Their understanding of the place of rights in capitalist and imperialist relations is an important reason for this. This book takes the concepts, histories, ideals and practices about rights as they exist within social movements at face value and as a given, as the point of departure for the critique of rights. I examine the assumptions that social movements and activist scholarship make about rights and how those assumptions influence actions for social change. My purpose is to provoke rethinking and re-engagement with social justice in ways that are grounded in the economic, political, cultural and ideological realities of life today – in other words, my purpose is to bring rights back to earth from the exalted world of normative ideals down to our world – the world of transnational, monopoly finance capitalism, a new kind of capitalism that has re-scripted a new regime of rights that is different from rights in the seventeenth and eighteenth centuries. When we speak about rights we can no longer assume that the rights we speak about are the same as those that prevailed during the early stages of capitalism. I endeavour to examine the resilience of rights in people's imaginations, to make sense of how and why social movements use rights and to understand the gaps and contradictions in the theories and practices of rights in philosophy, law and politics.

Social movement responses to four issues, which I think are central to rights-based democracy, namely representative democracy, accountability of public officials and political leaders, property rights and governance are woven into the structure of the arguments and inform the analysis of rights throughout. The purpose of the book is to move away from explication of the *correct* meanings of rights in philosophy, politics and/ or law, or as normative ideals in social struggles, and instead, to draw attention to what rights *actually do* in the *real* world. I will leave it to the readers to judge whether or not I have succeeded in my endeavours.

PART I

The Rights Resurgence

1

Social Movements, Law and Liberal Imaginations

During most of human history, historical change has not been visible to the people who were involved in it, or even to those enacting it. Ancient Egypt and Mesopotamia, for example, endured for some four hundred generations with but slight changes in their basic structure ... But now the tempo of change is so rapid, and the means of observation so accessible, that the interplay of event and decision seems often to be quite historically visible, if we will only look carefully and from an adequate vantage point. (Charles Wright Mills, *The Power Elite*, 1956, pp. 20–1)[1]

This book is about rights, not 'human' rights. Throughout this book 'human' in human rights is used in inverted commas, so as not to reduce rights, a broader concept, to 'human' rights, and also to remind the reader not to lapse into reading rights as 'human' rights from sheer force of habit. The book is about what is entailed in reducing rights to 'human' rights.

SOCIAL MOVEMENTS AND RIGHTS

At least since the 1990s the motto of most contemporary social movements appears to be 'every wrong must have a corresponding "human" right'. Even a cursory survey of contemporary social movements is enough to see that the clamour for more 'human' rights continues to expand. The expansion of rights continues notwithstanding the contradictory, even antithetical, right claims. The 'human' right to water comes hand in hand with new proprietary rights to water, the 'human' right to food with property rights to land titles, rights of homosexuals to marry with rights to religious beliefs opposed to it, the right to wear a hijab *and* the right to set up nudist colonies, rights of indigenous peoples *and* to private property, right to self-determination *and* security, rights to privacy *and* transparency, right to statehood *and* integrity of existing state boundaries, cultural *and* political rights, rights of migrants *and* 'sons of the soil', rights to health, the internet, even the 'human' right to happiness. After the United Nations (UN) was established at the end of the world wars in 1945, the Universal Declaration of Human Rights (UDHR) enumerated twenty-eight rights. Today, it is estimated that international law recognises more than three hundred rights.[2] Typically, an excellent diagnosis of a problem is followed with a proclamation of a new right and mobilisation for struggles that demand legalisation of that right. Eventually, notwithstanding the scepticism of many about the efficacy of rights, right claims seek out law courts. In the seventeenth and eighteenth centuries right claims inspired millions of disempowered men and women in Europe to rebel against the oppressive European feudal order under which they lived at that time. Today the demands for evermore rights and the reasons why diverse actors advance them are less straightforward.

Consider the recent demand by New Social Movements (NSM), by which I mean social movements that emerged in the Euro-American countries in the mid 1960s and in the Third World two and half decades later in the early 1990s, on one of the most important questions for people around the world today: land. The International Land Coalition (ILC) formed in 1995 is a global alliance of just about every type of organisation: G7 and Third World states, International Economic Organisations (IEO) and International Organisations (IO), bilateral and multilateral aid and development organisations, International Non-Governmental Organisations (INGO), national Non-Governmental Organisations (NGO), grass root social movements, and global, regional and international land alliances like the Via Campesina.[3] The ILC argues, correctly, that the roots of rural poverty in the Third World lie in land alienations and displacement. The solution to the problem is the demand for 'human' rights to land titles, fair compensation for land acquisitions and resettlement and rehabilitation of displaced people.[4] The ILC fuses diverse voices, interests and standpoints and brings about a convergence in the positions of actors as varied as the World Bank and Via Campesina, Group of 7 (G7) and Group of 77 (G77) states, and INGOs and anti-imperialist social movements. The glue that holds the convergence together is their common commitment to the language of rights. Rights are no longer adversarial as they were in the seventeenth and eighteenth centuries. Far from challenging existing orders or authorities and inspiring historical transformations in the dominant architecture of global power, the world's most powerful economic, political and military alliances – the IEOs, the IOs, the G7 states, the corporations, influential 'think tanks' and INGOs, even the North Atlantic Treaty Organization (NATO) – champion rights alongside the disempowered, the working people, the unemployed and the discriminated. From coalitions such as the ILC at least it would seem as though we live in a world where lions and lambs have at long last recognised their common claims to water, forests and land and tigers have become vegetarians. What kind of micro and macro processes produced this convergence? Answers to these questions must await the chapters in Part II of this book. What is important here is to grasp what is entailed in the claims for 'human' rights to land and the reality of our relationships to land.

Land is, quintessentially, a *relationship*. Land is not a 'thing'. It is a bond that ties people to nature and to each other. Land is the glue that holds people and nature together to form *places*. Historically, rights transformed places into property.[5] It transformed a *relationship* into a *thing*, a commodity. The transformation characterises capitalism as a distinct type of social system. The European Enlightenment transformed land as the ordering mechanism in feudal Europe to commodity production as the ordering mechanism in modern Europe. The breakup of feudal land relations and the transformation of land into a commodity exchangeable in the market place was an essential condition for capitalism to advance in systemic ways.[6] The modern concept of rights owes it birth to that moment when land was transformed into a commodity and hundreds of thousands of people were evicted from the places they called their 'homeland'. New theoretical concepts and legal mechanisms were needed to reconstitute society where both nature and labour could become saleable commodities. The concept of individual rights was pivotal to reconstituting society ordered on land relations to a society ordered on commodity exchanges. The idea of individual alienable rights to land provided the theoretical, political and legal underpinnings for the transformation.

The idea of land rights helped found new social institutions for land transactions including modifications to contract laws, land surveying, state departments like the land registry entrusted with overseeing land transactions, new land laws and land transactions as a source of revenue for the state in the form of stamp duties, inheritance taxes and such. Land rights enabled new right claims by states such as the legal principle of eminent domain. Property rights to land came with its 'human' component – the right to fair procedures for land acquisitions, fair compensation and fair dispute resolution mechanisms.[7] Thus, property rights to land were the first among rights to be instituted in transformations from feudalism to capitalism. Property by its very nature is the very *opposite* of glue that binds nature and people. Being necessarily alienable and transferable, it *unbinds* people from land and nature more generally. Right claims conceal what is entailed in our relationship to land and nature. Indeed, right claims facilitate the transformation of places into properties and homeland into home-market. Yet, even the more radical movements on land such as indigenous peoples' movements that are opposed to the very notion of land, forests and water as property frequently end up supporting the idea of 'human' rights to land.

Speaking for the radical Mapuche movement in Chile, a spokesperson for the Council of All Lands (Consejo de Todas las Tierras), Aucán Huilcamán, relied on the UN Declaration on the Rights of Indigenous People as the legal justification for the creation of an autonomous, self-governed Mapuche region.[8] Why do indigenous peoples whose land claims arise from being synonymous with Time's claim to places find the need to invoke an international statute enacted in remote places like the UN headquarters in Geneva as recently as 2005 to make their claims sound 'reasonable'? Social movements sometimes argue that right claims are nothing more than conceptual vehicles that validate ethical and moral claims. The need for legal justifications to validate their land claims invite us to consider why ethical claims are articulated as legal claims in the first place. Further, are right claims strictly ethical claims with no ramifications for law and politics? Right claims as ethical justifications do not lead us to questions why the UN Declarations on Rights of Indigenous People was adopted, who the actors driving the adoption were, and the timing of it coming as it did in the wake of sweeping neoliberal reforms of international order.

In a similar vein, the declaration of the Keepers of the Water movement, an alliance of the indigenous Dene peoples in northern Canadian provinces, begins with the statement:

Water is a sacred gift, an essential element that sustains and connects all life. It is not a commodity to be bought or sold. All people share an obligation to cooperate to ensure that water in all of its forms is protected and conserved with regard to the needs of all living things today and for future generations tomorrow.

In the next paragraph the declaration continues with the statement:

> All peoples in the Basin have a fundamental human right to water that must be recognized nationally and internationally, and incorporated into domestic law and policy. Progress towards the realization of the right to water must be monitored, and appropriate institutional mechanisms developed to ensure that these rights are implemented.[9]

The same can be said about campaigns for incorporating forests, seas, and everything else that is brought under a regime of 'human' rights. Right claims as ethical and moral claims divert attention from the context, the actors and the mechanisms at work in the rights resurgence underway manifestly since the 1980s. The powerful indigenous critique of individual property rights in nature ends up reifying the dualism of property and 'human' rights on which liberal rights are founded.

The voices that converge in the rights discourse, as in the ILC example above, are far from harmonious. Indeed, the rights discourse today is a cacophony of discordant voices. Each actor in coalitions to promote this or that right, such as the ILC, has a different understanding of rights, of its history, its philosophical presuppositions, and above all expectations. Each actor canvassing for this or that right is located within a distinct type of institutional setting and carries a particular ideological orientation to rights. Arguments about rights in international coalitions and campaigns take the form of 'my version of rights is better than yours ...'. This argument is analogous to the argument 'my god is better than yours', an argument that ultimately relies on faith, a belief that cannot lead a rational engagement about god, yours and mine. As Brewster Kneen observes,

> Whether it be in reference to human rights or property rights, the right to life or abortion rights, farmers' rights, right to water or intellectual property rights, the word itself seems to have become a sort of essential – if powerless – invocation.[10]

At the same time, there is growing disenchantment with rights among critical scholars and social movements alike.[11] The disenchantment with rights is not new. It goes back at least to the nineteenth century. By the nineteenth century, as European feudalism became history and rights revealed new realities, the euphoria about rights died down. With rights came new class polarisations, new forms of poverty, displacement, dis-possession, large bureaucracies, states, armies and wars.[12] In the United States (US), ideas from the European Enlightenment inspired the expansion, construction and consolidation of the American state on the backs of the lands and resources of indigenous peoples and the labour of African slaves. Rights to trade freely, far from abolishing slavery, *revived* and *modernised* the ancient institution of slavery.[13] In Europe, expro-priation of indigenous lands and slave labour were located in far-flung colonies removed from the sights of ordinary people on the streets of European cities. In the US, liberalism did not have to struggle against an existing feudal order. Instead in the US liberal capitalism came hand in hand with colonial expropriation and slave labour located in the *same sites*, where slavery and expulsion from land occurred in full view of all the actors as part of the same processes of nation building and liberal constitutionalism. The mythology of rights should have broken down first and foremost in the US. Instead the US became the bastion for rights where the ideology of rights remains strongest even as it wages wars, displaces people and drives them to destitution around the world.

The mythology of rights *did* break down in those parts of the world where capitalism *also* broke down towards the turn of the twentieth century. Since the Paris Commune at least, rights were challenged both in theory and practice by the socialist movements in Europe, movements of indigenous and black Americans and anti-colonial movements. These challenges to rights occurred against the backdrop of crises of capitalism. At least since the 1960s Euro-American capitalism has undergone a series of crises that shows no signs of abating. While radical scholars and social movements have become more sceptical about rights, their critique comes hand in hand with a critique of the Old Social Movements (OSM) of the early twentieth century. Disenchanted with socialism *and* liberalism and unable to embrace the critique of imperialism whole-heartedly in its totality, rights scepticism flounders and gropes for theoretical moorings.

The irony is that the environmental crises everywhere, the ever deepening poverty and destitution in Third World societies and the general crises of human alienation, call it aesthetic, emotional, whatever that we see everywhere impels us to ask the very questions that dominated discourse in the seventeenth and eighteenth centuries. What is a human being's relation to land and nature, to law and state, to one another? Can land and nature be commodities like shoes or clothes? Can people live without ties to places? Are relations between people formed on the basis of economic self-interest alone? Can a person's inner life flourish when their material 'real' life is driven by economic self-interest? These questions dominate contemporary consciousness, debates and concerns within social movements, academia and popular media. Such questions invite us to challenge European Enlightenment's answers to the questions. Instead, most social movements turn to right claims in evermore qualified and conceptually nuanced forms. Why is it that social movements and critical scholars are unable to 'let go' of their invocation to rights even when they recognise that those rights have always been an essential precondition for capitalism and colonialism, for displacement and dispossession throughout capitalism's history? This book addresses these questions.

WHY DO 'THEY' WANT RIGHTS?

The answers to our problems are directed by how we frame our questions. Or, in Marx's words '[t]o formulate a question is already to solve it'.[14] The question about rights is usually framed as: 'what do *we want* rights to do in *our* world?' Consequently, the answers lead to aspirational statements that are disconnected from a comprehensive understanding of the way the world works and the complicity of right claims in it – the various actors, mechanisms and processes that drive the trajectory of rights. In the domain of ideas, rights remain secure and insulated from the reality of dramatic, disconcerting and violent changes in the world around us. The question for social movements and critical scholars wanting to change the world we live in is to ask, what do rights actually *do* in this world? Who are the actors promoting it and why? What mechanisms do the proponents of rights adopt and what does that mean for those that aspire for a just and humane world? In other words, to rephrase the question as 'why do *they* want rights?' instead of 'what do *we want* from rights?' The question for social movements and critical scholars, at least, is, 'can more rights help us walk the road of human emancipation?' By reformulating questions about rights as 'why do *they*: the US and G7 states, the IEOs and IOs, the INGOs and NGOs want rights', this book addresses what *they* want from rights and what *we* hope to get from rights.

Two aspects of right claims in the post-World War II (WWII) order become clear when questions about rights are reframed contextually. The first is the internationalisation and universalisation of rights and the second is the de-politicisation, juridification and legalisation of rights. Juridification and legalisation invariably presuppose institutionalisation. Institutionalisation, legalisation, de-politicisation and international-isations more generally are key components of post-WWII liberalism whether of the Keynesian or the neoliberal type. The chapters in this book address these key components of post-WWII liberalism.

LAW AND THE PURSUIT OF HAPPINESS

Something more has happened to the idea of rights in the post-WWII years than simple proliferation. Consider the pronouncement in the American Declaration of Independence made in 1776 by the thirteen states that declared independence from Britain. The American Declaration upholds 'the pursuit of happiness' as an 'inalienable right', one of three 'self-evident' truths together with rights to life and liberty.[15] For the signatories of the American Declaration in the eighteenth century 'pursuit of happiness' was a statement about their aspirations for greater freedom in the new nation that they were in the process of establishing. They drew their inspiration from their European homelands, ancient European philosophers and the more recent European Enlightenment thinkers.[16] In the nineteenth century the 'right to happiness', in the US at least, took a juridical turn as courts were called upon to interpret and apply the right in cases of breach of personal freedoms such as challenges to prohibition laws, dress codes and such.[17] In the twenty-first century, in contrast, the 'pursuit of happiness' as an 'inalienable right of Man' has surreptitiously metamorphosed into a '"human" right to happiness'. From an aspirational statement inspired by certain philo-sophical precepts in European intellectual history in the seventeenth and eighteenth centuries, to a justiciable utilitarian principle of personal liberty in the nineteenth century, the 'right to happiness' today is a sta-tistically measurable goal designed to guide *international* policy makers.

On 19 July 2011 the United Nations General Assembly (UNGA) adopted a resolution titled 'Happiness: towards a holistic approach to development'.[18] The resolution called on member states, UN agencies and International Organisations to 'develop new indicators, and other initiatives, ... as a contribution to the United Nations development agenda'.[19] Even as the target date for achieving the Millennium Development Goals (MDG) drew to a close in 2015, with questionable outcomes one must add, the development of the 'human' right to happiness was well underway. MDG set 2015 as the deadline to end extreme poverty, environmental distress, provide universal education, gender empowerment, end child mortality, promote basic maternal health, and combat diseases like HIV and malaria. The failure of those targets notwithstanding, the UN has initiated measures to advance the 'human' right to happiness in the Sustainable Development Goals 2030 (SDG) that takes the place of MDG 2015.[20]

The following year, on 28 June 2012, the UNGA adopted another resolution declaring 20 March as the International Day of Happiness.[21] Consequently, happiness was on the agendas of every IO, IEO, UN agencies, regional organisations and states with reporting requirements and action points. Since 2012 the UN has published the *World Happiness Report* each year.[22] The report is produced by a consortium of think tank centres located in leading Anglo-American universities and led by influential academics with close nexus to nodes of power internationally and within states. Academics leading the research include John F. Helliwell, based in the Canadian Institute for Advanced Research at the University of British Columbia, Lord Richard Layard, a Labour peer in the UK and Director of the Well-Being Programme in the Centre for Economic Performance at the influential London School of Economics, and Jeffrey D. Sachs, director of Columbia University's Earth Institute, a special advisor to the UN Secretary General Ban Ki Moon on development, advisor to Eastern European and Latin American states in 'transition' to democracy and named by *Time Magazine* as one of the hundred most influential men in 2004.[23]

The *World Happiness Report* develops a 'scientific' methodology for measuring happiness and involves an array of pollsters, statisticians, sociologists, social psychologists, development studies scholars and practitioners and policy 'wonks' who produce a happiness index for the use of policy makers.[24] The OECD has published *Guidelines on Measuring Subjective Well-being for National Statistical Offices* for the use of bureaucrats in member states.[25] On 14 April 2010 Antonio Tajani, the then Vice President of the European Commission with responsibility for industry and entrepreneurship, in his opening address to the European Tourism Stakeholders' Conference in Madrid, told the delegates,

The Lisbon Treaty has for the first time given the European Union specific powers to act in a sector as important for the economy and for individuals as tourism. ... Today, taking holidays is *a right*. As the person responsible for Europe's policies in this economic sector, it is my firm belief that the way in which we spend our holidays is an excellent indicator of our quality of life. ... Our unrivalled tourism resources must become fully accessible to those for whom travelling is difficult: the elderly and persons with reduced mobility. ... Concerning accessibility, similar attention must be paid to young persons and families at a disadvantage who – for various reasons – also face difficulties in exercising their *full right to tourism*. ... As Commissioner for Transport I successfully defended passengers' rights. The next step is *to safeguard their right to be tourists*.[26] (Italics added)

Mr Tajani's inspiration came from the medieval European philosopher, St Augustine.

Allow me to close by quoting a towering figure in western thought: St Augustine, in his capacity as a great philosopher. Referring to the topic of 'travel', which is foremost in the minds of all present in this room, he said: '*The world is a book, and those who do not travel read only a page.*'[27]

Mr Tajani of course did not add that for St Augustine travel was a means to knowledge not pleasure. St Augustine could not have envisioned taxpayer-funded holidays for the elderly and disabled as a 'human' right to happiness to revive the sagging fortunes of Europe's tourism industry. More importantly for the discussion here, the 'human' right to happiness far from being idealistic rhetoric is a calculated strategy for expanding the tourism and related industries by relying on legal treaties and health and welfare legislation in European Union (EU) member states. The tourism industry was naturally delighted by the 'human' right to happiness. It is equally true, however, that for many Europeans, Tajani's argument will appear fair. If the rich can take holidays, Europe's less privileged should also have the right to holidays.

While the EU Commissioner advocated the 'human' right to tourism for poor Europeans, the poor in the poor countries campaigned for rights to food sovereignty in the face of mounting pressures by the WTO to end food subsidies for the poor and to open up agriculture to global agribusiness. If the right to minimum living standards was the goal in the MDG, the failure of the MDG to meet those goals leads to the new 'human' right to happiness that will feed into its successor: SDG

2030. The 'human' right to happiness delinks the economic situation of a person from a subjective feeling about their lives. If a poor person *perceives* herself to be happy why fuss about growing income inequality, exacerbating income gaps, cutbacks to education, health and pensions? Conversely, if rich people are also unhappy, then the causes of happiness can be attributed elsewhere to non-material causes and the vulgar, even sickening disparities in the human condition around the world need not weigh on our conscience as much.[28]

The World Happiness indices, the 'scientific' data and country profiles on happiness of citizens, feed into social policies of states, IEOs and IOs. In the process the meaning of rights and of happiness, *both*, undergo profound transformations. Happiness, which for centuries meant a state of being in which there was minimal dissonance between a person's inner world (emotional, psychological, spiritual, whatever) and outer world (social, communal, institutional and such), is now an aggregated set of statistics that guides social policy making by states, international organisations and corporations. The greatest happiness of greatest numbers, as Jeremy Bentham famously wrote, articulated the individualistic aspirations of European Enlightenment thinkers for an expanding capitalist state. In the twenty-first century, the utilitarian pursuit of happiness as a state building project and constitutional principle is transformed into an affirmative action policy for the world's most powerful organisations and states for intensified liberalisation and globalisation.

Like MDG projects, it can be expected that SDG projects will be contracted out to a plethora of private enterprises, NGOs, academics and experts. The signs are already there. Corporations regularly include 'wellbeing' programmes and 'work-life-balance' training for their staff as part of employment and collective bargaining policies. 'Life coaching' is now an expanding industry replete with professional coaches, training institutes and certification requirements. A 2012 study by the International Coaching Federation found that there were around 47,000 professional life coaches working globally and the industry's annual revenue was around US$ 2 billion.[29] An international 'right to happiness' could well expand the coaching industry.

At the ideological level, however, the powerful proponents of 'human' right to happiness seldom justify the right to happiness in terms of economic benefits to themselves. Instead they claim to being responsive to the critique of liberalism and Enlightenment Thought, and the dehumanisation under capitalism more generally, developed by indigenous, feminist, environmental and other social justice movements. Their responsiveness in turn creates a *general* environment for the acceptance of the 'human' right to happiness. The activities of powerful economic actors are mediated, as we have seen above, by academic institutions and think tanks that induct, indeed entice, networks of indigenous people, feminist, environmental and social justice activists desirous of defending ecologically sustainable communitarian ways of life into engaging with the quest for alternatives in particular ways. In other words, it opens up avenues for powerful corporations to appropriate and truncate alternate world views and 'mainstream' them within an international neoliberal economic order. The justifications for 'human' rights by the powerful economic actors and the oppositional movements elide in new ways. The emphasis on norms by both types of actors obscures the capacities of the actors to institutionalise and operationalise rights. Social movements frequently complain that rights are not enforced. The truth is rights *are* enforced, just not in the way that social movements think they ought to be.

In 2009 the World Economic Forum (WEF) set up the Global Business Initiative on Human Rights. The initiative consolidated the predecessor initiative launched by seven major corporations in 2003 called the Business Leaders Initiative on Human Rights and chaired by former President of Ireland and former UN High Commissioner for Human Rights, Mary Robinson.[30] The 2003 initiative decided to 'mainstream' human rights in business.[31] These initiatives claimed to respond to social movement protests against corporate abuse and the criticism that neoliberal reforms had given corporations a free reign around the world. Nevertheless, their initiatives set the context for the 'human' right to happiness enabling corporations to redefine 'human' rights in particular ways that enable service sector industries like tourism and human 'resource' development to expand.

The 'human' right to happiness is often dismissed as 'mumbo jumbo' by social movements and critical scholars. The right appears nonsensical or utopian only if we leave out of consideration the economic actors, the legal persons and *their* reasons for canvassing the right. Framing happiness as a 'human' right is the key to the transformation of an ontological human attribute into a commodity for sale in 'sustainable' development projects. The right to happiness conceals the fact that happiness is an ontological attribute of being human. Ontologically, as an attribute of human life, even in the most destitute and inhumane conditions human beings will seek joy, solidarity and form human bonds within the limitations imposed by their material and social conditions. As the film *Salaam Bombay* shows, street children in Mumbai are also happy, form communities and human bonds.[32] The ontological attribute of life that impels human beings to seek joy, solidarity and form human bonds, i.e. the sociality of human life, is now appropriated by an epistemology reliant on numbers and quantitative reasoning to be incorporated into profitable development projects in which states, corporations and international organisations can invest and harvest returns.

The quantification processes and 'scientific' methods render the theoretical, political, legal and social moves through which happiness becomes a 'human' right invisible. Once tabled on the agenda of rights, the debate takes on the dualistic form of happiness is/is not a 'human' right. Framed in this way the debate prevents the rights agenda from transcending the dualist framing to get to questions about the nature of happiness and the economic, social and cultural preconditions for it. Instead happiness translates into a set of entitlements and expectations from corporations and states that must be recognised by law. Yet who can argue with the proposition that every human being, rich or poor, has a right to be happy? Who can argue with that proposition even when half the world's population goes to bed hungry?

From the above discussion it is possible to see how an examination of a new right, an apparently nonsensical one at that, reveals the economic, political, legal, institutional, ideological and cultural issues entailed in rights. Thus, whether it is a tangible commodity like land or an intangible commodity like happiness, rights are deeply complicit in constructing market relationships for both types of commodities. Social movements, however, do not consider the two types of rights as constitutive of the totality of a regime of rights. Instead, 'human' rights to land are considered 'serious' matters whereas the 'human' rights to happiness remains a side-show in the analysis of rights.

RIGHTS WITHOUT REMEDIES?

A frequent refrain among social activists and activist scholars is that the problem is not with rights per se but that they are not enforced. Rights are not enforced according to activists and critical scholars because of lack of political will. Framing the problem of rights in this way assumes that law-makers find the political will to make the law but lose it thereafter. Why are rights legislated but not enforced? In his *Commentaries on the Laws of England* William Blackstone, the renowned eighteenth-century English jurist, judge and Tory politician, enunciated the legal maxim: 'that every right when with-held must have a remedy, and every injury its proper redress'.[33] Blackstone's commentaries in England were invoked by his contemporaries in the US Supreme Court against the officers of the US state in the historic *Mardbury v. Madison* decision in 1803. The essence of the decision turns on whether there can be rights without remedies. The decision affirmed the Common Law principle that every wrong must have a remedy. Justice Marshall who delivered the unanimous decision on behalf of the US Supreme Court reasoned,

> The very essence of civil liberty certainly consists in the right of every individual to claim the protection of the laws whenever he receives an injury. One of the first duties of government is to afford that protection.[34]

Relying on Blackstone's commentary, Justice Marshall observed that the US government was a government of law not men, and 'it will certainly cease to deserve this high appellation if the laws furnish no remedy for the violation of a vested right'. The ideas and ideals in *Mardbury v. Madison* lives on in popular legal imaginations. The problem with these ideals is that they presuppose a certain type of state founded on clear boundaries between public and private law, between state, economy and civil society, a state founded on clear boundaries between the executive, legislature and judiciary. These presuppositions have become highly problematic since the beginning of the twentieth century, as we shall see.

In classical liberal thought political freedoms were the key to unlock economic freedoms. Political freedoms were necessary to challenge feudal constraints on property and democracy was a necessary condition for economic freedoms and to defend market interests. In the post-WWII era of transnational monopoly finance capitalism the relationship between politics and economy is reversed (see Chapters 6 and 7). Economic freedoms and economic institutions are seen as the necessary conditions for political freedoms and democracy. Milton Friedman, a leading neoliberal thinker, makes this point explicitly, reversing the position of Bentham and other radicals who conceptualised political freedoms as the condition for economic freedom in the eighteenth century.[35] Friedman turns classical liberalism on its head. Should social movements not question the ramifications of these inversions of classical liberalism for rights which are so central to defining the relationships between economy, state and civil society? As Philip Mirowski writes, neoliberals seek to transcend the contradiction between lack of democratic control and the persistent need to provide a source of popular legitimacy by *'treating politics as if it were a market and promoting an economic theory of democracy'* (italics in original).[36] Should social movements not revisit the role of rights within an *economic theory of democracy*?

Locked in seventeenth and eighteenth-century imaginaries, social movements and critical scholars continue to assume that having rights will provide legal remedies and bring justice. International law for a start is law without judicial remedies. International judicial forums like the International Court of Justice or the International Criminal Court require the states to consent to their jurisdiction. The requirement of consent gives the mechanisms for resolving conflicts between states a quasi-arbitral character. The distinction between arbitration by consenting parties and public justice is an important one in classical liberalism. Nevertheless, international law operates as the international standard that overlays domestic law with particular understandings of rights that must be legalised and judicialised in certain ways within national jurisdictions (as the chapters in Part II show).

The post-WWII era has seen a vast expansion of quasi-judicial forums like ombudsman, tribunals, independent regulatory bodies set up to 'self-regulate' an industry or sector and administrative authorities making decisions without appeal. These mechanisms provide ad hoc justice in that they do not develop the law or add new meanings to rights and remedies. Public justice following judicial procedures is limited to certain types of cases, generally, related to property or crime. If justiciability of rights is problematic, might it not be that the problem is as much with rights as with justiciability?

In the international domain, economic matters take the legal form of contracts between states or between states and IOs and IEOs. In such international contracts 'the will of the state' is read as the 'will of the people'. The distinction between citizens and state is the bedrock of classical liberalism. Nevertheless, international contracts bind the states even after the people of the state have changed their 'will' through representative politics. Alvarez writes that there are 'nearly three hundred

IOs – regional and global' and 'forty institutional dispute settlers' that address 'virtually every field of human endeavour ... modelled on ... Western models of governance and free markets, and functionalist needs as the drivers of international cooperation'.[37]

These legal remedies are very different from the promise of public justice that rights made in classical liberalism. Alvarez observes how Woodrow Wilson's statements sound prescient in today's context.

President Wilson's address [to the League of Nations] was particularly prescient given current concerns over the 'democratic deficits' of IOs [International Organisations]. ... He [President Wilson] noted that since it is 'impossible to conceive a method or an assembly so large and various as to be really representative of the great body of the peoples of the world,' the best alternative was to have each government be represented by two or three representatives, though only a single vote, so that a number of voices would speak from time to time for each government.[38]

Internationalisation of rights appears to have changed the fundamental concept of rights and democracy. The absence of real representation of people in international bodies or delegating/subcontracting the details of substantive law and law enforcement to unelected bureaucrats, experts, think tanks and 'reputed' scholars has become acceptable practice even to social movements campaigning for public accountability. These changes in practices of governance and their ramifications for rights and justice are underplayed in rights-talk amongst critical scholars and activists. Why are rights legislated but not enforced? Perhaps it is because increasingly rights are normative standards to guide administrative actions and less and less the basis for justice.

SOCIAL MOVEMENTS AND LIBERAL IMAGINATIONS

Contemporary debates, critical and mainstream, in philosophy, law and politics, speak, invariably, about 'human' rights and not simply rights in its generic form. The prefix 'human' to rights is relatively recent in the history of rights, one that appeared during the world wars and the efforts to resurrect capitalism and liberalism after their collapse. Nonetheless, post-WWII, 'human' rights invoke ideas about rights in ancient, medieval and early modern European civilisation to justify them as 'inalienable' and intrinsic to being human. This way of engaging with rights fixes the concept of 'human' rights as a timeless, placeless concept and obfuscates the changing historical and social character of rights. As abstract ideas, rights-talk in ethics and politics is unable to connect rights to the reality of life and people today. 'Human' rights-talk within social movements today remains largely a clash of ideas and ideals. As Samuel Moyn writes, 'the phrase implies ... the most elevated aspirations of both social movements and political entities – states and interstate'.[39]

The resilience of 'human' rights in the imaginations of social movements is not because other utopias have failed as Moyn argues, but rather it lies in liberalism's capacity to generate an unending series of new hopes and a feeling of agency even when rights consistently fail to deliver on promises and rarely empower transformative social change for the oppressed, as we shall see. In contrast, when working and colonised peoples in the socialist movements and national liberation struggles challenged the idea of rights, and liberalism more generally, their challenges led to revolutionary structural transformations in the architecture of global power. The subsequent reversals and setbacks in those challenges to liberalism ought not to undermine the significance of that moment for structural social change (see Chapter 8).

Liberalism is first and foremost the ideology of capitalism. It is a world view comprising a complex of ideas, assumptions and beliefs in philosophy, jurisprudence and political theory and praxis about individual and economic freedoms. Underpinning the complexes of ideas in liberalism there is a mode of reasoning that elsewhere I have called 'epistemological economism'.

> Epistemological economism refers to a merchant's world view inscribed in the very structure of reason such that it extends an accountant's logic to every sphere of human life. Statistical reasoning, empiricism, cost-benefit enumerations resembling ledger-book classifications – costs in one column, benefit in another – become integral to the way socio-political-cultural questions are analysed. The merchant's world view is no longer limited to trade and commerce but extends to all spheres of social and cultural life. Labour, an attribute of being human, is transformed into a tradable commodity like shoes and furniture. Social problems are aggregated numerically to become comprehensible, as in statistical analysis. Even philosophical arguments must be 'weighed' so that they may 'profit' society in definite ways.[40]

Liberalism's core commitment is to *alienable* property as an inalienable right. Johann Wolfgang von Goethe wrote in the early nineteenth century,

> When I hear people speak of liberal ideas, it is always a wonder to me that men are so readily put off with empty verbiage. An idea cannot be liberal; but it may be potent, vigorous, exclusive, in order to fulfil its mission of being productive. Still less can a concept be liberal; for a concept has quite another mission. Where, however, we must look for liberality, is in the sentiments; and the sentiments are the inner man as he lives and moves. A man's sentiments, however, are rarely liberal, because they proceed directly from him personally, and from his immediate relations and requirements. Further we will not write, and let us apply this test to what we hear every day.[41]

The resilience of liberalism and rights in the imaginations of social movements lies in its ability to sustain the belief that sentiments can be un-problematically translated to political action.

European Enlightenment thinkers took rights as an ethical and moral concept in ancient European philosophy[42] and used it as a trope for a utilitarian economic and political philosophy supportive of emerging capitalism. As a trope, rights were pivotal to building institutions that replaced feudal institutions. The prefix 'human' to rights has invisibilised the institution building role of rights. At the same time, the invisibilisation of rights from its utilitarian purposes has rendered the institutional, legal and ideological conditions for transnational monopoly finance (TMF) capitalism unintelligible to social movements. Therefore, the prefix 'human' to rights is an important shift in the old and new rights-talk. It continues to evoke ethical and moral sensibilities and conceals its utilitarian purpose from view. It should not appear paradoxical therefore that the World Bank and displaced people, both, defend 'human' rights.

As Jewei Ci points out, liberalism sees the economy as morally neutral and generates a 'human' rights discourse that is related to but independent of the economy. Liberalism, according to Ci,

> ... redescribes the existing behaviour of economic actors within morally neutral framework of capitalist ethic. What happens here may be described as willing after the fact.

Quoting from Koslowski Ci writes,

> … '[c]apitalism as a system of contractual freedom and technical innovation, historically required the weakening of rigoristic morality and the toleration of external effects.' Willing after the facts is willing one's self-interest, not willing moral freedom. It testifies to the power of bourgeois ideology that the case is often thought to be otherwise, that the positions of the horse and carriage are reversed without being noticed most of the time.[43]

The feeling of agency stays with individuals as does the moral sentiment, but only as a feeling and sentiment. Social movements therefore continue to press for this or that right, argue about 'human' rights of subaltern people even as transnational corporations, IEOs, G7 states and IOs continue to use 'human' rights for building institutions and embed them within the global architecture of power. For example, the critical scholar Oche Onazi argues correctly that states and social movements have different understandings of 'human' rights.[44] From there he draws the conclusion that the concept of legal pluralism very much aids the subaltern view [of 'human' rights] because

> legal pluralism helps to paint a picture of human rights as a system founded on diverse sources of legitimacy. This view of legal pluralism in my opinion appears not only to liberate human rights from their state-centred world view but also opens up the possibility of reading them in social and other imaginative terms. Seen this way, I argue that human rights would thus effectively recognize the aspirations and, indeed, the agency of the poor, marginalized or oppressed.[45]

In this argument, there is no recognition of what the actors proposing state-centric view of human rights might be doing with it and what the 'subaltern' need to do to counter it. More importantly, pluralism presupposes the possibility of co-existence of state-centred and subaltern views. It unhinges rights from citizen-state relations and transforms it into a normative concept without moorings in the materiality of the world. Challenges to 'human' rights remain as a contest of norms in the domain of ideas (see Chapter 3).

The purpose here is not to belittle the efforts of social movements or critical scholars. Struggles present activists with difficult ethical choices.

Action is always in the present. Action mediates between the past and the future. Action presents activists with what I have called the 'temporal tension' in rights:

> By temporal tension I mean a tension between the situation that activists have inherited which is not of their own making but which nonetheless circumscribes what they can or cannot do, and the ways in which their actions, and responses to the situation reify, modify or change future structural contexts.[46]

The temporal tension usually takes the form of an ethical dilemma in decision-making about the extent to which the present is to be prioritised over the future. In other words, 'do we live to fight another day' or 'do we die for what we believe in today'. Social movement stories are replete with stories of martyrdom. In the absence of an understanding of the place of rights within contemporary TMF capitalism and the legal and institutional context for rights, a utopian understanding of rights including ideas about subaltern rights do not offer easy choices. The temporal tension then is at the same time the source for continued disillusionment about rights in practice which co-exists with their idealisation in theory (see Chapter 8). The purpose of this book is to contribute to making more enlightened decisions when activists are confronted with the 'temporal tension' in rights-talk.

2

What's Wrong With Rights?

Men are free to make history, but some men are much freer than others. Such freedom requires access to the means of decisions and of power by which history may now be made. It is not always so made; in ... the contemporary period ... the means of history-making power have become so enlarged and so centralized. It is with reference to this period that I am contending that if men do not make history, they tend increasingly to become the utensils of history-makers and also the mere objects of history-making. (Charles Wright Mills, *The Sociological Imagination,* 1959, p. 181)[1]

THE FALL OF THE WALL AND THE RIGHTS RESURGENCE

1989 was a 'happening' year, astonishingly so in retrospect. It was the year when the Berlin Wall was pulled down, when Poland and Russia conducted their first Euro-American-style multi-party elections, when the Tiananmen Square events, known as the '89 Democracy Movement' played out as millions of Chinese gathered at the square to demand freedoms inspired by Euro-American liberal democracies, the year when Romania, the former Czechoslovakia, Hungary, countries across Central and Eastern Europe with the exception of the Balkan states witnessed a resurgence of movements for rights, democracy and constitutionalism not seen on the European continent since the revolutions of the seventeenth and eighteenth centuries. Eastern and Central European states responded to the implosion of the former Soviet Union in different ways but everywhere the end results were similar. Euro-American-style democracies brought constitutional changes guaranteeing multi-party elections and individual freedoms: formal rights to speak, organise, assemble, protest, freedom of conscience, non-discrimination, fair trials and right to life. At the same time, the Second World: Eastern and Central Europe and Russia, reinstated the right to property and introduced what I shall henceforth call the 'LPG reforms' – Liberalisation-Privatisation-

Globalisation. These reforms prioritised the global political economy over local people.

Elsewhere in the Third World, like the other LPG – Liquefied Petroleum Gas – the LPG reforms proved incendiary as new inequalities, poverty, class polarisation, ethnic tensions and wars pitted citizens against states and people against people. The Third World did nothing to dampen the rights resurgence in the Second World where new ruling elites willingly remodelled institutions of the state on Euro-American constitutional models to qualify for membership of the EU. Most Eastern and Central European states were welcomed, not just into the EU, but also into the NATO military alliance. The end of the Cold War, far from ending all wars as many had hoped, expanded and consolidated the most powerful military bloc known in human history. NATO expansion, LPG reforms and the rights resurgence walked hand in hand. Social movements, critical scholars, public intellectuals, working people around the world simply did not see this handholding, the connections between the promise of freedom and democracy offered by one hand and the promises of endless riches by the other, one hand waving the flag of 'liberty, equality, fraternity' and the other waving a bayonet. Such is the power of promise. This book explores the extraordinary power of promise that ideological liberalism has over our imaginations and how it conceals from view the handholding of economy and politics bonded together by a regime of rights, a regime that promises everything to everybody in the contemporary world of transnational monopoly finance (TMF) capitalism.

1989 was a euphoric moment for the capitalist Euro-American world. The US which, as the leader of G7 states, had led capitalism to partial victory in World War II (WWII) now led them to complete victory in the Cold War. Speaking at the Olin Center for Inquiry into the Theory and Practice of Democracy at the University of Chicago in 1989, Francis Fukuyama told his audience:

> The triumph of the West, of the Western *idea*, is evident first of all in the total exhaustion of viable systematic alternatives to Western liberalism. ... What we may be witnessing is not just the end of the Cold War, or the passing of a particular period of postwar history, but the end of history as such: that is, the end point of mankind's ideological evolution and the universalization of Western liberal democracy as the final form of human government.[2] (Italics in the original)

Fukuyama was the deputy director of the US State Department's policy planning staff when he made the speech and was previously an analyst at the Rand Corporation, an influential US think tank with a track record for policy research on military and international affairs.[3] Fukuyama's pronouncement, 'capitalist triumphalism' as it came to be called, was heavily criticised by scholars and activists coming from a range of theoretical and activist perspectives on the 'Left' used here in the broadest possible sense.[4] But their critique did not dare challenge the normative order prefigured by rights-based democracy. Tearing down the Iron Curtain to liberate the people there from socialist tyranny was the finale in the epic struggles against socialist rivals of the liberal capitalist world order. The epic war between the Free World founded on formal rights and democracy and the dark world behind the Iron Curtain was a struggle with a long history going back nearly a century and a half, or a century, or seventy years depending on whether we see the beginning of the struggles as the Paris Commune in 1871, or the Russian Revolution in 1917, or the emergence of the socialist and Third World blocs after the end of World War II. These events deconstructed liberal capitalism and challenged a world order that the ancestors of modernity had established during the Age of Enlightenment in the seventeenth century as the ideal normative order for all times and all peoples. Epics according to Bakhtin, valorise the past; they wall off the past from the world in which the singers and their audience live.[5] When the curtain fell on the historic drama it had walled off the epic struggles from the world in which the viewers of the drama lived in 1989. Bakhtin writes,

> ... tradition isolates the world of the epic from personal experience from any new insights, from any personal initiative in understanding and interpreting, from new points of view and evaluations. The epic world is an utterly finished thing, not only as an authentic event of the distant past but also its own terms, and by it its own standards, it is impossible to change, to re-think, to revaluate anything in it. It is completed, conclusive and immutable, as a fact, an idea and a value.[6]

The denouement to the epic struggles in the Cold War meant evil socialism was vanquished and rights and democracy were unchallenged as an inviolable Western tradition. In 1989 when the curtains fell on the modern epic and brought the performance on the European stage to a close there was nothing else for the audience to do except to go home and attempt to live as best as they could by the ideals of the tradition that their European ancestors of modernity had established. From that moment rights violations invariably happened 'out there' somewhere in Africa, Asia, Latin America. The US, UK, Europe, Canada, Australia, New Zealand became 'mature democracies' now charged with helping the infantile ones to grow up. The spatial hiatus entailed in the distinctions between 'mature' and 'immature' democracies, this book will show, has skewed the critique of rights. Beyond the European stage where the finale in one epic of democracy was played out, in the distant continents of Africa, Latin America and Asia, the epic of rights and democracy was being re-scripted in new ways unnoticed by critical thinkers in the West (see Part II of this book).

THE RIGHTS RESURGENCE AND THIRD WORLD DEBT

In the Third World, which is in reality the two-thirds world, the 1980s was the decade of the debt crisis. In Venezuela there were public protests, referred to as the *Caracazo* against austerity and unemployment in 1989. The *democratically* elected president, Carlos Andréz Peréz, who won on the promise of reducing austerity, buckled to pressures from the International Monetary Fund (IMF) and introduced price increases as part of an IMF debt relief package. The measures brought thousands of people out on the streets of Caracas and elsewhere in the country to protest against the government for retracting from its democratic mandate.[7] The previous year, in 1988, over 20,000 people in Argentina had staged a protest rally against an earlier round of austerity measures introduced by the government. The 1989 rally was the twelfth since Argentina made the transition from dictatorship to democracy in 1983.[8] Notwithstanding popular opposition, the government remained in power and so did the austerity programme.

In Nigeria opposition to austerity programmes imposed by the IMF triggered a national strike and clashes with government troops. Nigeria was in the process of transition from dictatorship to democracy. The *New York Times* reported,

[W]hat is most worrisome, Western diplomats and some Nigerians say, is that a continued breakdown in order could tempt the military to delay a return to civilian rule.[9]

Nigeria experienced a spate of anti-austerity strikes prior to and after 1989, in 1986, 1988, 1990, 1992. On independence from France in 1960 and Britain in 1961, the Republic of Cameroon adopted a multi-party electoral system. In 1966 it adopted a one-party electoral system and in 1990 it reverted back to multi-party system.[10] Cameroon's problems with its electoral process mattered little to international financial institutions and to the former colonial powers Britain and France. Piet Konings writes,

Decisions about privatisation in Cameroon are taken by the Bretton Woods institutions and implemented after secret consultations with a small group of national technocrats representing the government. Power, in other words, is increasingly located outside the political community as conventionally defined by democratic theory, and beyond the reach of the democratic control of Cameroonian citizens.[11]

Niger was no different.[12] In the wake of LPG reforms, in 2002 political groups in the poorest regions in four countries, Nigeria, Cameroon, Chad and Niger formed Boko Haram, a movement that viewed all Western education as *haram* or forbidden.[13] Presumably, in the absence of any other kinds of knowledge or education, Western or otherwise, and where liberalism becomes synonymous with Western knowledge in the minds of the uneducated and disenfranchised poor, it was difficult for some at least to make sense of the re-scripted versions of rights and democracy that was being enacted in their name and in their nations. Boko Haram and others, most likely, relied on intuition to recognise something was not right in the theory and practices of rights and democracy when they declared Western *education* to be *haram*. If democracy was about the will of the people, why did their will matter so little? By 1990, the international financial institutions had sixty countries under the discipline of one hundred and eighty-seven structural adjustment loans.[14] Austerity was everywhere.

The debt crisis was a moment of profound constitutional and institutional changes throughout the world, indeed the most far-reaching since the establishment of the UN order at the end of WWII. The drivers of these legal and institutional changes were the demands by global bankers and investors for a regime of *international* property rights. Yet few associate the debt crises with the rights resurgence, or make the connections between property rights and the demands for political, social and cultural rights. But the debt crises enabled the establishment of the international property rights regime (see Chapter 6) and 'good governance' regimes to manage the political, social and cultural dimensions of the change within states. Social movements believed that it was possible to keep the good from global governance and throw out the bad. Chapter 7 analyses the coming together of the two types of rights, property and socio-political, in global governance.

The debt crises created cracks in the Third World state apparatuses. The cracks provided opportunities to introduce LPG reforms that enabled Western corporations and financial institutions to wrench the states, pull them apart, and initiate full-blown institutional and constitutional transformations of states and societies there. The LPG reforms came wearing the mantle of accountability, participation and empowerment. In the context of the debt crises and the LPG reforms that followed invariably, rights and democracy presented a confusing picture. Most actors, social movement activists, critical thinkers, trade unions, scholars, First, Second and Third World states, International and Regional organisations, corporations, banks, financial institutions, debtors, investors, borrowers, lenders, everyone competed with each other to establish the rights that best suited their interests. Their engagement with the internationalisation of the regime of rights further embedded voluntarist thinking that is at the heart of the concept of rights (see Chapter 3).

Democracy promotion rhetoric blamed the economic crises of the socialist countries on socialist ideology. In the Third World it blamed the economic crises on dictatorships and state-led development in the post-WWII era. In both cases the primacy of ideology concealed the real economic crises of the capitalism in the 'Free World' and the end of post-WWII recovery in the Euro-American states. LPG reforms began first and foremost in the US and the UK, the hubs for post-WWII world economy, during the Reagan and Thatcher years in the early 1970s, long before those reforms were internationalised. In the old script of liberalism, the European Enlightenment gave a very marginal part to the colonial world and people as foot soldiers in the epic of democracy. The new script was different. The Third World was the stage for the re-scripted epic where full-blown institutional transformation of states was experimented and embedded. If the Eastern and Central European states became the battleground for liberal ideology, the long history of colonialism and imperialism in the Third World had put in place state structures that provided the conditions for institutional changes and made it the theatre for staging the re-scripted epic. The first sites for colonial governance, the Latin American states, also became the first sites for institutional restructuring in the 1980s. At the time, in the 1980s, most critical thinkers and anti-globalisation activists in the West never imagined that the LPG reforms would return to haunt Europe and the US in the form of austerity and structural adjustments as in Spain, Greece, Portugal, Italy, or as Brexit in the UK or the Trump phenomenon in the US.

The new script retained rights and democracy as virtues from the old European Enlightenment script, but introduced new characters: international law, IOs, the UN, the IEOs, international courts, international and regional organisations, and most importantly, a much stronger and more powerful tribe – the Allies and Axis states integrated into the G7 with a new invincible hero, the US with its unparalleled military technologies and destructive capacities. The integration of Allies and Axis powers in economic blocs like the G7 and the Organisation for Economic Co-operation and Development (OECD), and military blocs like NATO are absent characters in the old script. These new characters speak the language of old European Enlightenment but the old lines spoken by new characters in the re-scripted epic present a different drama. They change the meaning of popular sovereignty, political representation and above all the state as the pivot for economic and socio-political actors, as will be shown.

'DEMOCRACY PROMOTION' AS US FOREIGN POLICY

'Democracy promotion' in US foreign policy is not entirely new. It has a history going back to Woodrow Wilson's presidency (1913–21). The Carter presidency (1977–81) signals the moment when US foreign policy began doing overtly what it had hitherto done covertly. From the mid 1970s 'democracy promotion' became an *overt* foreign policy, a prescription for institutional reforms that Third World states perforce had to introduce. In the 1950s and 1960s covert actions by the CIA were important foreign policy tools.[15] Covert interventions in the Second and Third World states by the CIA eroded the credibility of the US in the Third World. More importantly, it corrupted the US state machinery from *within*. US defeat in the Vietnam War signalled the beginning of the political crisis in the 'belly of the beast' so to speak, the US administration. The Watergate scandal in the early 1970s made the corruption and corrosion of the state apparatus public. The Carter presidency signalled the need for the US to govern differently. Internally, the Carter presidency signals a moment when the US Congress became progressively more assertive vis-à-vis the Executive than it had been earlier. Since Carter, regardless of their party affiliations, successive US presidents have adopted democracy promotion as the cornerstones of their foreign policies with small variations in style and emphasis. The hand of the market in the wake of the economic crises remained invisible in democracy promotion.

Looking beyond the surface of the political crises triggered by the defeat in Vietnam and the Watergate scandals, democracy promotion as a foreign policy instrument came at a time of the most severe economic crisis for the US and indeed for TMF capitalism since the end of WWII. For the US, the late 1960s was the beginning of an enduring and deepening series of economic, political and ideological crises. It was the decade of the debt crisis, challenges from the Organization of the Oil Producing Countries (OPEC), the first and second oil shocks, economic recession, inflation, fiscal deficits, the suspension of the US dollar's gold convertibility, the end of the faith in the US dollar's invincibility, the collapse of the Bretton Woods agreement on fixed exchange rate systems pegged to the US dollar, increasing competition from the EU and Japan and demands for New International Economic Order (NIEO) by the Third World. In a televised address to the nation on 15 July 1979 on the energy crisis, President Carter linked the energy crisis to the wider crisis afflicting the nation, which he attributed to a 'crisis of confidence' that threatened to 'destroy the social and political fabric of America'.[16] President Carter at least did not put the problems of the US into disciplinary boxes neatly labelled as 'Economics' and 'Politics'. For most people in the US and G7 states Carter's statements were justifiable for pragmatic economic reasons and uncontroversial. In contrast, the CIA's activities were perceived as political opportunism, unethical, excessive and controversial. Such perceptions become possible because liberal ideology invites us to believe that economics and politics are distinct spheres that can be disconnected or reconnected at will[17] (see Chapter 3).

The series of economic and political crises challenged the leadership role of the US within the G7, OECD alliances and TMF capitalism more generally. Doing overtly what it had done covertly in politics and silently in economics called for restructuring the apparatuses of governance within the US and internationally. Democracy promotion through bilateral projects directly funded by the state through the United States Agency for International Development (USAID) and overseas development programmes were hardly designed to bring about changes in the international order. The CIA could bring about political changes and install dictatorships, but was hardly in a position to establish international property regimes, governance mechanisms and legal and political institutions for TMF capitalism to function in systemic ways. The economic crises exposed in all its nakedness the absence of international law and institutions that protected global bankers, investors and traders (see Chapters 6 and 7). The 1970s may be seen as the decade of institutional 'brainstorming' within the US administration when various mechanisms to promote democracy overseas were proposed, discussed and explored. The National Endowment for Democracy (NED) was America's eventual solution.

The NED was established and fostered under the Reagan presidency (1981–89). Under Reagan, democracy promotion acquired a distinctive neoliberal orientation, an orientation that has endured, not least because it was embedded in the institutions of state and society in ways that took the policy far beyond the Reagan era. A key tenet of neoliberal thinking is that international relations are relations between private actors developed through voluntary associations and transactions. The state's role in international relations is that of a facilitator of private transactions and relations.[18] The other neoliberal tenet is 'rolling back the state' from substantive activities and instead directing its activities to regulating markets and society indirectly by using financial instruments as (dis) incentives. The neoliberal orientations during the Reagan era lent itself to long chains of 'contracting out' of state functions to private actors. Democracy promotion activities were 'freed' from state monopoly and contracted out to a vast array of social actors in the US including private foundations, NGOs, humanitarian organisations, think tanks, universities, experts and others with elaborate mechanisms for funding, accountability and engagement regulated by 'turning on' or 'turning off' the funding sources or appropriating the 'products': the knowledge, social movements and media and channelling them selectively towards foreign policy aims of the US state. The NED triggered the NGO revolution. As their roles became controversial, non-state interventions splintered into social networks, social movements, grassroots movements, protest movements, each with a particular orientation to NGOs. Chapter 8 examines the extent to which the liberal imaginations of social movements on the political Left, their understanding of rights and its place in capitalist social relations contributed to the development of legal and institutional frameworks for TMF capitalism.

In an influential speech to the British Parliament in 1982 Reagan said the objective of democracy promotion was to 'foster the infrastructure of democracy'.[19] The meaning of this becomes clear in the objectives for the NED spelt out by the US Congress when it approved US$ 31.3 million for two years to set up the endowment. David Lowe, the Vice President of NED for Government Relations and Public Affairs, in his history of the NED sums up those objectives as

> ... encouraging democratic institutions through *private sector initiatives*; facilitating exchanges between private sector groups (particularly the four proposed Institutes) and democratic groups abroad; promoting nongovernmental participation in democratic training programs; strengthening democratic electoral processes abroad in cooperation with indigenous democratic forces; fostering cooperation between American private sector groups and those abroad 'dedicated to the cultural values, institutions, and organizations of democratic pluralism;' and *encouraging democratic development consistent with the interests of both the U.S. and the groups receiving assistance.*[20] (Italics added)

Hereafter democracy was to be about building particular types of institutions in other countries. 'This is not cultural imperialism', Reagan told the British Parliamentarians, but a means for 'protection of diversity' and further that as a nation it was important to make a commitment 'in both public and private sectors – to assisting democratic development'.[21] The phrase 'democratic development' is now part of the vocabulary of social sciences, social movements and national and international policy makers. 'Let us tell the world that a new age is not only possible but probable', Reagan said.[22] Curiously, the slogan 'Another World is Possible' was to echo around the world in the 1990s as the slogan of the new anti-globalisation movements (see Chapter 8). Social movements went along with democracy promotion, initially at least. They did not make the connections between markets and rights, norms and reality, rights and institutions, and most importantly the reasons why actors canvass rights from different institutional locations.

The NED epitomises the idea of 'rolling back the state' in international relations. The NED is registered as a non-profit organisation with independent legal personality distinct from the state. The board members, chairman and president are drawn from the two main political parties in the US, the Republican Party and the Democratic Party. Board members include trade union and business representatives, foreign policy specialists and two members of the Congress from the two main political parties. The NED is accountable to the US Congress which authorises the funding.[23] The NED is anything but 'non-governmental' except that it has an independent legal personality. The independent legal personality distances it from the state, transforms it into a 'private' body, and insulates it politically from successive governments. The NED is widely criticised by scholars and activists but few have grasped the effects of the NED's independent legal personality and what it means for the public/private divide on which the edifice of liberal law stands, points expanded in Chapter 3.

The NED comprises four core institutes which receive funding from the US Congress. The Center for International Private Enterprise (CIPE) was set up by the US Chamber of Commerce Foundation (previously National Chamber Foundation), a wing of the US Chamber of Commerce. The CIPE works with business leaders, policy makers and journalists to promote democratic institutions. Projects funded by the CIPE include 'democratic governance', 'access to information', 'combating corruption', entrepreneurship, setting up business associations, corporate governance, legal and regulatory reform, women, youth, informal sector and private property rights and corporate citizenship.[24] All these issues were to become components of the Good Governance Programmes legalised and institutionalised by the World Bank in the 1990s. Over the past thirty years such programmes have spread a common vocabulary that associates democracy with private enterprise and rights with 'efficiency' and individualism. Democracy movements have made access to information, transparency, corruption and governance the focus of their struggles over the decades oblivious of the actors promoting them (see Chapter 7).

The second institute is the Free Trade Union Institute (FTUI). The FTUI was created in 1977 by the American Federation of Labor and Congress of Industrial Organizations (AFL-CIO), the largest federation of trade unions in the US. After affiliating with the NED the FTUI's mission broadened in scope and breadth.[25] By 1983 the AFL-CIO had a track record of promoting US foreign policy overseas, including funding the Solidarity movement in Poland which was instrumental in the overthrow of the communist regime there, undermining unions with socialist inclinations in Europe, and subverting militant unions in Third World countries.[26] The third affiliate organisation is the National Democratic Institute for International Affairs (NDI) set up by the Democratic Party. The NDI works with political parties around the world that share its principles. According to the NDI brochure, amongst other things it has worked in seventy-five countries with more than three hundred citizen groups to provide assistance in election monitoring, electoral reform, citizen training programmes, political party building and helps ministers, prime ministers and presidents' offices and local governments to function more efficiently.[27] The fourth affiliate is the International Republican Institute (IRI) (formerly National Republican Institute for International Affairs). Like the NDI, the IRI works with political parties and groups to promote its own brand of democracy (see Chapter 4).[28] The four affiliated institutes in turn use the funds they receive from the US Congress to support a wide range of NGOs, organisations, voluntary groups, political groups, academics, universities, think tanks and other segments of society in the US for their international work.

Between them the four organisations cover nearly every segment and every type of political group in the First, Second and Third World states. These initiatives *create* new right-bearing actors, the 'civil society' organisations and groups as conduits for extended chains of contractual arrangements for US foreign policy. Spontaneous actions by civil society actors were the foundations for democracy in classical liberalism. Adam Smith's famous 'invisible hand of the market' referred to spontaneous actions by a vast array of people buying and selling in the market place that formed the basis for economy and society according to him. The NGOs and civil society organisations created by networks of NED-funded organisations are by no means 'spontaneous' voluntary associations of individuals with common interests, and the 'invisible hand' here is not that of buyers and sellers but rather that of an imperial state with global reach (see Chapter 5). Civil society today is not the civil society that European Enlightenment thinkers wrote about in the seventeenth and eighteenth centuries. The discourse of civil society drowns these distinctions in a cacophony of moral outrage about 'human' rights violations (see Chapter 3).

Congress approvals for NED funds have soared from US$ 31.3 million in 1983 to US$ 112 million in 2012.[29] Over and above the funds provided to the four organisations the US Congress earmarks discretionary funds to be used in political sensitive hotspots. Special funds targeting particular countries were approved for support to Solidarity in Poland, to opposition groups in the Balkans during the Serbian elections in 2000, to pro-Western opposition groups in Eastern Europe after the implosion of the former Soviet Union, and in Chile, Nicaragua, South Africa, Burma, China, Tibet, North Korea, amongst many others. Since the events of 9/11, the NED has approved special funding for Muslim countries in the Middle East, Africa and Asia.[30] The NED works with a wide range of private foundations in the US and international and regional organisations. The NED model has been replicated in different forms by other G7 states. The British government set up the Westminster Foundation for Democracy in 1992 which focuses on Eastern Europe and the Commonwealth countries; the Australian government established the Centre for Democratic Institutions located in the Australian National University in 1998 which focuses on the Asia-Pacific region; the EU has recently set up the European Endowment for Democracy in 2013. The NED supported the establishment of the World Democratic Movement, a network of activists, scholars, policy makers, practitioners and funders to promote similar regional and national networks around the world struggling for freedoms. The NED established the Center for International Media Assistance (CIMA) and the International Forum on Democratic Studies which publishes the influential *Journal of Democracy*. The materiality of the rights resurgence becomes apparent in retrospect. But the power of promise is such that not many questioned where the material wherewithal for the rights resurgence came from, so quickly and rapidly at that.

The proliferation of organisations and the downward chain of contracted out projects permeate every aspect of political, cultural, intellectual and social life (see Chapter 3 for the place of contracts in liberalism). They bombard social movements, trade unions, intellectuals and cultural workers seeking real answers to the social, economic and political problems confronting their nations and peoples with a way of framing those issues, and with a vocabulary that is difficult to escape or avoid. They promote a 'one shoe fits all' approach in an attempt to standardise institutions and tailor institutional changes to the interests of the G7 states and global economic interests. The careers and professional standings of many in different professions become tied to the funding and recognition by institutions leading the changes as also the work of many sincere and dedicated workers who opt to work with voluntary organisations, social movements and NGOs in the hope of bringing about real social change in their societies.[31] Indeed, the very distinction between state and private activities becomes skewed. Yet this distinction is the bedrock of classical liberalism. This bombardment has led to deep divisions within scholars and social movements. Within anti-globalisation movements against IEOs like the World Bank, IMF and WTO in the 1990s these divisions created the 'fix-it' and 'nix-it' camps. 'Fix-it' or 'nix-it', the fealty to rights remains as strong as ever.

The networked model of 'democracy promotion' supports engagement with the normative aspects of rights and democracy as a discursive and conceptual problem and invisibilises the materiality of rights: its anchor in the new post-war national and international institutions and the actors and mechanisms driving the rights resurgence. This point is a thread that runs through all the chapters. The NED has matured into the hydra of political and social movements. Yet the apparent autonomy of the NED and the networked 'contracting out' model for 'democracy promotion' renders the long hand of US and G7 states invisible in rights and democracy movements. The invisible hand of the market is joined by the invisible hands of imperial states masquerading as 'civil society'. Indeed, civil society itself becomes embedded in contractual relations and exchanges in the market place of economic, political, social and cultural humanitarianism. The common vocabulary, themes, organising strategies, demands, even the naming of movements ought to raise questions in the minds of activists and engaged scholars at least. How come so many democracy movements become colour coded for example: the green (Iran), orange (Ukraine), rose (Georgia), purple (Iraq), blue (Kuwait), yellow (Philippines) and saffron (Myanmar) revolutions; or they are named after nature as for example the tulip (Kyrgyzstan), cedar (Lebanon), grape (Moldova), jasmine (Tunisia and China), and lotus (Egypt) revolutions? Who named these so-called revolutions in this way? So-called because none of these revolutions have identified the real social contradictions in their societies or proposed solutions for the real problems confronting their peoples. Many believe that the spread of vocabulary, ideas and names are inspired by the internet and technology. If we accept that the internet and technology are not divine interventions, who are the actors who are able to mobilise the most sophisticated technologies to spread a coherent set of ideas? Is the rights resurgence anchored to the materiality of the world at all?

INTERNATIONALISING G7 FOREIGN POLICY

Unlike CIA activities located in the invisible depths of the US state apparatus, democracy promotion as foreign policy entails changes in the international order. 'Human' rights were put on the agenda of international relations by President Roosevelt (1933–45) during the interwar period. From its inception the inclusion of 'human' rights had a moral and economic rationale. Roosevelt's Four Freedoms included 'good business' and international leadership for the US after the end of the world wars.[32] The Atlantic Charter signed between the UK and the US in August 1941 on international arrangements after the end of the world wars included rights of people. The Declaration on the United Nations made in January 1942 included 'human rights in their lands as well as in others'.[33] It is important to note that the prefix 'human' appeared during negotiations over peacetime arrangements between two imperial powers conducting a world war. The world wars concluded with a partial victory for the Allies, however. The victory against Axis powers became possible because, contrary to expectations of the Allies, the former USSR defeated Hitler. In the East, China defeated Japan and contrary to expectations, the Chinese Communist Party continued the revolution after the defeat of Japan. Democracy promotion in 1945 did not work as it did in the 1970s. Chiang Kai Sheik, a US ally in the war against Japan, fled to Taiwan and established the Republic of China on a small island. The Allies did not recognise the communist government on the mainland, a continent with a billion people, for twenty-five years until the onset of economic crises in 1971. China's seat remained vacant in the UN Security Council leaving Russia as the sole dissenter. The implosion of the Empire system made it difficult for Britain and France to govern their colonies. The partial victory of the Allies meant that the Atlantic Charter's vision for the world order could be realised only partially. Besides, in 1945, capitalism too required reconstruction of the economic, social, legal, institutional and ideological infrastructures destroyed by the world wars. This reconstructed world order is crucial to differentiating the concept and meaning of rights in the European Enlightenment writings and in the twentieth and twenty-first centuries. This difference is another thread that runs through the book.

During the negotiations on the UN Charter in 1944 the former USSR and China emphasised sovereign equality of states whereas the US and the UK focused on the economic organisations, the specialised agencies and their relationship to the UN Economic and Social Council (ECOSOC). The compromises forced by the turn that the world wars took at their concluding stage meant that the text of the UN Charter emphasises 'human' rights *and* sovereign equality of states throughout. Competing interpretations of the two ideas and the relationship between 'human' rights and sovereign equality continue to be controversial and contested in the UN's deliberations, as we shall see. The period from the end of WWII until the end of the Cold War, formally in 1989, may be seen as the continuation of the world war agenda through political means and localised wars. During this period the US led the proceedings in the UN to draft and adopt the Universal Declaration of Human Rights (UDHR). The UDHR remained a non-binding declaration because of disagreements within the US as conservatives feared it could compromise US sovereignty and subject domestic segregation policies against African-Americans and policies towards indigenous peoples to international scrutiny. Equally, there were disagreements externally with the socialist bloc over the meaning of rights and their internationalisation and institutionalisation in the post-WWII international order.[34]

Between the end of WWII and the Cold War the focus of the Allies was on building the legal and institutional infrastructures for TMF capitalism on the ground by reconstituting economic relationships between states and between states and private actors. That included integrating the Axis states into TMF capitalism and the formation of the G7 as a coalition in world affairs: economic and political; operationalising the IEOs: the WB, IMF and the General Agreements on Tariffs and Trade (GATT); establishing frameworks for foreign investments, international financial transactions, transnational corporations; developing and expanding the international development agenda for the Third World as the global economic strategy for neo-colonialism especially during the three UN Development Decades; military expansion and formation of blocs like NATO; establishment of military bases around the world; innovation of new financial securities; international currency trading; international dispute resolution mechanisms; international technical and social standards; and much more. Much of these initiatives occurred during the Cold War. By the time of the debt crisis the institutional infrastructures for TMF capitalism were well established. The debt crisis provided the opportunity for restructuring the post-WWII *political* arrangements, of which state sovereignty was an important component. A new regime of rights was the core of these changes. Yet the inability to see the connections between rights and markets, states and ideology meant people, many radical ones even, were prepared to participate in the new regime even when they were uneasy about the ground from beneath the sovereignty principle and rights to self-determination slipping away. The chapters that follow consider the sovereignty question during the re-scripting of different rights.

Although the US was instrumental in inserting promotion of 'human' rights as a goal of the UN in the UN Charter adopted in 1945, it had not ratified important international conventions concerning 'human' rights due to internal opposition.[35] The partial victory of the socialist revolutions and national liberation struggles meant that the right of nations to self-determination and the sovereign equality of states became the founding principle of the UN Charter. It is possible to speculate that the back-pedalling on 'human' rights by the US was also due to its covert actions to prop up dictatorships in so many states. The reverse side of the partial success of the socialist and national liberation struggles also means the partial defeat of the Euro-American Alliance during WWII. The economic crises of the late 1960s introduced a new urgency in turning the partial victory into a complete one and to prise open Second and Third World states and markets, and renewed determination to complete the legal and institutional changes commenced after the end of WWII, as we shall see. In his speech to the UN General Assembly (UNGA) in 1977 Carter signalled the need for a change of direction in the UN. Referring to the commitments to 'human' rights in the UN Charter, Carter told member states, '[t]he United States has a *historical birthright* to be associated with this [promoting 'human' rights] process'[36] (italics added). To demonstrate US commitment to human rights he promised to seek Congressional approval to sign the International Covenant on Economic Social and Cultural Rights (ICESCR) adopted in 1966, the International Covenant on Civil and Political rights (ICCPR) adopted in 1966, the Genocide Convention adopted in 1948 and the Convention on Elimination of All Forms of Racial Discrimination adopted in 1965. He told the UNGA that the US was on the way to removing all travel restrictions for US citizens, something the US had been pressuring the former Soviet Union and Eastern European states to do since the end of WWII, but imposed on its own citizens. He proposed the establishment of a UN Office of the High Commissioner for Human Rights (UNOHCHR) because, as he put it, the 'strengthened international machinery will help us to close the gap between promise and performance in protecting human rights'.[37] The UNOHCHR was set up in 1993 with an additional office in New York.[38] The speech began a process within the US for ratification of the international treaties which it had refrained from doing until then. The US signed the ICCPR in 1992, the Genocide Convention in 1988 and the Elimination of Racism treaty in 1994 with reservations to protect US national interests. It rejoined the United Nations Educational, Scientific and Cultural Organization (UNESCO) in 2002. These ratifications of international 'human' rights instruments occurred after the dissolution of the former USSR. Although the US did not sign the ICESCR, the Vienna Declaration and Programme of Action (VDPA) adopted in 1993 incorporates the provisions of the ICESCR, giving socio-economic rights a neoliberal market-friendly orientation.

'Democracy promotion' was not limited to bilateral foreign policy for different states but extended to its UN policy as well. The UN World Summit on Social Development marks a milestone in restructuring the relations between states, economic institutions and civil society actors in the new internationalised regime of rights. In 1995 Vice President Al Gore announced a significant shift in the delivery of US overseas assistance at the UN World Summit on Social Development. The US Agency for International Development (USAID) would from then on, Gore announced, channel 40 per cent of its overseas development assistance through US and local NGOs and not through states as it had done previously. The three objectives of the initiative were to empower small businesses and entrepreneurs, to strengthen the role of NGOs in development programmes and to bolster democracy at local levels. 'All three are linked by a single idea – that families and individuals, when given the power and opportunity to change their lives, will do exactly that', Gore told the Summit.[39] The Summit added 'empowerment' and 'civil society empowerment' to the expanding vocabulary of 'democratic development'. Hillary Clinton compared the NGOs to the abolition-ists, the suffragettes and the civil rights campaigners.[40] What Gore and Clinton forgot was that the abolitionists, the suffragettes and civil rights leaders were not funded by parliaments and international organisations or by the slave-traders, property-owning men and white supremacists. Furthermore, Gore and Clinton forgot to add that the abolitionists, the suffragettes and civil rights did not speak from the pulpits of imperial power, indeed those leaders challenged important pillars of power on which the institutions of the state rested at that time including the institutions of class, race and gender.

NGOs in the G7 states, who were hitherto the good Samaritans working from humanitarian impulses on the fringes of society, found themselves catapulted to centre-stage after the UN World Summit on Social Development. They became the voice of a diffused and diverse 'global civil society', the voice of the voiceless in the emerging rights regime. (We will return in Chapter 8 to the question of what the 'global voice' amplifies and how.) In turn, the G7 NGOs brought with them the groups and networks they worked with in the Third World. A large contingent of NGOs, 1300 of them, participated in a UN World Summit setting a precedent for a new model of governance that was emerging in which the NGOs had an important part. A new kind of corporatist tripartism was taking shape in the international domain. Earlier the International Labour Organization (ILO) was the only recognised tripartite body in the international legal order. In the ILO states, employers' organisations and trade unions participated as representatives of organised sectors of society recognised under domestic law. In the new tripartism business interest groups, NGOs and international organisations spoke for the people of the Third World not as representatives but as the voice of morality and compassion, what each one of them must do to help 'those poor people out there'. NGOs claimed to be the new 'global civil society' that mediated between the Third World poor and a global alliance of states and corporations and financial institutions. Part II throws light on NGO responses in re-scripting rights. Not surprisingly, debates ensued within social movements about the meaning of 'global civil society' and the distinctions between NGOs, INGOs, social movements, grassroots movements, people's movements, protest movements and similar terms, each term reflecting a particular theoretical orientation to NGOs and the neoliberal reforms underway. These differences notwithstanding, all supported the 'human' rights agenda and affirmed the idea that people could be empowered by legal rights.

In 2004 George Bush proposed setting up a new United Nations Democracy Fund (UNDEF) as a multi-donor trust-fund with contributions from different states.[41] His reason for the trust-fund was very similar to NED's, i.e.

... to help countries lay the foundations of democracy by instituting the rule of law and independent courts, a free press, political parties and trade unions. Money from the fund would also help set up voter precincts in polling places and support the work of election monitors.[42]

The trust-fund model enabled G7 and other developed countries interested in democracy promotion as international policy to pool resources to pursue their interests through the UNDEF. Like the NED, the UNDEF was a funding organisation advised and supported by the funders, states, NGOs and private foundations.

Although the formal UNGA resolution on the creation of the trust-fund was more diplomatically worded reiterating, in typical UN-speak, universal values, freely expressed will of the people, self-determination, respect for sovereignty and the interdependence of human rights,[43] important shifts have occurred in the institutional arrangements for democracy promotion internationally. The point may be exemplified by examining the composition and mechanisms of the UNDEF. The advisory board for the UNDEF in 2011–13 comprised the seven largest contributors to the trust-fund; the US, India, Sweden, Germany, Australia, Poland and Chile; representatives of two US foundations: the former Commissioner of the New York City Mayor's Office for International Affairs and head of the Global Cities programme of Bloomberg Philanthropies; Mr Jeffrey Wright, an American actor and founder of Taia Peace Foundation and Taia Lion Resource; Action Aid International, an international charity with close relations to corporations;[44] and Avaaz, a global online campaign group with its main hubs in the UK and the US.[45] Avaaz was co-founded by Moveon.org, a US online campaign group associated with the US Democratic Party.[46] Under the leadership of Ricken Patel, a Canadian-British citizen, Avaaz rose to prominence very quickly as one of the largest online campaign networks.[47] Avaaz claims to be a movement of non-political 'practical idealists'[48] who promote a 'global web movement to bring people-powered politics to decision-making everywhere'.[49] Avaaz has played a controversial role in several hotspots including Syria.[50] Of the thirteen members of the UNDEF advisory group only six are states and seven are private foundations and INGOs.

These new institutional arrangements point to a new type of democracy where the boundaries between public and private actors and institutions are blurred and the architecture of power becomes hard to decipher.

In this new hydra-headed organisational model it becomes difficult to speak of organisations and movements without examining their chains of connections, networks and linkages. The architecture of power becomes invisible and tangled in a maze of legal persons, i.e. entities established by law. In the new networked model of democracy, real people/natural persons, traditionally the pivot of liberal democracies, are transformed into a set of photographs on the websites and glossy organisational brochures of NGOs, states and UN agencies. Who speaks for who can no longer be discerned only from the spoken and written words of different international actors. It must be discerned from what the actors do and how they do it, as will be highlighted in the pages that follow.

The new brand of 'networked' democracy today looks very different from the movements for democracy in the seventeenth and eighteenth centuries when rag-tag bands of peasants and workers, disaffected intellectuals, disempowered merchants uprooted, root and branch, the institutions of nobility and aristocracy, monarchy and papacy that were entrenched in European societies for centuries. The new brand of networked democracy is very different from the adventurous merchants who set out to 'discover' new frontiers for trade and occupation. There are no further discoveries to make – only development of new methods of appropriation from lands and people already 'discovered' and occupied. The democracy promotion we are seeing today is about standardising institutions around the world for more 'efficient' governance. It sounds and feels like a more refined version of the 'administrative reforms' of colonial governments in the early twentieth century.[51] Rights today are galaxies away from the rights of the seventeenth and eighteenth centuries not least because capitalism itself has transformed over the past one hundred years. Rights and democracy today are part of a package that includes NATO expansion, LPG reforms and regime changes. It is democracy re-scripted by the largest economic, military and ideological powers that have ever existed in human history. The re-scripted democracy alters, transforms the meaning of rights and severs it from the philosophical, political, historical, ethical and juridical moorings of the European Enlightenment.

BRINGING RIGHTS BACK TO EARTH

This chapter has presented an overview of the problem posed by the question in the book's main title: *What's Wrong With Rights?*

The theoretical premises suggested in the two opening chapters are considered more systematically in Chapter 3. The real problem with the rights resurgence is that it failed to establish the *relationship* between the normative order and real social relationships, i.e. the *relationship* between property rights and 'human' rights, the ideology of rights and political-economy, law and institutions, the history and geography of rights. Consequently, social activists found themselves having to catch the tiger by its tail, to fix the problems of TMF capitalism using moral arguments and legal persuasion. Part II takes up the changes in two political rights, electoral democracy (Chapter 4) and representative politics (Chapter 5) and connects them to the macroeconomic context for those changes, the development of property rights (Chapter 6) and global governance (Chapter 7).

The conundrum of rights in the contemporary world of TMF capitalism invites us to challenge European Enlightenment's answers to social questions generated by capitalism. Instead, most social movements cling on to right claims, qualifying their claims and adding new nuances to their qualifications. Chapter 8 reflects on the challenges and questions critical scholars and activists must consider in their practices. The central questions for contemporary social movements struggling for justice and social change is not a general understanding of rights in the abstract but a historically and politically situated one, not rights and capitalism generally but rights in the epoch of TMF capitalism. The question for social movements today is rather: who re-scripted rights and why? It is about 'concrete analysis of concrete conditions', as Mao said,[52] and the importance of understanding 'the how and the why of things', as Lenin put it.[53] This task in the twenty-first century requires a counter social philosophy. This book hopes to make a modest contribution to the development of a counter social philosophy that enables us to see our world with a lens that helps us to make better sense of it.

3
Rights in the 'Epoch of Imperialism'

In actual history, those theoreticians who regarded power as the basis of right, were in direct contradiction to those who looked on will as the basis of right ... If power is taken as the basis of right, as Hobbes, etc. do, then right, law etc. are merely the symptom, the expression of other relations upon which State power rests. ...

... one can divorce right from its real basis, whereby one obtains a 'ruling will' which in different epochs becomes modified in various ways and has its own, independent history in its creations, the laws. On this account, political and civil history becomes ideologically merged in a history of the rule of successive laws. This is the specific illusion of lawyers and politicians... . (Marx and Engels, The German Ideology, pp. 106, 107)[1]

THE EPOCH OF IMPERIALISM

What do rights actually do in the real world? Framing the question about rights in this way as *rights-in-action* draws attention to the different actors advocating this or that right, their motivations for doing so, their theorisation and re-theorisation of rights in particular contexts, the mechanisms they adopt for achieving their goals and the outcome of their deliberations and interventions for the world. In other words, the question brings rights from the exalted world of ideas to the murky world of contesting actors, mechanisms, theories and practices. Bringing rights down to earth requires, first and foremost, an understanding of the world we live in *today*. The world we live in is a world of transnational corporations, global financial markets, militarised states, economic and military alliances of the most powerful states, environmental destruction, extreme wealth polarisation unknown in history and mass destitution in entire continents the likes of which humanity has never seen before. It is not enough to locate rights in capitalism in general terms. Bringing rights back to earth requires locating rights in the type of capitalism *we* live in today, a capitalism that has undergone *qualitative* transformations since the turn of the twentieth century. *What do rights do in such a world?* This is a concrete historical question that arises in a specific historical context.

Historically, rights in their modern form emerged concurrently with capitalism. Capitalism evolved in Western Europe over several centuries. In the fifteenth and sixteenth centuries capitalism grew within the womb of a disintegrating feudal order. Feudal societies are founded on land as the organising mechanism, the lynchpin of the social order. In contrast, commodity production is the organising mechanism, the lynchpin of capitalist societies. The edifice of capitalism as a society organised around commodity production rests on the tripod of Economy, State and Civil Society as distinct types of institutions. The relationships between these institutions are established and mediated by law. The legal order that establishes capitalism as a social order is distinctive and not comparable with legal systems in earlier social orders even if they resonate with some aspects of the past or use certain vocabulary inherited from the past. In the seventeenth and eighteenth centuries, spearheaded by European merchants and intellectuals, commodity production became systemic, in that it dismantled feudal laws, ideology, institutions, modes of thinking and being in the world and established capitalism as the social order. The debates, theories, sciences, technologies, philosophies, politics, practices encompassing the systemic social transformations that replaced the feudal order are understood within the epistemological rubric of the European Enlightenment. Capitalism has evolved ever since but the evolution is marked by *qualitative* transformations at crucial junctures in its history. The capitalism of today is not the same capitalism that existed in the seventeenth and eighteenth centuries. The qualitative changes mark different stages of capitalism.

The early stage of mercantile capitalism laid the foundations for capitalism as a social system by establishing the ideological, philosophical, legal, institutional, scientific, technological, cultural and social foundations, i.e. the social infrastructures for commodity production. Mercantile capitalism transformed into industrial capitalism from the late eighteenth century until the end of the nineteenth century. Industrial capitalism, marked by the Industrial Revolution and the Empire system, was national in that the nation-state provided the institutional umbrella for economy and civil society, competitive in that it was marked by rivalries between capitalists and other capitalist states and industrial in that it was driven by manufacturing. This youthful National-Competitive-Industrial (NCI) capitalism restructured and reconstituted the infrastructures for commodity production in the NCI stage, building on the foundations laid during the mercantile stage. By the turn of the twentieth century NCI capitalism collapsed under the weight of its own economic expansion, internecine rivalries and nationalism resulting in two world wars, economic crises and institutional breakdown. The breakdown of capitalism in the early twentieth century afforded opportunities for a wide range of social movements that challenged capitalism including socialist movements in the heartlands of capitalism, Western Europe and the US, the anti-colonial movements, movements of indigenous peoples and much more.

The capitalism that was reconstructed from the ruins of the world wars was *qualitatively* different, indeed the very opposite of the youthful NCI capitalism. The ageing capitalism that was reconstructed during and after the world wars was transnational (the opposite of nationalist capitalism), operated as monopolies (as opposed to competitive enterprises) and driven by finance and banking sectors (as opposed to manufacturing). Lenin, writing during the birth of these qualitative transformations which began at the turn of the twentieth century, described this new stage of TMF capitalism as 'the epoch of imperialism',[2] a phrase used throughout this book interchangeably with TMF capitalism. For Lenin, imperialism is an entire epoch not limited to the moment of its birth before and during the world war years, or reducible to economic relations exclusively. Imperialism as an entire epoch has not received the attention and emphasis it deserves in the vast scholarly and social movement literature on Lenin's writings about imperialism. Imperialism as an entire epoch entails, necessarily, a set of ideological, philosophical, legal, institutional, scientific, technological, social, cultural and other preconditions and presuppositions that are required for the economic relations under TMF capitalism to become systemic. An answer to the question *what do rights do in this world* must be located in the specific stage of capitalism, which for *us* is TMF capitalism. Rights scholarship and education at all levels reinforces classical conceptions of rights by drawing on European Enlightenment thinkers, constitutional histories and legal precedents to reinforce right claims in the *contemporary* world. This anachronistic understanding of rights warps interventions for social justice.

Capitalism is a generative mechanism that drives the manifest changes in society. Periodisation of capitalism helps to relate the transformations in the nature of capitalism to the manifest changes in the social infrastructures of capitalism. Throughout this book the term 'social infrastructure' is used to include a wide range of social conditions including the ideological, philosophical, legal, institutional, scientific, technological, social and cultural amongst others needed for capitalism to operate in systemic ways. To bring rights down to earth it is important to develop the analytical tools necessary to make the connections between the drivers of change and the manifest systemic changes. Human beings, as the philosopher Roy Bhaskar argues, are concept-dependent beings. Human beings inherit a repertoire of concepts that helps them to make sense of the world. Concepts are not fixed however. Concepts need to be constantly reviewed, revised, renewed, adapted and challenged to enable us to negotiate our way in a constantly changing world. To do that, concepts must be understood within the geo-historical contexts that produced them and the contexts that transformed them. This is as true for the concept of rights as any other.

If capitalism emerged and evolved in Western Europe what can we say about the rest of the world? As a social system founded on commodity production capitalism is an ever expanding phenomenon seeking to make, buy and sell commodities. Capitalism is constituted by internal relations at the national level and external relations at the international level with other states and enterprises. Capitalism has always relied on exploitative (neo-)colonial relations externally as much as it has relied on exploitative class relations internally. The former is necessary for sourcing resources needed for production and consumption at the cheapest possible prices and the latter for extracting maximum productivity from labour. The nation-state remains the key institution that mediates internal class relations and external (neo-)colonial relations of capitalism.

Internally, the nation-state acts as a state unto its diverse and divided citizenry, making laws and maintaining itself as a centralised apparatus with capacities to command and control. Externally, vis-à-vis other states, it acts as a nation, speaking with a singular will in the name of all its citizens. The nation-state includes, must include, ideological, philosophical, legal, institutional, scientific, technological, cultural and social functions. The nation-state requires finance from economic actors, popular support to the extent feasible and possible, a police and military apparatus, personnel and bureaucracy to operate as a centralised institution and speak as a nation in international affairs with a single *will*. It needs ideological domination that commits its diverse citizenry to the state for whatever reasons. The three-nodal constitution of capitalism on the axes of capital-class-colonies also characterises the epoch of imperialism. Capitalism would not be capitalism without the three-way relations. Unfortunately, scholars and social activists alike focus attention on manifest changes in the imperial-colonial relations and treat colonialism as a thing of the past, a relation that ended with the implosion of empires during the world wars. If we consider colonialism as a categorical relation of capitalism, as its external relations, comparable to class relations internally, it becomes possible to go beyond a semantical understanding of colonialism and address the substance of relations between imperial-capitalist states and subordinate nations, and their transformations throughout the different stages of capitalism. During different phases of capitalism, the *character* of the relationship between capital-class-colonies has undergone major reworking. Institutional relationships with the colonies during the NCI stage under the Empire system were restructured in the epoch of imperialism. Class relations and colonial relations must be understood in their historical specificities during each of these stages. Periodised understanding is all the more necessary for social justice movements seeking to change the world as it enables them to understand the continuities and the changes in the world.

The modern nation-state has also undergone transformations in form and substance during each stage of capitalism including the epoch of imperialism. The modern nation-state is a legal entity, a creature of the constitution and a right-bearer. It cannot, however, be reduced entirely to its juridical features, a fallacy that is deeply embedded in social movement thinking. The reconstitution of the state in the epoch of imperialism has transformed the institution from political sovereigns in the seventeenth and eighteenth centuries into risk managers in a global political economy in the twentieth century, a reconstitution considered at length in Chapter 7. Social movements need to grasp what is entailed in these transformations when they make right claims. The legal attributes of nation-states at a general level notwithstanding, states have different capacities and different *wills* that arise from their geo-historical substance which shape their institutional architectures.[3] These distinctions between form and substance of states, the juridical and institutional attributes of states become particularly relevant in the epoch of imperialism, as the chapters in Part II show.

From its inception capitalism has an internationalist as well as a nationalist character. Historically, a particular capitalist nation has played a leadership role in the international expansion of modern capitalism during different stages of capitalism. Leadership of capitalist states entails the capacity to lead in developing the social infrastructures necessary for capitalism during that epoch. For example, the Dutch Republic 'liberated' itself from Spanish rule and established itself as the international centre for trade and commerce during the mercantile period. The Dutch Republic led capitalist development by acting as the entrepôt for merchants, innovating commercial instruments for commodity trade, shipping, inventories, patents, merchant banking, and institutions like the modern central bank, stock markets and commodity markets. Above all, the Dutch Republic led the way in the innovation of a new type of state (novel in largely feudal Europe) – as a federation of a number of political units united by economic interests with decentralised political and cultural institutions.[4] These innovations by the Dutch Republic provided the institutional and political conditions for the development of social infrastructures during the epoch of mercantilism in other European countries.

Britain played a leadership role during the epoch of NCI capitalism, leading the innovations in the social infrastructures for the Empire system in the eighteenth and nineteenth centuries. The US took over the mantle of leadership of the capitalist world during the world wars and continues to lead the G7 states, the OECD states, Second and Third World states and international affairs more generally in the epoch of imperialism. US exceptionalism is written into the architecture of the epoch just as Dutch and British exceptionalisms were written into the architectures of the epochs of mercantilism and industrialism. The chapters in this book illuminate the leadership role of the US in shaping the normative, legal and institutional aspects of rights in the current epoch.

Rights belong to the normative world however. If dissolved into political economy, the legal and institutional preconditions and presuppositions of political-economy of capitalism become invisible. If, on the contrary, the distance between rights in the normative world and the changes in the political economy remain too wide, rights lose their connectivity to the real world. For rights to remain connected to the real world at all times, our understanding of rights must remain tuned into and sensitive to the changes in the political economy without dissolving one into the other or treating them as distinct unrelated domains. Interventions for structural economic and political changes presuppose an understanding of the 'nature of the beast' as it were, how capitalism functions, how it responds and what makes it tick. Knowledge of the linkages between the normative world of rights and the real world of capitalism in the epoch of imperialism is necessary for social movements to evaluate what is necessary and what is possible in actions for transformative social change.[5] Having considered the epoch of imperialism as the generative conditions for rights in the contemporary world we can turn to the normative world of rights.

LIBERALISM AND THE POWER OF PROMISE

Why are rights so resilient? The answer to this question lies in liberalism's power of promise. The resilience of liberalism in popular imaginations may be attributed to the fact that rights, a founding concept in liberal thought, promises the possibility of something but does not guarantee the thing itself. The right to property does not guarantee a home to a homeless person. Quite simply, it means if a person has money they may buy property if they choose to. The right to life does not exclude the death penalty, it simply means, in order to take a person's life certain procedures must be followed. The lure of rights invites people to act in particular ways by inviting them to believe that the promise of rights will be realised. Liberal societies invite people to hand over their possessions, land, labour, natural resources, money, whatever on the promise that by doing so they could improve their conditions tomorrow.[6] The possibilities held out by rights are invariably constrained by context and institutional locations of people. Besides, tomorrow is always uncertain and unknowable. Yet liberalism's power of promise is such that the uncertain possibilities of tomorrow are more alluring than the certainty of the present.

This power of promise that makes tomorrow more alluring than today is founded on the hiatus between the real world and the thought-world in liberalism. In the thought-world, the critique of rights, the reformulations, restatements and reinterpretations of rights, remain battles of ideas that take place in the minds of individuals. In the minds of individuals, the threads that connect ideas to reality become at best opaque and tenuous and at worst they appear transcendental and exalted. The battlefield of ideas, when disengaged from reality, can be an exciting one however. In the world of ideas anything is possible, even 'Another World is Possible'.[7] The world of imaginations is not constrained or bounded by the limitations of the real world. This way of battling problems of the real world in the imagined world of ideas is the hallmark of liberalism.

Liberalism as a mode of thought presupposes that ideas are products of human mind and human reason. Liberals argue that in order to change the world, we need to refine, reinterpret and reformulate ideas, theories and philosophies. Inevitably, therefore, liberals seek the source of ideas in other thinkers of the past going back to Socrates and beyond. Nothing disrupts and contaminates beautiful thoughts as much as the real world, and this applies to our ideas about rights. How social movements understand the *relationship* between the thought-world and the real world, the concept of rights and what they do in the world, marks the difference between liberal and non-liberal modes of thought. Unable to grasp the relationship between rights and what rights do in the world, critical scholars and social movements lapse into the hypocrisy argument to explain the gaps between the normative and real world of rights.

Hypocrisy arguments juxtapose what liberals say, or have said, and what they do or did, i.e. the professed values and real actions. For example, John Locke, the patriarch of classical liberalism who argued for rights, citizenship and freedoms, including the right to rebellion as universal rights, did not include slaves, the 'rabble' and 'vagabonds', i.e. the urban poor and pauperised peasantry in England in his concept of the universal 'Man'. He was a shareholder in the Royal African Company, a world-leading British company engaged in the slave trade, and as secretary of the Council for Trade and Plantations he was engaged in expansion of colonial settlements and expulsion of indigenous peoples from lands in the Americas from 1673 to 1674.[8] More recently, Hannah Arendt, a critical philosopher writing in the post-WWII political environment of social revolutions and national liberation struggles, celebrated the colonisation of North America and the republican government that the American Revolution established as 'perhaps the greatest, certainly the boldest, enterprise of European mankind' and argued that the problem with slavery is inherent in the institution itself and not the 'perversion of heart' or 'dominance of self-interest' of the

American settlers.[9] Why did the settlers choose an institution that was inherently inhuman and repressive?

These types of juxtapositions highlight the paradoxical nature of the theoretical claims that liberal, even critical thinkers make and their responses to the problems of the real world. Paradoxes signal the existence of unresolved theoretical and methodological problems. Often an easy road to take from the hypocrisy critique is to attribute moral inadequacies and ethical lapses to individuals. To argue that the most prominent thinkers in modern history were hypocrites says little about the enduring influence of their thought decades, even centuries later, or about the reasons why they excluded so many aspects of social reality from their universal theories or why they found it necessary to articulate their interests in universalist terms. Ethics is by no means an unimportant or a secondary issue. Ethics is, however, necessitated by social relationships, and social relationships in turn are a condition for human existence. In other words, ethics too have a basis in the materiality of this world where human beings must evaluate social relationships and locate one's actions within them in ever changing social contexts. The idea that human existence occurs in distinct spheres makes our economic modes of existence, capitalism and market relationships of themselves morally neutral.[10]

In the liberal world view a human being lives in multiple spheres of existence: economic, social, cultural, familial and so on. Ethics is one of the many spheres of human existence. In this view of human existence, the relationships between different spheres of existence must be, can only be worked out in the thought-world where there is freedom to combine and permutate theories, ideas and concepts. In the real world, people do not live their lives in distinct spheres. Rather they experience life as 'unity in diversity', a unified conjuncture of all the spheres converging at particular moments in time and place in specific ways. In the liberal mode of thought it is for us as individuals to determine what combinations and permutations of relationships between the economic, social and personal spheres we wish to establish. Such liberal modes of thought are voluntarist fallacies that obfuscate the reasons why some ideas become powerful and others do not. To illuminate the nexus between the theoretical arguments and the social forces driving those arguments, this book highlights the positions from which influential theorists driving changes in the international order speak and write.

DIVISION OF LABOUR: THE THOUGHT-WORLD
AND THE REAL WORLD

Rights are concepts, however, and belong to the thought-world. If human beings are concept-dependent, then ideas, concepts and theories are essential as guides to action. When the distance between the conceptual world and the real world of life, work and activities become remote, ideas appear to acquire autonomy. It becomes possible to speak of ideas as if it were a product of the thought-world. The more disengaged ideas are from reality, the less useful they become to those who wish to change the world. For people who are happy with the state of the world or only marginally dissatisfied with it, the distance between the conceptual and real world does not matter. Social movements and activist scholars, it is fair to assume, are unhappy with the state of the world as it is and engage with rights with a view to changing the state of affairs. Locating rights in the materiality of the world is a challenge for social movements and activist scholars therefore.

Marx and Engels attribute the apparent autonomy of ideas and their disconnection with the materiality of the world to social division of labour in the historical development of societies.[11] Division of labour confines human lives, their modes of existence, to particular segments of society and produces a gap between consciousness born of experience and the reality of the world.[12] The division between mental and physical labour is most significant as it produces a segment in society, a social class that specialises in knowledge production. Scholars turn language into an independent domain and give thought an independent existence in that domain.[13] Interconnections between empirical knowledge produced in each segment of society is made speculatively in the realm of thought-world by refining and changing the content of words in the domain of language.[14] Making connections between thoughts and reality is not about changing the meanings of words but about grasping the interconnections between different segments of the social division of labour as they really exist. Division of labour, Marx and Engels argue, is the same as private property – the first refers to activity and the second to the product of activity.[15] The gap between consciousness and reality produces what they call the 'illusion of the epoch'.[16]

Since the beginning of the twentieth century further divisions of mental labour have expanded exponentially, with fissiparous divisions of natural and social sciences into numerous disciplinary specialisations, emergence of new disciplines (e.g. sociology, psychology, management, media studies and many others), sub-fields within disciplines and expertise in specific aspects within a sub-field of a discipline. Each science, discipline, sub-field and expertise produces its own vocabulary, methodology and thought-world. The divisions in mental labour have come concurrently with an exponential expansion of divisions of labour in the real world: the worlds of Fordist and post-Fordist production within industry, international division of labour within global commodity chains, the divisions between banking, trade and manufacturing sectors, further sub-dividing into banking, insurance and finance sectors, and so on. Thought itself becomes private property framed by rights like copyrights, patents and databases to be bought and sold. These divisions in processes of production, distribution and consumption have come together with the expansion in scales of operation of the activities.

Beginning as local activities of merchants in the fifteenth century, the scale of production, distribution and consumption has expanded throughout the history of capitalism. Mercantilist capitalism and divisions of labour within emerging modernist states expanded the scale of production and led to the Empire system. The Empire system expanded the scales of production, distribution and consumption by introducing new divisions of labour within empires between capitalist centres and colonial peripheries as appropriate for NCI capitalism. The end of the world wars inaugurated a new phase that integrated the capitalist states – the Allies and Axis powers – and further expanded the scale of production, distribution and consumption based on new and more extensive international divisions of labour. The 'Free World' and the 'socialist world' became two main camps after WWII. The end of the Cold War opened up the possibilities of further restructuring of production, consumption and distribution and new divisions of labour on global scales.

The more fissiparous the divisions of labour get, the greater is the segmentation of markets. The demand for evermore rights discussed in Chapter 1 mirrors the segmentation of markets and the consequent fragmentation of social relations. The structure of social movements also mirrors the segmented markets and fragmented societies. The chapters in the book expand on the ways in which right claims hem-in social transformations within liberal imaginations pre-empting the emergence of new alternatives. The international divisions of labour present difficult questions for social movements that have a communitarian vision for society and seek to unite movements with diverse interests. The expanded divisions of labour on global scales presuppose institutional orders facilitative of transnational activities in *each* market segment. Transnational corporations, global financial markets, foreign direct investments, international financial institutions, International Organisations, international law, international division of labour are some of the hallmarks of twentieth-century capitalism. Rights, one must imagine, must be located within these historical developments if they are to remain close to the ground and connected to modes of existence of people. The 'illusion of the epoch' suggests otherwise.

THE 'ILLUSION OF THE EPOCH' OF IMPERIALISM

The illusion of the epoch of imperialism suggests that it is possible to reconcile liberal democracy and TMF capitalism and that the two are not inherently incompatible. Many social movements direct their energies to environmental, labour, economic, cultural, indigenous peoples or other problems. Often, social movements and activist scholars identify, correctly, the causes of social problems and the actors responsible for the state of affairs as in the case of land rights discussed in Chapter 1. Their critique highlights injustices based on empirical research and deconstruction strategies that are often pertinent and many are excellent. Their prognosis, however, canvasses refinement or restatement of rights and gets mired in contradictions and inconsistencies. The tension between diagnosis at the empirical level and prognosis at the conceptual level is symptomatic of the mismatch between conceptual lenses used to understand the world and the realities of TMF capitalism. It reveals inadequacies in the theories and concepts used to understand and explain reality. Have rights to racial equality ended racism? Have labour rights ended slave labour in new forms under new names? Do improved regimes of rights bridge the reality gap? Or does racism, slavery, discrimination of women reappear in new forms, become invisibilised and ever more subtle with the redefinition of rights? Should we settle for incremental improvements in the conditions of life or should we take a more 'root and branch' approach to social justice? These types of questions dominate debates within social movements. Rights have become a conundrum as arguments circle around various binaries: economic versus 'human' rights, individual versus collective rights, European versus non-European rights, moral versus legal rights, theories versus practices of rights, normative versus institutionalised rights and so on.[17]

Critical scholarship on rights continues to grow and deconstruct rights. Social movements often seek to craft their political, organisational and campaign strategies based on correct diagnosis but become cautious or uncertain about their prognosis for the future. Hand in hand with the expansion of the deconstruction of rights, there is increasing angst about alternatives and divisions within movements about the directions social movements should take. In the 1990s and early 2000s, these debates within anti-globalisation movements often crystallised as the 'fix-it' or 'nix-it' positions referred to in Chapter 2.[18] The 'fix it' or 'nix-it' arguments were responsible in a large measure for the critique of rights during that period. Political movements in contrast, against repressive governments for example, reaffirmed and reargued the case for rights. Rights scepticism on the one hand and rights affirmation on the other have made social movements increasingly uncertain about the efficacy of their right claims. Frequently, excellent diagnosis of problems ends up with prescriptions for greater monitoring, vigilance, protests and active direct participation in political and social protests. In doing so, they base their prognosis on the 'illusion of the epoch'.

The 'illusion of the epoch' is founded on boxing in economic issues from political issues and political issues from ideological and cultural ones. The 'illusion of the epoch' makes it problematic to establish the inter-relationships between the domains of economics, politics and ideology in ways that explain contemporary realities. This book argues that the 'illusion of the epoch' is no longer possible, if ever it was. Rights-based democracy as understood in classical liberal theory and contemporary imperialism is fundamentally incompatible as the chapters in Part II show. The 'illusion of the epoch' leads social movements to believe that by refining or reprioritising rights it is possible to reconcile imperialism and social justice. In contrast to previous epochs, in the epoch of imperialism, capitalism's capacities to expand atrophies. The atrophying of capitalism raises *new* questions about the future of societies and peoples. Atrophying capitalism means rights no longer have the capacity to do what they have always done historically. *What have rights always done?*

WHAT HAVE RIGHTS ALWAYS DONE?

Rights are conceptual tools that create legal subjects capable of forming contractual relationships. If there is no capitalism without commodity production, and no commodity production without commodity exchanges, there cannot be commodity exchanges without contracts and no contractual relations without two right-bearing parties who are entitled to give and receive, buy and sell. The fissiparous divisions of labour means more and more social relationships must be established externally through contractual relations between different segments of society. To say anything can be bought and sold – one's body, a woman's womb, child-care, carbon emissions, risks, ready-meals, debts, whatever – is to say all those things can be the subject matter of contractual agreements. Contracts presuppose the existence of one party who possesses something and able to exchange it and another who is able to receive it in exchange for something else. Contracts are abstract legal forms however. In themselves contractual forms have no specific content, no material or immaterial goods or services that form the substance of contracts. Rights are the recognition by law and state of tangible and intangible things that right-bearing parties may exchange.

Rights in liberal theory are conceptual 'empty shells'.[19] Nevertheless, following Ian Shapiro, they have an underlying grammar.[20] The grammar of rights involves a set of assertions about entitlements that are both formal and relational. Rights invariably involve assertions about i) the subject of entitlements, ii) the substance of entitlement, iii) the basis of entitlements and iv) the purpose of entitlements.[21] These assertions presuppose philosophical ideas about human life (subject of entitlements), human relationships with nature and labour (substance of entitlements), the justifications for entitlements (basis for entitlement) and objectives for claiming entitlements (social purpose of entitlements). The grammar of rights enables the 'empty shell' to be filled and refilled with different subjects, substance, basis and purposes at different times in varying combinations. However, the underlying grammar is the grammatical structure of the language of contracts.

For right-bearing subjects, freedom means the freedom to determine the basis and purpose of contracts. Liberal theories generally distinguish between contractarian and utilitarian traditions in rights. Whereas the contractarian tradition is generally seen as being more engaged with rights, the utilitarian tradition is considered to be instrumentalist in character. This distinction has framed much of the debates within social movements about what rights ought or ought not to be. As Shapiro notes, the distinction is misleading as '[t]he nature of the term "right" is such that reference to the substance and purposes of rights is inevitably entailed by its use'.[22] The chapters in the book illuminate how the 'empty shell' of rights is understood and used by different actors for different purposes.

Rights presuppose institutions capable of giving effect to them. Social movements frequently claim that it is possible to change asymmetrical social relations *within* existing institutions. For example, rights transform one's capacity to work into one's property which can be exchanged for a price in the labour market. Collective bargaining rights may appear to increase the price of labour when wages increase but do little to alter the modes of appropriation that create the conditions in the labour markets in the first place. Rights have the capacities to organise and reorganise modes of appropriation depending on what types of rights are invoked by who and when.

In themselves rights are also abstract legal forms. In theory, anyone can enter into a contract with anyone else to exchange the things over which they have an established right. In practice, however, they must have something to give in return for something else. Rights transform social relationships based on ties to land and people, nature and culture into exchange relationships based on market transactions. In classical liberalism, the freedom to contract and to be the subject of rights is synonymous with human freedoms and therefore inalienable. The identity of buyers and sellers becomes warped as the division of labour expands, commodities become 'virtual' or fictional and exchanges become international, as for example trade in futures, risks, debts or currency, or at the personal level, surrogacy, sperm and organ trade.[23]

Rights in the thought-world appear exalted precisely because they are abstracted from the world of ownership and exchange, production and consumption, buying and selling. In the liberal mode of thought rights are deeply ideological because they conceal rather than reveal what rights actually do in the real world. On the one hand, critical scholars and activists complain about commodification that puts money value on everything. On the other hand, they affirm the rights to tangible and intangible 'things'. Right claims assert that people have an inherent right to the things that are regularly appropriated from them: life, labour, nature, culture and so on. These right claims are in fact mirror images of commodification in that both presuppose proprietary relationships to the thing. They do not challenge the idea of social relations as contractual relations but rather the argument takes the form: 'we are entitled to own this thing, not you'.

CONTRACTS AS SOCIAL RELATIONS

When rights are brought down from the exalted world of liberal critique in the battlefield of ideas to the world of TMF capitalism it becomes apparent what rights actually do/have done in the world. They create contracting subjects and endow them freedom of exchange. Rights are located *within* social relations, not outside them. Employment, fracking, homosexual relationships are social relations between people and between nature and people. Pre-capitalist societies validated social norms entailed in social relationships by drawing on transcendental sources: god, traditions, ancestors, whatever. Capitalism substitutes transcendental sources with law to validate social relations. Law establishes social relations between people and between people and nature by establishing rights. Social movements (except those that call for armed struggles as the means to social justice) argue that social relations can be changed by changing the law. This is akin to putting the cart before the horse as the saying goes. Following Evgeny Pashukanis, social relations precede legal relations. Merchants engaged in exchanging goods and commodities first, the law of contracts regularised and systematised their activities later. Indeed, social relations create the necessity for legal relations and conditions them.[24]

European Enlightenment thinkers used contracts as the metaphor for *all* social relationships. In the post-WWII era contracts are no longer a metaphor in social philosophy. Rights in the post-WWII world order are international in scope and established by *real* treaties and contracts. Contracts form the *real* basis of the post-WWII order. International contracts between states and between states and International Organisations set the framework and the plenary conditions within which nation-states must enact laws and people exercise their democratic freedoms. Sir Henry Maine argued that societies progressed from status-based relationships to contract-based relationships. If this is true, then post-WWII societies have reached the pinnacle of contract-based relationships.

Pre-capitalist societies were founded on the organic unity of nature and people.[25] Pre-modern rights and social institutions were 'corporatist' in that they were founded on ascending and descending order rights and obligations between constitutive components of larger social units: estates, tribes, clans, nations considered as a whole. European Enlightenment thinkers challenged these status-based relationships arguing that contractual relations are freer as they are between individuals and provide individuals with choices. Capitalism as a system based on commodity production ruptured the relations between nature and people, displaced people from places, and dissolved communities into disaggregated individuals. Pre-modern rights allocated a *place* to people and nature whereas modern rights *displace* people and nature.[26] Commodity production reconstituted relations between people and nature and people *inter se* as exchange relations based on property rights. Labour itself became a 'natural' private property endowed in the body of a person and could be bought and sold and used to acquire other forms of property.

Rights in classical liberalism mirror the wider historical transformations. Rights in classical liberalism introduced dualistic relations between nature and people and between contracting individuals which in turn introduced all sorts of dualisms in society and social theory. Classical liberalism is founded on the dualism between state and citizen, national and international, economic and social, public and private, nature and culture, body and mind, material and moral, science and art as distinct domains. The dualistic institutional architecture characteristic of earlier periods of capitalism has undergone radical transformations in the epoch of imperialism. In the epoch of imperialism, in contrast, *integration* and *interrelatedness* are the keywords.

The global scales of operations in the 'epoch' of imperialism are made possible by legal 'persons': transnational corporations, International Organisations, global think tanks, international standard-setting organisations, universities and so on. These legal 'persons' are *also* right-bearing persons alongside natural persons. The principal contradiction in rights in the epoch of imperialism *is* between rights of legal 'persons' and natural persons. The revolving doors between these legal 'persons' – the corporations, states and NGOs and such – have made conventional assumptions about citizen-state relationships and representative democracy problematic. States today are no longer Adam Smith's 'night watchman'; instead they are risk managers in a global economy, an argument expanded in Chapters 6 and 7. Public contracting, public-private partnerships and such have rendered the boundaries between public and private law opaque. The corporatist structure of post-WWII capitalist states integrates all segments of society as 'stakeholders' in the economy including corporations, states, labour and civil society organisations into a totality. Polanyi argued that classical capitalism dis-embedded the economy from society and set up antithetical relationships between the two. TMF capitalism re-embeds *society into economy*. TMF capitalism integrates Economy-State-Civil Society, the institutional tripod of capitalist societies in the seventeenth and eighteenth centuries. The integration subsumes the place of right-bearing natural persons within those of legal 'persons'. *This subsuming is the problem of rights in the epoch of imperialism.*

The reconstitution of relations between Economy-State-Civil Society began during the world war years when the need to mobilise the entire society for war, the large-scale scientific and technological innovations needed for war and the collaboration of corporations and military establishments integrated institutions. The gigantic military-industrial-technology-finance-media complexes we see today are the result of institutional *aggregation* not disaggregation of different components of society as was the case with classical liberalism. These distinctions between liberalism before and after the world wars are expanded in the chapters in Part II.

Rights in the context set out above are not only about individual freedoms to contract between formally equal subjects. Rights operate on multiple scales – at the macro levels of relations between legal persons – states, corporations, International Organisations, trusts, civil society organisations, NGOs – and at micro levels as relations between natural and legal persons. In relation to legal entities, corporations, states, NGOs, trusts and such, rights are about freedom of contracts. The subjects of contracts are qualitatively different from small groups of individuals engaged in trade or manufacture of goods and commodities in the previous periods of capitalism. Contracts between legal persons in the epoch of TMF capitalism organise and reorganise the *whole of society*. Within legal 'persons'/entities, i.e. within corporations, states, other types of organisations, rights operate on a micro-scale to assign individuals a place within those institutions. For example, employment rights assign an individual a place within a corporation at the micro level whereas WTO agreements or public sector contracts enable corporate entities and states to order and reorder entire societies through contractual agreements at the macro level.

For the individual, their assigned place, although formally contractual, resonates with the pre-capitalist relations of ascending and descending rights and obligations of the feudal era. The epoch of imperialism brings back corporatist forms of the feudal era under new conditions of divisions of labour within corporations, within states and within the international order. In the epoch of imperialism rights have embedded individuals/natural persons in ever narrower divisions of labour that limit entitlements, make freedom an illusion and choice a wishful desire. In contrast, they endow legal persons with extensive freedoms to alter and change the conditions for human life at the 'will' of legal 'persons'. The corporatist conception of the world, as the chapters in the book show, is captured in popular imaginations by phrases like 'our common world' and 'one world' popularised by the Brundtland Commission report, 'we the people of the United Nations' in the preamble to the UN Charter, and the imagery of a 'borderless world' and the 'global village' since the 'fall of the Wall'.

The dualisms that rights introduced in the past have longer and more tenacious roots in ancient European intellectual traditions that deserve at least a passing mention not least because they lubricate the transitions in liberal modes of thought during different historical periods. The Platonic division of the world into a transcendental world of perfect ideas and the real world as an imperfect imitation of the perfect idea is a peculiarly European cosmology and lubricates the transition to modern liberal thought. Dualist European cosmologies echo through the European Enlightenment which appeared with the rise of European capitalism. The hiatus between the lofty ideals in rights-talk and the stark inequalities in the real transactions between people that we see today has deeper roots therefore.

Non-European civilisations had very different cosmological conceptions that guided the establishment and transformations of social institutions. 'Had' is used here in the past tense because European capitalism transformed history into world history and dispersed its ideas and modes of thought around the world. The authenticity of European cosmology and its impacts on non-European social orders have been challenged for as long as colonialism and capitalism have existed. A comparative cosmology is beyond the scope of this book. The point is raised here to alert the reader to the fact that the concept of rights, indeed even the word 'rights', is absent in many non-European intellectual traditions.[27] The point is flagged up here also because a large proportion of time, space and resources devoted to engagement with rights within social movements today are in relation to the problems of the Third World where abject human misery and dehumanisation makes social justice and social transformation an urgent necessity.

INTERNATIONALISATION AND LEGALISATION OF RIGHTS

The extension of a regime of rights to the Third World is, in historical terms, relatively recent. Most Third World countries and its peoples did not have rights under the Empire system. The *internationalisation* of rights began during the world war years and embedded in the 'New World Order' after the end of WWII. While some form of international law existed prior to the world wars, its scope and meaning was restricted by the supremacy of the sovereignty principle on the one hand and the fact that it applied primarily to relations between European nation-states on the other. The establishment of an *international institutional* order founded on states as right-bearing subjects in international law is a distinctive product of the world wars.

The League of Nations kick-started the process of institutionalisation as a way out of capitalism's worst economic crisis. The imperatives of internationalisation, a necessary condition for TMF capitalism, created the need for institutionalisation. Internationalisation presupposes the existence of right-bearing subjects with capacities to enter into *international* contractual relationships. The League was a historic first in establishing an institutional framework for international law. International Organisations and international law, as we know them, bear the imprint of the world wars. The New World Order at the end of WWII formalised the institutional framework for the nascent TMF capitalism that emerged at the turn of the twentieth century bringing down, in the process, the institutional edifice of NCI capitalism. The world war years were a period of frenetic institution building whereas the period after the crises of the late 1960s was a period of frenetic law-making.

Prior to the world wars it is difficult to speak of international law as we do today. The dominant international institutional order was the Empire system under the four Great Powers: the UK, France, Russia and Austria.[28] The world wars retained the Great Power structure of power under the Empire system but changed the composition of the Great Powers replacing Austria with America and included China in the 1970s ending prolonged disputes about its status. The world wars universalised the institution of the state as a legal entity and formalised its juridical attributes in the Montevideo Convention on Rights and Duties of States, 1933.[29] The Third World was incorporated into the international interstate system as and when formal and juridical decolonisation occurred beginning during the world wars and peaking in the 1960s.

The League and later the UN drew heavily on the law and policies of Empires to craft the new international legal order.[30] From its inception the post-WWII International Organisations established a 'corporatist' world order that conceptualised the world as a totality founded on asymmetrical distribution of powers between states *inter se* and states and institutions. These are qualitative changes for which there are no precedents in classical liberalism.

Rights have always been the mechanism for establishing institutions. During the mercantile periods rights were instrumental in establishing modern institutions like the nation-state, capitalist private property, standing army and police, modern markets and such. International rights establish international institutions. What is the place of rights in the post-WWII world which is the theatre for activism and activist scholars today? Who were the actors who advocated internationalisation of rights and why? What were the imperatives for legalisation of international relations and internationalisation of rights? How did Third World social movements engage with the idea of rights historically and how do they engage with it now? What has brought about the changes in their understanding of rights if at all? How did the socialist critique of liberalism inform the socialist movements? And how did their understanding of rights transform or reify the institutional order? Did the old Empire system simply vanish? Where did ideas of 'human' rights and global governance, so widely used today, materialise from? Such questions invite us to examine the rise of new liberalisms of the Keynesian and neoliberal types during and after the world war years and to interrogate the extent to which classical and post-WWII liberalisms share or deviate from philosophical assumptions, political and social practices, and more importantly shared understandings of freedom and democracy in the European Enlightenment of the mercantile era and in the epoch of imperialism. Since the 1990s movements for social justice have tended to be critical of neoliberalism but remain ambivalent about Keynesian liberalism. The chapters in this book highlight the synergies between the two liberalisms in the post-WWII era.

THE 'HUMAN' IN RIGHTS

The prefix 'human' to rights is a post-WWII phenomenon. Critical scholars argue that 'human' rights emerged variously in 1945 with its incorporation in the UN Charter, in the 1970s in the course of US-led democracy promotion programmes and in the 1990s after the 'fall of the Wall'.[31] These dates reveal particular theoretical orientations that are important. It is not necessary, for the purposes of this book, to digress into the history of 'human' rights. It is important to note, however, that the prefix 'human' to rights is accepted un-problematically by mainstream and critical scholars alike. The prefix 'human' to rights conceals what is entailed in rights in the epoch of imperialism.

European Enlightenment thinkers wrote about rights as a complete concept that included property rights as well as social ('human') rights. They engaged with the relationships between property and social questions to develop general theories about rights. Indeed, their starting point for engagement with rights was to provide explanations and justifications for the origins and (unequal) distributions of private property. Arguing against feudal property privileges on the one hand and justifying its appropriation in the wake of widespread displacement from land and pauperisation of the peasantry on the other, European Enlightenment thinkers turned to labour and labour theories of values to provide unified justifications for property and social rights. Indeed, as John Locke argued, labour itself was the justification for private property, the reason why some were entitled to more wealth than others. By the turn of the twentieth century capitalist property relations had become a 'natural' condition of the world and needed no special explanations or justifications. The rise of the corporatist state during the world war years, and immediately thereafter, incorporated labour and indeed the wider society into corporate property relations as 'stakeholders'. The natural human person now confronted an unparalleled rival in the legal corporate person.[32]

Neither the justifications for private property nor labour theories of value were of much concern in the reformulation of rights in the twentieth century. Instead the focus of social theory shifted to the legal personality of corporations on the one hand and market governance on the other. In the early years of the post-WWII era a great deal of legal and social science research and practice was devoted to developing the basis for recognition of corporations, governance of large organisations, and the basis for attributing personhood to legal entities. During the interwar period capitalists, socialists, fascists and anti-imperialists alike opposed classical liberalism, obviously from different perspectives and for different purposes.[33] As early as 1924, John Maynard Keynes, the English aristocrat and economist whose theories and political interventions played a critical role in the revival of capitalism from the ashes of the world wars, pronounced that laissez-faire liberalism was dead.[34] The rise of specialist fields of Law and Economics in the 1930s and 'human' rights in the 1940s as two distinct spheres in law and regulation introduced a disjuncture in property/economic rights and social/'human' rights.[35]

Even as Keynesian liberals reconstructed post-WWII institutions during and after the world wars, networks of economists, philosophers, sociologists, corporate personnel and industry think tanks began reworking and recasting legal relations in classical liberalism in networks like the Walter Lippmann Colloquium (CWL) and the Mont Pelerin Society (MPS) that became champions of neoliberalism. After the end of WWII influential institutions like the Chicago School of Economics and the London School of Economics became the crucibles where classical liberalism was re-scripted and re-enacted in the new avatar of neoliberalism.[36] These developments introduced what appeared on the surface as antithetical: economic rights versus 'human' rights. Equally, reinterpretations of liberalism forced the natural person to accept the corporate person as an 'equal' in the eyes of the law at least and live with it. The natural and legal persons, both, shared 'equally' property rights and increasingly 'human' rights. The transformation of the corporation from an association of merchants to safeguard against trading risks during the mercantile era to an autonomous personified being in its own right with human 'will' is an attribute of TMF capitalism. More than in any other jurisdiction the US Supreme Court played an instrumental role in investing corporations with constitutional rights and recognising natural and corporate persons as right-bearing citizens, something classical liberalism invested only in natural persons.[37]

Scientific and technological innovations in communication and management sciences and organisational and social psychology during the world wars were driven by militarism. Military imperatives gave birth to a number of new disciplines and new knowledge necessitated by the need for command and control of not only the war apparatus of the military but of the wider society for the mobilisation of economy and society for the war efforts. These innovations and disciplinary knowledge were shared by states and corporate persons.[38] Endowed with capacities for centralised command and control by scientific developments, twentieth-century corporations could henceforth, like the states, act as autonomous persons, with an independent 'will' vis-à-vis states, other corporations, other legal entities and above all, natural persons.

These legal, institutional, scientific and technological developments are necessary preconditions for transnationalisation of corporations and their capacities for monopolistic practices. Equally, these developments generate rights conundrums for activist scholars and social movements.

Post-WWII, liberalism whether of the Keynesian and neoliberal type, reverse a keystone in classical liberalism. Competition was the 'holy cow' of classical liberalism. States did not bail-out private economic actors or set up public sector undertakings and public-private partnerships. Post-WWII recovery was founded on the economic and institutional integration of Axis and Allied countries. The integration centralised coordination of economic policies in informal, quasi-legal and legal forums like the G7, OPEC, the Bank of International Settlement, organisations of industry regulators such as the Basel Committee of Bank Regulators and the International Organisation of Securities Commissions to coordinate and manage the regulatory aspects of TMF capitalism, as discussed in Chapters 6 and 7. The post-WWII corporatist states *partnered* the transnational banking and financial institutions and monopolistic corporations. These developments reversed the role of the state as referee between numerous competing economic and social actors within the nation-state. In the past 'state capture' by economic actors was considered deviance from norms. States as risk managers, public entrepreneurs, as *partners* in TMF capitalism *is* the ideological reversal of property rights in classical liberalism.

Hiving off property rights from 'human' rights promotes normative understandings of rights and obfuscates property rights. The obfuscation has led to widespread practices of *moral* evaluations of social problems and of rights as negative/positive binaries: property rights (negative)/'human' rights (positive); markets (negative)/people (positive); G7 states (negative)/Third World states (positive). These evaluations mystify the relations between the binaries and the unifying forces that hold the opposites together. The disjuncture between property rights and 'human' rights eased the process of internationalisation and institutionalisation of rights in the post-WWII era. The internationalisation and institutionalisation of property rights occurred in tandem with the internationalisation and institutionalisation of 'human' rights yet the interconnections between them were obscured by the disjuncture between property and 'human' rights. Consequently, where connections between 'human' and property rights are made, the attempt is to synthesise 'human' rights with changing forms of private property and the rights of new economic actors. For example, critical scholars and social movements have argued that 'human' rights can and should be read into the Articles of Association of the World Bank and IMF, that corporations are bound by international 'human' rights law, that states should pay heed to the 'human' rights in international diplomacy and so on (see Chapter 7).

The irony of these 'human' rights claims against corporations and economic actors is that the more legal 'persons' are required to behave like natural persons, to respect and comply with 'human' right responsibilities, the greater is the acceptance, recognition and reification of the hypostatised legal 'person' as an equal of the natural person. In other words, the more corporations are treated as if they are human, as personified entities and right-bearers, the more they become effectively 'human' and a rival to the natural person. The legal 'person' is a fictional person however. It does not share the ontological attributes of human life. For example, it is not subject to birth and death, it does not rely on nature to live, it does not have an emotional/psychological life and ethical evaluations are not conditioned by social relationships.[39] To put justice and freedom centre-stage of social movements it is necessary to probe the hiatus between property and 'human' rights on the one hand and the metonymical uses of legal and natural personhood on the other.

SOCIAL MOVEMENTS AND SOCIAL CHANGE

Definitions of social movements and distinctions between them abound in the literature on Social Movement Studies (SMS).[40] Social movements are zealous about maintaining their distance from NGOs. Third World social movements are zealous about marking the differences between them and the international counterparts. The chapters in this book consider all types of interventions for social change as 'social movements' and use specific terms like 'NGOs', Old Social Movements (OSM) and New Social Movements (NSM) or protest movements to draw attention to particular differences in their responses in a given context. The distinctions usually made in SMS literatures are not important for the purposes of this book which is to locate rights and its uses in the epoch of imperialism. Besides, there are many overlaps and synergies between different types of movements, too many to be mapped within the space of this book. Instead the book takes different types of inter- ventions by the NGOs, social movements, protest movements, networks and so on as part of a spectrum of liberal views about social change. There are three reasons for this. First, the distinctions between different types of interventions for social justice are based primarily on the differences in their modes of organising.[41] Protest movements focus on the importance of grassroots mobilisations to challenge power. Social movements organise campaigns on various issues and participate in networks but stay away from participating in the institutions of power, i.e. gaining a 'seat at the table'. NGOs canvass to bring about changes by working within institutions. This book is about rights. Regardless of their modes of organising, to the extent that all three types of interventions for social justice are informed by liberal thinking, the differences in their understanding of the nature of rights is one of degree and methods of organising.

Second, although distinct in the way the three types of interventions operate, at the macro level, the conditions for rights are set by legal 'persons' and the international contracts they enter into. There are synergies in the way different types of interventions use rights as well as differences therefore. The chapters draw attention to the synergies and/or the differences in the typologies of social movements as and when those differences become necessary to illuminate the arguments. Lastly, the label 'social movements' is problematic for considerations of rights and liberalism. Classical liberalism argued for protection of *political rights* to enable groups with diverse interests in society to compete and contend with each other and mobilise political actions in the public domain to influence the state. The undermining of the state and sovereignty principle, the corporatist integrated institutions with revolving doors between states, economic actors and civil society organisations, in the post-WWII order also undermines politics and the public sphere.

The shift in the language from *political* to *social* movements is not simply semantic but rather signifies the systematic undermining of politics in the epoch of imperialism. The NSMs that emerged in the leading centres of G7 states in the late 1960s used the term 'social' movements to distance them from the OSMs which were first and foremost movements for political change. The shift was part of legalisation of Economy-State-Civil Society relations since the late 1960s which until then were primarily political. The NSMs' critique of TMF capitalism is, not surprisingly, ambivalent about rights and its uses in the epoch of imperialism. Their differences notwithstanding, NSMs generally do not engage in political interventions to bring down TMF capitalism, through force or peaceful means.[42] OSMs in contrast do not subscribe to liberal modes of thought and continue to struggle for political change as if the 'nature of the beast' remains the same as it was one hundred years ago when socialist and anti-colonial movements intervened to pull down crisis-ridden NCI capitalism. The theoretical and organisational problems of OSMs are radically different in that they are not located in liberal imaginations. Instead the theoretical and organisational problems of OSMs relate to reassessments of the struggles for socialism and national liberation, a task that must await consideration another time.

Social movements in the Third World more than anywhere else are grounded in the social realities they are seeking to change. They are, for that reason, more anti-imperialist and historically grounded. The extraordinary levels of concerted global 'knowledge offensives' by knowledge institutions in the G7 states have 'bombarded' Third World social movements with conceptual and theoretical arguments that put them on the defensive even when they are sceptical about rights. Third World social movements associate liberal rights with historical experiences of colonialism and Empire. Yet they are unable to 'walk away' from rights. Third World social movements criticise the economics and politics of rights but embrace its ethics. It is precisely the hiatus between economics, politics and ethics that reifies rights. Liberalism, expelled through the front door, returns through the backdoor in Third World social movements. In the epoch of imperialism the struggle against capitalism *is* the struggle against imperialism and its ideology of rights.

PART II

Re-scripting Rights

4

International Election Monitoring: From 'Will of the People' to the 'Right to Free and Fair Elections'

Whenever those states which have been acquired have been accustomed to live under their own laws and in freedom, there are three courses for those who wish to hold them. The first is to ruin them, the next is to reside there in person, the third is to permit them to live under their own laws, drawing a regular payment from the state, and establishing within it a governing group which will keep it friendly to you. Because such a government, being created by the prince, knows that it cannot stand without his friendship and interest, it tries hard to support him. Therefore he who would keep a city accustomed to freedom will hold it more easily by the means of its own citizens than in any other way.
(Niccolò Machiavelli (1469–1527), *The Prince*, p. 11)[1]

Dominant narratives describe rights in evolutionary terms. First generation rights refer to seventeenth- and eighteenth-century rights on democracy and civil liberties, second generation rights to socio-economic rights introduced after WWII and third generation rights to group and collective rights arising from challenges to individualism of rights by Third World and indigenous peoples in the 1970s. Whatever happened to the so-called first generation rights four centuries later? This chapter examines representative democracy and elections and the next considers citizens' authority to revoke their mandates to public officials and political leaders to govern, both foundational ideas in European democracies. The emergence of the new 'right to free and fair elections' including its broader variation as 'right to democratic governance' as a legal right in international law[2] was made possible by the support of NSMs, INGOs and NGOs ostensibly to give effect to the 'will' of Third World peoples. The right to free and fair elections, this chapter argues, does the opposite. It rolls-back the rights to national self-determination, the basis for democracy in the Third World and rolls-in principles of imperial governance in new legal formats.

SOVEREIGNTY, SELF-DETERMINATION, INTERNATIONAL ELECTION MONITORING AND THE THIRD WORLD

The Emergence of International Election Monitoring

National elections are, as Arturo Santa-Cruz says, now international events – and 'international election monitoring (IEM) an institution-alized practice in world politics'.[3] IEMs became possible according to Santa-Cruz because of the 'synergy created by domestic and transnational actors that made the rapid consolidation of the IEM TAN [transnational advocacy networks] possible'. Furthermore, Santa-Cruz writes,

> ... what is more remarkable about this network is the way it contributed to *the redefinition of the issue it implies: sovereignty*. By making explicit that the people's right to free and fair elections (and more fundamen-tally, to democratic governance) transcends state boundaries, the IEM TAN promoted an understanding of sovereignty in international relations that, while not novel, *had fallen into oblivion*. IEM activists were thus recuperating the *social nature of sovereignty – even at the international level*. The international system has been partially altered by the practice of nonstate actors. But this has not been an anti-state quarrel. On the contrary, the activities of the IEM TAN can be seen as state affirming; *their aim is to make the world be constituted by the right kind of states*, not by organization other than states, or a world government. The IEM TAN *directly engages the state*.[4] (Italics added)

How did IEM transnational advocacy networks acquire their capacities to become influential enough to redefine an idea so entrenched in popular consciousness as sovereignty; an idea that national liberation struggles around the world fought so hard to defend not so long ago? In what sense did democratic governance 'fall into oblivion'? Statements like the above presuppose a particular understanding of 'human' rights and democracy within and outside the UN and make assumptions about the character of international law and International Organisations. The 'social nature of sovereignty' was an assumption that the European Enlightenment thinkers made when they developed the philosophical idea of social contract as the basis for a secular democratic state. Whether it is possible to extrapolate the idea of the 'social' in classical liberal theory to an interstate system based on the elusive notion of an 'international community' of states founded on unequal distribution of power within IOs is questionable. More importantly, extrapolating the 'social' into a very different historical context dismisses the birth and contested history of self-determination and sovereignty in the UN, international law and IOs since the world war years as irrelevant to our understanding of the rise of IEMs.

Sovereignty and the Third World

The principle of sovereignty in the Third World is closely tied to the principle of national self-determination and developed in the crucible of the world wars amidst competing conceptions of self-determination.[5] Vladimir Lenin, leader of the Russian revolution, argued that national self-determination was a *political claim* that oppressed nations make in the epoch of imperialism; it is not a legal right. Woodrow Wilson, president of the US during WWI, argued that the right of nations to self-determination was a *legal* right that applied to states externally in international law against other states and internally to the political systems within independent states.[6] Implicit in Wilson's idea of self-determination is the conception of states as juridical entities with certain types of national institutions and constitutions. States may be recognised as sovereign if they meet certain formal criteria for statehood set out in the Montevideo Convention on Rights and Duties of States, 1933: territory, population, government and capacity to enter into relations with other states.

Until the end of the world wars two-thirds of the world did not have sovereignty or self-determination. The struggle against colonialism and imperialism articulated freedom from colonial rule as the demand for self-determination. National liberation struggles did not demand the *legal right* to self-determination – they demanded the real thing – that the colonial rulers should relinquish power, pack up and leave. National liberation movements understood self-determination as a *political* demand of oppressed nations for freedom from national oppression. The meaning of national sovereignty in the Third World derives from the anti-colonial struggles therefore. In contrast, European sovereignty emerged from religious wars and economic rivalries between competing nations. The principle of sovereignty established equality between nations in external relations and principles of representative democracy established individual rights as the basis for citizen-state relations internally. Representative democracy removed divine rights and theology as the source of sovereignty and replaced it with popular sovereignty as the source of the state's authority. Popular sovereignty relies on the *philosophical idea* of social contract to justify representative democracy. The metaphor of contracts mirrors the real social relations of capitalism in Europe. This was not the case in the Third World. National liberation struggles were not economic wars fought under the banner of religion. It was the opposite.

Third World states whether under direct or indirect rule, whether protectorates or semi-colonies, suffered from oppression *as a nation*. Colonial rule gathered a diverse variety of races, nationalities, religions, tribes, cultures and social formations under the institution of a centralised administrative state – the colonial state. Struggles for national independence were based on an alliance of a wide variety of social groups that united to overthrow colonial rule.[7] Although possessed of the legal attributes of states, colonial states were substantively and structurally different from the institutions of the nation-state founded on individual rights and representative democracy in European history.[8] National liberation struggles argued that the state was not an 'empty vessel', an abstraction that was antithetical to civil society as Marx said. The Chinese Communist Party under Mao Tse-tung went the furthest in theorising the Third World state. Mao's thesis on what came to be called the 'four-class alliance' against imperialism argued that national liberation struggles must unite all those classes that were oppressed by imperialism on the basis of a minimum programme to gain freedom from national oppression and establish a 'people's democracy'. Mao's thesis on anti-imperialist statehood was influential across Asia, Africa and Latin America. There were other examples of alternative anti-imperialist conceptions of statehood. What is common to them is that in the Third World a wide alliance of anti-imperialist groups was the basis for state formation. The struggles over competing conceptions of sovereignty and democracy within the UN is precisely what led to the so-called 'third generation rights' in 'human' rights scholarship. Whatever one's views on people's democracy, four-class alliance or isolating comprador bourgeoisie, or tribe-based democracy as experimented in Libya, or combinations of modern and traditional systems of governance experimented in Zimbabwe, these theories of democracy and statehood developed to challenge imperialism are written-out of accounts of democracy, even denigrated.

Whatever one's views about Third World experiments with democracy, a few generalisations may be made about them. First, sovereignty in the Third World is not based on *philosophical* assumptions about social contract. They are based on *real* political agreements between diverse races, tribes, nationalities, classes, religions and social groups that were oppressed by the colonial state and joined forces in the national liberation struggles. Self-determination included freedom from colonial rule externally, as well as freedom to choose a model of governance that was most appropriate for the people living in states with colonial histories internally. The external and internal dimensions of sovereignty for Third World states is not comparable to the external sovereignty of European states as freedom from Church and internal state building based on individual rights and representative democracy to undermine feudal property and social ties. Democracy promotion by G7 states, covertly during the Cold War and overtly after it ended, targets breaking up the alliances on which Third World states are founded. Not surprisingly, democracy promotion of the NED type has exacerbated fragile alliances in the Third World and increased internal polarisation and ethnic and sectarian conflicts. Given the very different historical trajectories of sovereignty in the First and Third Worlds, the role of transnational advocacy networks in redefining sovereignty acquires new meanings.

Third World Sovereignty, Law and Liberal Imaginations

The right to free and fair elections operates on the liberal conception of statehood that sees a state as a juridical entity. Social movements assume that if liberal democracy worked for Europe and America it should work elsewhere. This assumption is fundamentally flawed. Empires did not replicate European states in the colonies – they could not have done so and remained imperialist states. Instead they modified and adapted European constitutional principles and created centralised authoritarian states.[9] These modifications to the institutional structure of the state rarely figure in the debates about democracy, law, and civil and political rights in the Third World. The idea of sovereignty in the imaginations of social movements remains anchored to seventeenth- and eighteenth-century liberalism as exemplified in Santa Cruz's statement about the 'social nature of sovereignty – even at the international level'.

The partial Allied victory limited to fascist states during WWII meant that the Allies could not keep the colonies and the Wilsonian idea was never entirely recognised by all UN members. The competing conceptualisation of self-determination had their imprint on the UN Charter in which the political right to self-determination sat side by side with civil and political rights from classical liberalism, and new socio-economic rights popularised by socialist movements during the world wars. Outside the UN *real* struggles continued on the ground in the economic domain over market access to corporations, investors, bankers and financiers and political wars between states throughout the Cold War. For a partial victory to become complete, and the Wilsonian concept of self-determination to be actualised, the *real* relations between states in economic and political fields had to change to enable institutionalisation and legalisation of the ideas. The economic crisis of capitalism in the late 1960s and late 1970s made the internationalisation, legalisation and institutionalisation of liberal conceptions of rights and democracy a matter of urgency.

Debates about sovereignty and self-determination within social movements take *doctrinal* principles in law as the point of departure to arrive at two types of *political* conclusions. The first political conclusion asserts that the right to self-determination has become a facade for states to violate 'human' rights. States act in their narrow self-interest and compromise ethics and universal norms.[10] The UN must intervene to promote 'human' rights within states even if it means weakening the principle of self-determination. The second political conclusion asserts that notwithstanding all the problems and controversies the right to self-determination principle in international law has given Third World states recognition and voice in international affairs which they did not have under Empires. It enables Third World states to negotiate better terms in the global political economy. The UN and the dominant states should respect the rights of Third World states therefore.[11] Both views disassociate political self-determination from economic self-determination and reify liberal modes of thought that sustain the hiatus between doctrine and social relations. The disconnected conceptions of political and economic self-determination were to play out in particular ways in the post-WWII years.

The Trusteeship Council, one of the principal organs of the UN, incorporated many principles and features of colonial governance in the new international law and institutional regime. The most important among them were the principles of governance under 'indirect rule' common in many parts of the British Empire.[12] Jan Smuts, a Boer War veteran who later a became a member of the British Imperial War cabinet and played a prominent role in promoting the Trusteeship doctrine in the League of Nations, was clear about the contribution that the British experience of colonial governance had to make in the emerging international order. Smuts wrote,

Where the British Empire has been so eminently successful as a political system ... the League, *working on somewhat similar lines*, could not fail to achieve a reasonable measure of success.[13] (Italics added)

Indirect rule is best summarised by the words of Smuts himself. Referring approvingly to Cecil Rhodes, considered the founder of the apartheid system in South Africa, Smuts wrote,

Rhodes' African policy embodied two main ideas: white settlement to supply the steel framework and the stimulus for an enduring civilisation, and indigenous native institutions to express the specifically African character.[14]

The Trusteeship Council's mandate was to oversee the transition from colonial rule to liberal democracy. The legal and institutional 'steel framework' for an asymmetrical international system was already written into the UN Charter at the end of WWII. The partial victory of the Allies in WWII meant that the Wilsonian conception had to wait seven decades to be fully operationalised. Hence the widely prevalent sense that liberal conceptions of democracy were 'in oblivion' for many decades. The story of how IEMs came to be 'institutionalised practices in the world' write-out what sovereignty means to two-thirds of the world. Liberal imaginations limit our understanding of sovereignty to the legal meanings of the word for one-third of the world. Self-determination is much more than a legal right, at least in the two-thirds world.

STEERING THE TRANSITION: THE IEM ACTORS

The practice of monitoring elections began with plebiscites during the world war years.[15] Generally, under the UN, the Trusteeship Council conducted and monitored elections in the colonies to oversee transitions from colonial to independent rule.[16] After independence elections were the responsibility of national governments and election monitoring the responsibility of citizens. International election monitoring was indeed in oblivion until it was resurrected in 1990 when the UN agreed to monitor elections in Nicaragua (see below). By the time the Trusteeship Council wound up its operations in 1994 after Palau became the last nation to be independent, the election monitoring role had returned to the UN, this time permanently as part of the UN's international obligations to *all* states. So did the vocabulary of 'transition' – transition now extended to transition from socialism to liberal democracy, from dictatorships to liberal democracy, from ethnic conflicts to liberal democracy and from 'illiberal democracy' to 'liberal democracy.'[17] IEMs turned the transitions from colonialism to independence on its head into international oversight over national independence. The practices of IEMs were developed by the US initially in the Philippines in 1986 and in Latin America during the second half of the 1980s[18] and eventually institutionalised in the UN system in their new 'decolonised' avatar.

IEMs became the first initiatives in US-led democracy promotion foreign policy after the NED was established. IEM programmes are amongst the earliest 'network' model of organisation developed under NED-funded programmes. The 'democracy community', as Thomas Carothers describes them,[19] comprise quasi-governmental organisations like the NED and NGOs devoted to promoting democracy around the world as well as major US universities, foundations, policy institutes, academics, experts, policy makers, mass media, and government departments like USAID, the State Department, the US Information Agency and the Defense and Justice Departments, the Carter Center founded by former President James Carter and a host of other private foundations and NGOs across the US too numerous to list.[20] The network model mobilises foreign governments, governmental, quasi-governmental organisations, NGOs and other actors around the world. The National Democratic Institute (NDI) affiliated to the Democratic Party, for example, receives funding from a number of foreign governments including from poorer states like Namibia and Yemen, governmental and quasi-governmental organisations and multilateral institutions. Key decision-makers are, however, from the Democratic Party.[21] Whether funds from countries like Namibia or Yemen are essential for NDI's work is a moot point. The method of organising, however, is important as it draws other governments, IOs, private foundations, corporations and individuals in hotspots around the world into networks that give effect to US foreign policy.[22]

The work of the 'democratic community' and the 'human' rights community has many overlapping areas and each reinforces the work of the other. One notable difference between the two communities is that many 'human' rights communities claim they do not accept government funding directly so as to maintain their neutrality. They do however accept funding from private foundations. Where the government outsources its work to NGOs or quasi-governmental organisations like the NED, the boundaries between governmental and non-governmental becomes difficult to monitor or track. These differences between the 'democracy' and 'human' rights communities notwithstanding, the 'human' rights community played a critical role in legalising and juridifying election monitoring. As early as 1984, a year after the NED was set up and three years before the first IEM mission to the Philippines, the International Human Rights Law Group (IHRLG), a US-based organisation, drew up guidelines for IEMs by synthesising the UN Charter, the UDHR and the ICCPR in a project funded by the State Department's USAID[23] (see below). Not surprisingly, the right to self-determination, the bedrock of the UN Charter, did not get a mention in the IEM guidelines.

To the 'democracy' and 'human' rights communities we must add another, the 'social movement community'. The social movement community is diverse and eclectic and any generalisation about them must be open to exceptions. Some general observations about the social movement community with regard to IEMs and the 'right to free and fair elections' are possible. The first is that social movement communities claim to work directly with people to organise oppositional movements against state oppression. Some do and others do not accept funds from governmental and quasi-governmental organisations directly although they may do so indirectly or unknowingly. Their opposition to state oppression feeds into the discourses of the 'right to free and fair elections' in particular ways. It would be fair to say most social movements in North America (excluding Mexico) and Europe share core values ingrained in the 'right to free and fair elections'. They believe 'globalisation' in the late 1980s or early 1970s (depending on theoretical orientations) is the cause of erosion of sovereignty; and further that because globalisation is a reality, IEMs are the only available vehicle for democratising Third World states. Furthermore, they believe the core values of the European Enlightenment can be brought back in the epoch of imperialism. Such beliefs have looser roots in Third World social movements where legacies of anti-colonial movements and armed struggles continue to articulate competing understandings of democracy.[24]

Social movement responses to IEMs present a complex political picture. In some countries popular movements against dictatorships invited IEM observers because of mistrust of their governments as for example in Chile.[25] In others, as in Mexico, IEMs came in the context of deeply divisive national politics alongside the Zapatista uprisings in the Chiapas.[26] In yet others, for example in Panama and Haiti, IEMs were part of a wider US-led political strategy for regime change.[27] Palestine was an extreme case where IEMs, it was hoped, would 'democratically' legitimise Israeli colonial occupation.[28] Whatever the case, three observations may be made about IEMs. Nearly everywhere transnational advocacy networks for IEMs relied on a section of the national elites and business interests for their work. Nearly everywhere their agenda went beyond ensuring particular elections were 'free and fair'. IEM reports typically called for restructuring the state apparatus and modifications of the constitutional arrangements for elections. Nearly everywhere LPG reforms followed IEMs. Where despite monitoring elections produced unacceptable results, as with the election of Hamas in Palestine in 2006 or Viktor Yanukovych in the Ukraine in 2010, calls for 'regime change' superseded IEM outcomes. IEM observers went to countries where the ruling governments were long-standing political allies of the US like Marcos in the Philippines and Pinochet in Chile as well as to countries where the government of the day was perceived as a threat to US interests as with Noriega in Panama and Ortega in Nicaragua. In the Third World, IEMs privileged social movements committed to liberalism and isolated those critical of it. IEMs came with a clear ideological orientation and that orientation was liberalism. The 1986 elections in the Philippines, more than any other, developed a model for IEMs that came to be used around the world.

CREATING AN IEM MODEL: THE PHILIPPINES

Eva-Lotta Hedman identifies four constellations of social factors that influence mobilisation for IEMs in the name of 'civil society', viz., 'the nature of regimes, the constellation of classes, the legacies of the Left, and the institutions of religion'.[29] A US colony until 1946, with two military bases and continued geopolitical significance for the US, and a political economy controlled by oligarchies, the Philippines provided the social and political context for internationalising the practices of IEMs in the 1986 elections. IEMs do not occur in a political vacuum. Frequently, they intervene in political contexts where politics is deeply fractured. Throughout the post-WWII era South-east Asia was a theatre of anti-imperialist movements and insurgencies and the Philippines was no exception.[30]

By the mid 1980s, in the wake of economic and debt crisis, the WB's structural adjustment programmes that demanded austerity measures and institutional reforms, the opposition to 'crony capitalism' from a section of the ruling elites, the divisions within the Catholic Church in the face of martial law since 1972 and widespread state violence against people under the brutal Marcos dictatorship, urban students and middle classes became increasingly receptive to the political programme of the Community Party of the Philippines.[31] In that context the IEM transnational advocacy networks adapted and internationalised the pre-existing National (Citizens') Movement for Free Elections (NAMFREL) model for election monitoring used in 1953. NAMFREL was formed initially in the early 1950s by a coalition of war veterans who had fought on the US side against Japan. The war veterans, organised as the Philippines Veterans' Legion (PVL) since the 1950s, had lobbied successfully for financial support from the US for their war efforts.[32] As an organised force with memory of NAMFREL experiences, the PVL played an important role in the revival of the election observation network in the 1986 elections. The war veterans were supported by the conservative Catholic clergy organised as the Catholic Action of the Philippines, the Philippines Junior Chamber of Commerce (Jaycees) and Lions Clubs International, a US-based charity founded by US businessmen to promote 'the principles of good government and good citizenship'.[33]

The US-CIA role in the 1953 elections in the Philippines through NAMFREL, which was the first election monitoring event in the post-WWII era, was covert. NAMFREL was revived on the intervention of the US Senate Committee on Foreign Relations in 1986 when Ferdinand Marcos ended martial law in force since 1972 and announced elections. In contrast to the 1953 elections, the US role in NAMFREL in the 1986 elections was open, conducted under the full glare of the media, with operational support from the US embassy in Manila, Congress appropriations for NED, democracy promotion as the new US foreign policy in place of covert dictatorships and the ideological rhetoric of the triumph of rights and democracy. The overt intervention of external actors brought with it certain types of public discourses of rights and democracy, including the 'right to free and fair elections', the network model of mobilisation and international alliances. These discourses of rights and modes of organising strengthened some political groups and weakened others in the country. Eva-Lotta Hedman and John Sidel describe the shift brought about by the IEM in the 1986 elections in the following words,

> ... the February 1986 'snap' presidential election brought the foreign correspondents down from the rebels' mountain and jungle hideaways and dramatically concluded the 'Revolution' story with a 'Democratic' dénouement.[34]

The overt nature of IEMs was crucial to internationalise, legalise and institutionalise election monitoring. The 1986 elections provided the first testing ground for IEM as a pivotal component of democracy promotion under an increasingly assertive US Congress. In November 1985, the US Democratic Party Senator Edward Kennedy proposed a Bill calling for election monitoring in the Philippines. The Bill did not pass. Instead, on the request of Richard Lugard, Republican Senator and Chair of the Senate Foreign Relations Committee, the US-based Center for Democracy sent a six-member delegation to the Philippines from 8–15 December 1985.[35] The delegation examined the feasibility of sending an election monitoring team to the Philippines during the elections in February 1986 and made eight recommendations that the election authorities in the Philippines must implement for the elections to be considered 'free and fair'. One of those recommendations was the accreditation of NAMFREL as election observer.[36] A second joint NDI/International Republican Institute (IRI) delegation focused on the procedures in place for free and fair elections. The delegation testified to the Senate Foreign Relations Committee on their findings about the procedures in place for the elections. Undeterred by the warnings of the Philippines Commission on Elections against 'external interference', the delegation recommended restructuring the Philippines Commission on Elections.[37] The NDI and IRI sent a joint team of forty-four election observers[38] and a twenty-member official US delegation led by Senator Lugar to observe the elections.[39] At a press conference in Manila Senator Lugar described President Marcos, a close US ally and the man who ruled the country under martial law from 1972, and the opposition presidential candidate Mrs Aquino, both, as 'two great leaders in this country', and called the Philippines 'one of the greatest democracies that our world has produced'.[40] If that was indeed true, then one must wonder what all the fuss about election monitoring was about!

Beginning with the presidential elections the Philippines held four elections between February 1986 and January 1988. Each one of these developed and trialled the procedures and practices for IEMs. Subsequent IEM teams were strategically selected to internationalise the Philippine experience. In the 1987 congressional elections in the Philippines the IEM team included opposition leaders from countries where elections of strategic importance to the US and G7 states were forthcoming including opposition leaders from South Korea, Haiti, Panama, Chile and Pakistan.[41] Since then, IEM teams regularly include opposition leaders from countries where the US and G7 states have strategic interests and where elections are either forthcoming or likely to be contentious. IEM teams do more than observe elections in a country. They promote networks of opposition leaders, election observers, like-minded NGOs, like-minded political parties with affinities to the two main political parties in the US – Democrats and Republicans. They 'educate' the political leaders of Third World countries in the new 'standards of civilisation'. The businessmen, clergy and international corporate leaders who contributed to the 1986 IEM in the Philippines introduced new organising skills to social networks, network governance and profession-alisation of IEMs.[42] This model of politics is not what people commonly have in mind when they speak of democracy and political freedoms. Instead in their imaginations, democratic politics is an expression of the 'will of the people'. In networked politics, the 'will of the people' is manufactured by powerful international alliances. The 'right to free and fair elections' is the device through which politics by international networks is organised, and the 'will of the people' manufactured.

The IEM in the 1986 elections in the Philippines organised three-quarters of a million Filipinos as elections monitors across the country.[43] This level of mobilisation effectively *created* a new type of 'civil society' that was international from its inception. The legacy of IEM in 1986 continued long after the 1986 elections. A proliferation of a large number of 'human' rights and other interest-based organisations adopted the international network model of mobilisation. Like the IEMs, many of these civil society organisations were conceptualised, designed and funded by NED's grantees and organisations linked to them. The NDI expanded the scope of its work to programmes for 'Citizen Participation' (to train voters and citizens in accountability techniques),[44] 'Debates',[45] 'Democracy and Technology' (to promote technology diffusion and cross-border information exchange and collaboration),[46] 'Democratic Governance' (to train and form networks of public sector officials, legislators and members of government including prime ministers and presidents of states, and local governments),[47] 'Gender, Women and Democracy' (to train and support women to participate in public offices and roles),[48] 'Political Inclusion of Marginalised Groups' (targets youth, people with disabilities, ethnic and religious groups, LGBT communities and others to participate in elections and other democratic activities alongside others),[49] and 'Political Parties' (to provide training and support in electoral campaigns to like-minded political parties around the world and multi-party electoral systems).[50] The IRI has comparable programmes for democracy promotion for like-minded social and political groups around the world.[51] Democracy promotion encompassed every aspect of political life of the citizens and the 'right to free and fair elections' was the vehicle for reorganising politics in the Third World. Social movements that distanced themselves from the NGOs, INGOs and IEM advocacy organisations were nonetheless caught in the conceptual vocabulary of 'representative democracy', 'right to free and fair elections' and the 'entitlement to democratic governance' even when they were uncomfortable about the sources of funding and the actors that were so aggressively promoting democracy around the world.

The new 'civil society' networks in the Philippines amplify the themes promoted by international democracy promotion projects. The Commission on Elections for the Philippines accredits a number of organisations that include local 'civil society organisations' (CSOs) as well and regional intergovernmental organisations and international NGOs.[52] Notable intergovernmental organisations accredited by the Republic of Philippines Commission on Elections include the Association of Asian Election Authorities, United Nations Electoral Assistance Division (UNEAD), USAID and International Institute for Democracy and Electoral Assistance (IDEA). Notable amongst the public-private partnerships organisations accredited by the Commission on Elections is ACE: the Electoral Knowledge Network. An analysis of IEM networks reveals a pattern of interlocking state, private, business and regional organisations and IOs that knit together bureaucrats, national and international NGOs, private sector businesses, think tanks, academics and UN officials in a dense web of relationships across the world. For example ACE was set up by nine organisations that include governmental, private and UN organisations: IDEA,[53] Electoral Institute for Sustainable Democracy in Africa (EISA),[54] Elections Canada,[55] the National Electoral Institute of Mexico (INE),[56] IFES,[57] the Carter Center,[58] UN Department of Economic and Social Affairs (UNDESA),[59] UN Development Programme (UNDP)[60] and the UN Electoral Assistance Division (UNEAD).[61] Some of these organisations have a double presence, in their own right as an organisation and as members of other networks. For example, international NGOs with accreditation by the Philippines Election Commission include the International Foundation for Electoral Systems (IFES), which is also the founding member of ACE. IDEA is independently accredited as IEM and also founder of ACE. This method of organising democracy in a country is anything but transparent to ordinary people in the Philippines or elsewhere. The interlocking relationships are invisible even for many social movements and smaller local NGOs which are often unable to map the maze of relationships where all speak in the name of 'the people' but somehow fail to discern their 'will'.

The internationalisation of election monitoring practices that began in the Philippines in 1986 was followed by increasing professionalisation of IEMs first trialled in the Philippines. IEMs created a global 'election industry' calling into existence 'election markets' – new election entrepreneurs, consultants, experts, trainers, NGOs and social scientists. Today IEMs are a feature of national election governance in most parts of the world outside the G7 states, except a few states like China. Corporate leaders played an important role in shaping the election monitoring 'industry'.[62] Whereas the national election monitoring model developed in the Philippines became the launch-pad for developing legal standards and professional practices to be used in IEMs around the world, it was the elections in Nicaragua in 1990 where the right to self-determination was re-scripted as the 'right to free and fair elections' in the very heart of the UN and the body of international law.

NICARAGUA: 'ELECTION OF THE CENTURY'

Institutionalising IEMs in the UN

In February 1990 Nicaragua held the 'election of the century'. For the first time, in August 1989, the UN, an international organisation founded on the legal principle of sovereign equality of states, agreed to monitor elections conducted by a sovereign state.[63] For over four decades since its formation in 1945, the UN had, following Article 2(7) of the UN Charter, refused to become involved in national elections in any country except when the elections formed part of the decolonisation process.[64] Article 2(7) of the UN Charter prohibits the UN and its member states from intervening 'in matters which are essentially within the domestic jurisdiction of any state'.[65] As late as July 1988 the Secretary-General Javier Perez was committed to this view and stated the UN 'does not send observers to elections'.[66] That conducting national elections is a core domestic responsibility of a state does not require elaboration. UN involvement in monitoring elections in a sovereign state was a fundamental shift in the two founding principles of international law: the sovereign equality of states and the principle of non-interference in the internal affairs of another state. These two principles cut across themes and values in classical liberal theory.

In Nicaragua, national elections overseen by IEM followed the failure of covert intervention. For nearly a decade, since 1981, the US conducted counterinsurgency operations against the revolutionary nationalist government of the Sandinistas by providing political, material, financial and organisational support to the opposition known as the 'contras'.[67] In 1979 the Sandinistas overthrew one of the most brutal US-supported dictators in Latin America, Anastasio Somoza Debayle. The Sandinista revolution was anti-imperialist in as much as it was a struggle against the centrality of US domination over the country throughout its history,[68] and also anti-authoritarian, a movement based on an alliance of diverse social classes and groups against authoritarian rule.[69] In mid 1986 the US Congress approved $100 million to arm and train the 'contras' from bases in Honduras, Panama and the US.[70] By the end of 1989 the Sandinistas had all but won the war against the US-backed 'contras' on the ground.[71]

The significance of the US role in the Nicaraguan elections, as William Robinson argues, goes beyond a quantitative analysis of external support to this or that opposition party as it

... obscures a phenomenon [i.e.] [t]he Nicaraguan elections were a contest, not between the Sandinistas and their domestic political opposition, but between the Nicaraguan Revolution and the United States.[72]

To this insight we can add another more important one. The Nicaraguan elections opened the pathway for internationalising and institutionalising IEMs.

Nicaragua, the International Court of Justice and International Law

The language of UNGA Resolution 2625 adopted in October 1970 on the Declaration on Friendly Relations and Co-operation is categorical. Resolution 2625 explicitly prohibits interference in 'civil strife in another state'.[73] In Nicaragua the US did just that. Faced with an aggressive undeclared war by the US, Nicaragua took recourse to legal action under international law. On 9 April 1984 the Republic of Nicaragua instituted proceedings against the US in the International Court of Justice (ICJ) alleging the US had violated its sovereignty, territorial integrity and political independence which were 'the most fundamental and universally-accepted principles of international law'.[74] According to Nicaragua, the US was 'recruiting, training, arming, equipping, financing, supplying and otherwise encouraging, supporting, aiding and directing military and paramilitary actions in and against Nicaragua ...'[75] On 10 May 1984 the ICJ gave a provisional order directing the US to 'cease and refrain from any action restricting access to or from Nicaraguan ports, and in particular, the laying of mines'.[76] The ICJ's final decision found that the US had indeed used force, interfered in the internal affairs of another state, violated the sovereignty of Nicaragua, disrupted peaceful maritime commerce, breached a friendship treaty between the two countries signed in 1956, and breached humanitarian law by producing a manual in 1983 for the use of 'contra' forces seeking to overthrow the government by armed force with US support, resources and training. The ICJ directed the US to cease and refrain from illegal activities and make reparations to Nicaragua. The US boycotted the proceedings after the ICJ judgment and did not file a response to the reparation claims.

Instead the US trialled the post-Watergate foreign policy to do overtly what the CIA had done covertly. The US Congress approved US$ 9 million through the NED to support the opposition presidential candidate Violetta Chamorro through the NID and IRI chain of grantee organisations.[77] For the quasi-governmental NGOs, US NGOs and think tanks, observing elections in Nicaragua was much more than ensuring that the governments respected the 'right to free and fair elections'. It was a regional diplomatic and foreign policy exercise to involve regional governments that were of strategic importance to the US, such as Venezuela and Costa Rica,[78] legitimise the proliferation of regional NGOs like the Center for Democratic Consultation[79] and the Center for Electoral Assistance and Promotion (CAPEL)[80] and create networks of diplomats.[81] Above all, it was a way of mobilising G7 states and Western allies in *US foreign policy*[82] and institutionalising IEM in the international order. To everyone's surprise, including the US, the 'election of the century' held on 25 February 1990 returned to power the US-backed Violeta Chamorro government.[83] In 1991 the newly elected pro-US Nicaraguan government's representative withdrew the state's claim for reparations before the ICJ for a decade of undeclared war.[84]

If the Philippines provided the model for setting up national alliances of 'civil society' organisations within the country, the Nicaraguan elections began the process of 'rolling back' the self-determination principle from international law and institutions. 'Rolling back' the ICJ decision is significant for two reasons. First, the ideological justification for IEMs and the 'right to free and fair elections' is to establish 'rule of law' as an international standard for governance. 'Rolling back' the ICJ decision is paradoxical in that 'rule of law' in the international order is established by violating 'rule of law'. Second, the ICJ decision had no influence on the UN's actions when considering its involvement in IEMs. To understand why this was so, it is necessary to understand the organisational dynamics of the UN apparatus, the nodes of power and influence in the organisation and the importance of strategic control of those nodes for US leadership of post-WWII imperialism.

IEMS ON UN'S AGENDA: US LEADS ROLLING BACK SOVEREIGNTY

IEMs on the UN Agenda

IEMs appeared on the UN agenda very tentatively at the end of 1988 but expanded rapidly in scope and scale in the following years.[85] In the UN the arguments were about re-scripting the primacy of right to self-determination in the UN Charter. The debates transformed the right to self-determination itself into a 'human' right. The new revisionist interpretation of the Charter inverted the status of right to self-determination as it was understood until then. The problem of sovereignty remained a sticking point in the deliberations over IEM in the UNGA. The IHRLG was amongst the first to lay the groundwork for the argument that 'the right to free and fair elections' and the authority for IEMs could be derived from UDHR, ICCPR and past UN practices in the context of transition from colonialism to independence and subjected to the 'human' rights agenda.[86] The report of the IHRLG is interesting for what it *omits* to consider in deriving the legal sources for the UN's authority to monitor elections in member states.

The IHRLG's report refers to past UN and Commonwealth election observer missions but *omits* to consider that UN election monitoring was limited to overseeing transitions from colonial rule. The report notes the considerable differences between member states of the Organization of American States (OAS) which sent eight election observation teams between 1962 and 1984. It *omits* to consider the reasons for resistance of some states to regional election monitoring.[87] The report draws on the ICCPR but *omits* to consider the provisions that subject the right to elections to the right to self-determination.[88] The report *omits* to consider UNGA Resolution 1514 adopted in the 1960s on the Declaration on the Granting of Independence to Colonial Territories and People, or Resolution 2625 adopted in October 1970 on the Declaration on Friendly Relations and Co-operation,[89] or ICJ Advisory Opinions, especially in the Western Sahara case.[90] The IHRLG for the first time made an explicit argument subjecting the political 'right to elections' to 'human' rights instruments in the UN, a line pursued by the US within the UN. It omitted to consider any provision in international law that did not sit well with this line. Coming from a US NGO, the arguments had the ear not only of the US administration but also Third World NGOs under dictatorships.

A year after IEMs appeared on the agenda of the UN in 1988, re-scripting international law on the 'right to free and fair elections' proceeded at a rapid pace. The following year the UNGA put *'Enhancing the Effectiveness of the Principle of Periodic and Genuine Elections'* as a regular item on its annual agenda and called on the Commission on Human Rights (CHR) to examine the tensions between the principles of sovereignty and the election monitoring role of the UN.[91] Simultaneously, the UNGA included *'Respect for the Principles of National Sovereignty and Non-interference in the Internal Affairs of States in their Electoral Processes'* as a separate agenda item at its plenary meetings.[92] These institutional manoeuvrings to shift the 'home' for considering 'right to free and fair elections' were crucial for rolling back right to self-determination and bringing it under the 'human' rights framework.

From 1991 until 2006 two parallel resolutions were passed, one on sovereignty and 'right to self-determination' and the other on the UN's role in election monitoring and 'the right to free and fair elections'.[93] The tenor of the two parallel resolutions provides striking contrasts. The resolutions on election monitoring advanced the election monitoring agenda by creating new organisational, legal and ideological conditions necessary to institutionalise international election monitoring, to develop norms for elections as the new 'standard of civilisation', to subordinate the sovereignty principle to international standards of democracy and to promote a revisionist ideology of rights and democracy where the 'will of the international community' is substituted for the 'will of the people'. In contrast, the resolutions on sovereignty were formal and repetitive, as if to assuage the misgivings of Third World states.

In 1991 the UNGA invited member states to submit their views on sovereignty and international election monitoring and in 1992 appointed a senior official to,

> ... develop an institutional memory, to develop and maintain a roster of international experts who could provide technical assistance as well as assist verification of electoral processes and maintain contact with regional and other intergovernmental organizations.[94]

In 1993 a full-fledged unit, the Electoral Assistance Unit (EAU), was set up to provide 'electoral assistance' on a 'case by case basis', the United Nations Trust Fund for Electoral Observation was set up and the UNDP established a separate fund for Technical Assistance to Electoral Processes. The UNGA resolved to redeploy personnel and resources to CHR to coordinate with the work of the EAU, recommended the publication of guidelines on electoral assistance and called for regular reports to the UNGA on implementation of its resolutions.[95] By 1995 the EAU's mission-creep had expanded far beyond monitoring whether or not elections were fair. The EAU was to provide 'post-election assistance to States that request such assistance, and to electoral institutions ...' and the reconstituted UNOHCHR was mandated to play an active role to

> ... support democratization activities ... including ..., assistance for human rights-related legislative reform, strengthening and reform of

the judiciary, assistance to national human rights institutions and ...,
reporting and international obligations as related to human rights.[96]

By 1998, the agenda of international election monitoring expanded to
'capacity building' of states and the election machinery within states, 'in
particular through the capacity of national electoral institutions'.[97] The
1998 resolution took the institutionalisation of election monitoring to
another level by regionalising election monitoring.[98] The Association of
the African Election Authorities, the Pacific Islands, Australia and New
Zealand Electoral Administrators (PIANZEA) Network, a semi-formal
association of electoral administrators working in the Pacific region,
was formed in 1997,[99] the Association of Asian Election Authorities
(AAEA) comprising twenty Asian countries[100] was set up in addition
to the OAU which had participated in regional election monitoring.
Annual meetings targeting knowledge communities, NGOs, experts and
media became regular UN activities.[101] By 2004 the UN was proactively
involved in promoting democracy, overseeing national elections and
engaging NGOs, experts, scholarly communities, states, regional organisations and international lawyers. International election monitoring and
democratisation in the UN went beyond interstate relations and became
a global 'public-private partnership' venture with consultants, law firms,
trust funds and technical assistance funds. In October 2005, the UN
formalised the public-private partnership in IEMs by developing a code
of conduct for monitors. The Declaration of Principles for Election
Observation and Code of Conduct for International Election Observers
was endorsed by an impressive array of public and private organisations
and US and European NGOs whose operations were intertwined with
US and EU political parties, funding and ideology.[102] The scope of 'right
to free and fair elections' now included a comprehensive set of reforms
to restructure Third World states. More importantly, the idea that the
popular will of the people to bring about political changes required
international oversight of some of the most powerful imperialist states
and the IOs was embedded within the UN, founded as it is on unequal
distribution of economic, political and ideological power.

In contrast, the parallel resolution on the UNGA agenda on '*Respect for
the Principles of National Sovereignty*' reiterated the UN's commitment to
the principle of state sovereignty, non-interference in the internal affairs
of states throughout 1991 to 2006 even as it continued to institutionalise
the election monitoring, democratising and 'capacity building' agenda.

The UNGA's 1993 sovereignty resolution urged all states to respect the principle of non-interference and 'the sovereign right of peoples to determine their political, economic and social system' and condemned acts of armed aggression or threat or use of force against 'peoples, their elected Governments or their legitimate leaders'. At the same time, the resolution clubbed the sovereignty issue with electoral principles bringing both under the agenda of 'Human rights questions'. By clubbing sovereignty and the right to free and fair elections and treating both as 'human' rights issues, the UN brought the problematic question of the primacy of self-determination over 'right to free and fair elections' firmly under the CHR's 'human' rights agenda.[103] After 2006 the agenda item on *Respect for Sovereignty* was formally concluded and the tension between sovereignty and 'human' rights was decisively resolved in favour of 'human' rights. Election monitoring had been institutionalised as an established norm and practice by the UN.

It fell to Boutros Boutros-Ghali's successor Kofi Anan to formalise the new rules of the international order. In 2005, he presented to the UNGA a report titled *In Larger Freedom*.[104] The report reconceptualised 'security', 'solidarity' and 'sovereignty'. With regard to security, it proposed that the UN subordinates state security, its primary function under the Charter, to the wider concept of 'human security'. The second proposal concerning solidarity subordinates the interstate system to the wider universal idea of 'human dignity'. Lastly, it modified the sovereignty principle by imposing a duty on the 'international community' to intervene to monitor democracy, transitional or otherwise.[105] Significantly, the report did not recommend changes in the distribution of power within the IOs which privileges the Permanent Five in the United Nations Security Council (UNSC) with a veto, and undermines the UNGA by limiting its powers to making recommendations.

These changes within the UN system render the ICJ decision on US violation of Nicaragua's sovereignty and ideas of 'rule of law' in international affairs redundant at best. Lenin argued that imperialism was about the economic, political and ideological domination of imperialist states over less powerful states and nations. The end of WWII established an interstate system founded on unequal distribution of power within the international system. The IEMs legalised and formalised the procedures for political and ideological domination. The 'empty shell' of rights was filled with a new legal entitlement (elections), a new political substance (rights of electors and elected), and established the basis (international law and IEMs) and purpose of entitlement (democracy promotion). The 'right to free and fair elections' is pivotal to the political and ideological developments that complement post-WWII institutions of TMF capitalism in the international order.

By 2014 international public and private organisations acting under the aegis of the UN had monitored over 100 elections worldwide.[106] Since its tentative beginnings in 1990 IEMs covered 70 per cent of elections in the 'non-established democracies', or more simply the Third World, by 1998. By 2004 the figures rose to over 81 per cent of elections.[107] Election monitoring is invariably what 'established democracies' do in 'non-established democracies'. Scholars, academics, legal professionals, consultants and NGOs have developed a complete array of indicators and standards for elections. Private US foundations like Freedom House produce State of Democracy reports based on indicators that provide normative assessments about states which then guide public and private policy makers.[108] We know that IEMs are, by now, firmly embedded in international law. The point of this analysis is to recognise who embedded them, how and why and what that means for political freedoms of ordinary people around the world.

US Leads Rolling Back Sovereignty

For the US, the end of the Cold War presented new opportunities to expand and redefine the role of the UNSC. John Bolton, the then Assistant Secretary of State for International Organizations under the new Bush administration, later US ambassador to the UN and a long-term critic of the UN, told the conference of the American Society of International Law in 1992,

> We began to see ways of using the United Nations and its peacekeeping functions in *dramatic new and expanded areas*.[109] (Italics added)

Trapped within their disciplinary conventions, academic writings on IEMs did not see the political significance of the continuities between two qualitatively distinct types of transitions: UN election monitoring to oversee the transition from colonialism to national independence and IEMs to oversee the transition from post-independence states to neoliberal states.[110] In contrast, US officials made that connection quite clearly. John Bolton, speaking for the Bush US administration, considered

Namibia to be the 'prime example'.[111] Referring to 'the successful transformation to independence in Namibia', Bolton continued,

> In addition to the traditional peacekeeping function of keeping
> combatants apart and then disarming them, the United Nations
> engaged in intensive police monitoring and in extensive observation
> of the Namibian elections leading up to its independence. ... That
> achievement was followed by the successful use of election monitors
> by the United Nations and by the Organization of American States
> (OAS) in Nicaragua ... Since those days we [sic] have been an explosion
> of peacekeeping activities.[112]

For Bolton, at least, 'intensive police monitoring' and 'extensive election
observation' were two sides of the same process and Nicaragua was the
continuation of decolonisation in Namibia.

For the Nicaraguan experience to be institutionalised and embedded
in interstate practices it was necessary to reinterpret the legal and
institutional framework on which the UN is founded. The Bush administration in the 1990s was very conscious of this need. Reinterpreting the
UN Charter was more methodical than what appeared on the surface,
a set of ad hoc and piecemeal responses to issues as they surfaced.
Bolton identified four clear goals for the UN, one of which was greater
involvement of the UN and regional organisations like the OAS in
election monitoring which was to be part of the *peacekeeping* role of the
UN under the Charter. Bolton told the conference,

> In the course of trying to work our way through the intellectual
> process of writing these resolutions, we have literally gone back to
> the State Department's law library and taken out volumes that have
> probably been gathering dust since about 1946. It would be helpful
> to have a more precise analytical framework within which to judge
> possible *additional UN activity*, but *we are already beyond the scope
> envisioned by the Framers of the UN Charter, and there is no sign of
> slowing down*.[113] (Italics added)

Bolton went on to add:

> I think that I could summarize our approach to peacekeeping by
> saying that it is now possible to state, with some justification, that the

UN Security Council is a *competitor in the marketplace of international problem solving*. For this administration [i.e. the Bush administration], that does not mean that every issue that comes up in terms of potential peacekeeping is to be solved in the United Nations, but it does mean that the United Nations is a competitor in a way that it was not five years ago.[114] (Italics added)

UN involvement in election monitoring was seamlessly fused with the UNSC's peacekeeping role. Elections in Third World states were no longer the political process through which people give their consent to be governed but rather the flip side of intrastate and interstate wars, a device to pre-empt civil wars and to bring them to a conclusion when they occurred. Every conflict in society was henceforth potentially open to international intervention. The ICJ ruling notwithstanding, the justification for UN participation in Nicaragua elections was that it was part of a regional peace initiative to end a decade-long civil war and therefore legitimately within the UN peacekeeping mandate.[115] That is not how the majority of the states, social movements and NGOs working for change understand the UNSC's role. For most people, and indeed most states, the UNSC is the neutral keeper of peace between states. For the US, however, the end of the Cold War meant the UN was one amongst several forums available for promoting its goals. Reform of the UN became an important focus of US foreign policy objectives. Beyond speech making, the US State Department appointed Richard Thornburg, US Attorney General and former Republican Governor of Pennsylvania, as Under Secretary-General of the UN for one year to oversee the reform of the UN in the areas of personnel, finance and peacekeeping.[116] Disenchanted with its nominee Boutros Boutros-Ghali's attempts to give the UNSC greater autonomy in peacekeeping after the end of the Cold War, the US conducted a vitriolic campaign against the extension of his term, threatening to use its veto if other UNSC members did not comply with the US decision to appoint another candidate.[117]

Boutros-Ghali in his book about his term as Secretary-General describes what he calls 'the "first conceptual" gathering after the cold war'.[118] The meeting on 31 January 1992 was special because it was the first meeting of the Security Council after the end of the Cold War and attended by the heads of states with their foreign secretaries. Boutros-Ghali describes how Boris Yeltsin of Russia waxed eloquent about how Russia had become a democracy, whereas François

Mitterrand of France promised 1000 troops at 48 hours notice to enhance the UN's peacekeeping role, and George Bush wanted regime change in Iraq and Libya.[119] The UNSC directed the Secretary-General to engage in 'preventive diplomacy',[120] a euphemism for interference in the internal affairs of a country. Boutros-Ghali adds, Premier Li Ping of China 'politely told me [Boutros-Ghali] to learn to distinguish between international wars and civil wars' and notes that 'most current conflicts were in fact *within* the borders of a single state' (italics added).[121] Maurice Bertrand, a veteran UN Inspector for decades, notes that after the end of the Cold War, Third World and socialist states naively believed that with the capitalist-communist blocs gone, with the withdrawal of Russian troops from Afghanistan, end of support to Nicaragua, Angola and Namibia, the UN would occupy the security vacuum and emerge as the voice of the 'international community' of states.[122]

US state practices in Nicaragua in the 1980s presented new doctrinal and theoretical questions for international law scholars and practitioners throughout the 1990s.[123] The debate prior to the 1980s was whether party pluralism was an essential feature of democracies. Nicaragua shifted the debate from democracy as a political question about the types of political systems to democracy as a legal question of 'entitlement to democratic governance' and the legal right to 'free and fair elections'.[124] Framed as a legal question, the debates centred on whether or not the UN Charter, the UDHR and ICCPR should take precedence over state sovereignty.[125] The US led the procedural manoeuvres within the UN to bring right to self-determination under the 'human' rights agenda. For the US, its UN foreign policy initiatives were part of democracy promotion as foreign policy. The UN initiatives were tried and tested for over a decade initially in Latin America where the US had influence in the OAS. It paved the way for the UN to become involved in IEMs and in the Conference on Security and Cooperation in Europe (CSCE) targeting Eastern European states which inaugurated the rights resurgence there.[126]

IEMS AND THE 'RIGHT TO FREE AND FAIR ELECTIONS' IN THE EPOCH OF IMPERIALISM

What's wrong with IEMs? IEMs internationalise, institutionalise and legalise what is essentially a political relationship between citizens and state. The political relationship between citizens and state is the foundations of statehood and representative democracy in classical liberalism. IEMs appear to play the role of a neutral referee. In the epoch of imperialism there are no neutral referees, at least not in international institutions. The international order is an interstate system based on unequal distribution of power. This much many may concede. Why do powerful imperialist states like the US wish to legalise and institutionalise IEMs and the 'right to free and fair elections' in the international order? The most obvious reason is of course that IEMs remove political power from the citizens and transfer at least part of it to IOs where imperialist powers wield special status and influence. After the end of the world wars imperialist states resorted to political, diplomatic and military strategies to install 'puppet' regimes in the Third World by supporting brutal dictatorships and coups around the world. The right of nations to self-determination and the principle of non-interference in the internal affairs of states in international law meant the political, diplomatic and military measures by the US-led imperialist bloc had little legitimacy. The 'right to free and fair elections' in international law legitimises interference in the internal affairs of states. The IEMs, institutionalised as public-private partnerships led by the US and European powers, give legal authority to intervene in internal affairs of states in a way the CIA coups or military interventions never did. They roll back the gains that national liberation struggles made towards freedom from national oppression which remains the pivotal mode of oppression in the epoch of imperialism.

The more important question is why did social movements in the Euro-American states embrace the 'right to free and fair elections' so warmly, and why did even those who were suspicious of the actors promoting democracy go along with it? The problem lies with liberal imaginations as much as the 'empty' conceptual shell of rights with a distinct grammar from which different institutional regimes could be constructed. Chapter 3 discussed how liberalism gives primacy to the thought-world over the real world. Euro-American social movements, almost universally, saw the right to free and fair elections as a grand idea and believed that by having the right ideas they can change the world. Ideas are right only when they are connected to the real world. The real world was somewhere else – out there in Africa, Asia, Latin America. Liberal imaginations pit 'evil' transnational corporations, financiers and investors in one side of the democracy ring against the 'desirable' democracy, political freedoms and civil liberties in the other as adversaries. Social movements believe they must take sides with the best ideas. They seldom asked the question: why does right to free and fair elections come hand in hand with LPG reforms? What is the connection between the economic transformations underway and the political ones, if at all?

In the Third World, generalising again, the IEM agenda divided political movements from social movements and OSMs from NSMs. If we recall the point made above, that national liberation struggles united a broad array of people against colonialism and the Cold War was a struggle to break that alliance, the LPG reforms dissolved society into diverse segments each with its own interests within specific global markets. Old OSM slogans like 'unite the many to defeat the few' appeared to lose the efficacy they once had. For each interest group democracy is a means for state-capture. Not surprisingly, LPG reforms, IEMs and 'right to free and fair elections' have exacerbated sectarian divisions within Third World societies.

The resonance of the vocabulary and grammar of rights with seventeenth- and eighteenth-century ideas of freedom, democracy and equality provide the trope that holds together wildly differing expectations from the IEMs for different actors. It has put social movements of all types on their back foot. How can anyone argue that the 'right to free and fair elections' was ideological and false, a fetish, without appearing to be against empowerment which rights claim to give and freedom from oppression which IEMs claim elections will bring. How can social movements convince the people that the right to free and fair elections is part of a package of neoliberal reforms and globalisation when liberalism's power of promise remains so alluring?

5

The Rights of Victims:
From Authorisation to Accountability

History proves that many States, so far from being originally independent, merely exchanged one suzerain for another. ... But, if the control of the Paramount Power were ... limited ..., it would be difficult to account for its rights to intervene to suppress barbarous practices, or to punish the personal misconduct of a ruler which did not amount to disloyalty. (W.S. Holdworth, The Indian States and India, 1930, pp. 411, 413)[1]

This chapter considers the authority to punish political leaders and public officials, which is the other side of the representative democracy coin in classical liberalism. The state's authority to act in classical liberalism required *authorisation* by citizens. Authorisation is a political act and signifies that the locus of political power rests with the citizens. Authorisation in politics, so central to representative democracy in liberal theory, was buried unnoticed in the post-WWII era. Its place is filled, instead, by *accountability*, a concept better suited to the institutional architecture of TMF capitalism. Accountability is conceptually and etymologically a very different idea from authorisation. Accountability is a concept grounded in accounting and involves a relationship between an account-holder and accountor.[2] Chameleon-like, the use of the term has expanded.[3] Used initially as financial accountability in the context of the nationwide economic and banking crisis in the US in the 1930s, the use of the term expanded to corporate accountability in the 1950s and to political accountability in the 1970s.[4] The use of the term has been internationalised and legalised since the 1980s. In the epoch of imperialism, the idea of *political* authorisation as the source of legitimacy for the state is converted into *accountability* of political leaders and public officials to international 'rule of law' far removed from the citizens. This conversion is brought about by the new international 'rights of victims' and the crime of 'abuse of power'. This chapter tracks these developments along three parallel trajectories: the 'war on drugs', recognition of rights of victims and abuse of power in the UN, and the establishment of the International Criminal Court (ICC).

FROM AUTHORISATION TO ACCOUNTABILITY

Doubts about the dependability of elected representative governments followed close on the heels of the right to free and fair elections and IEMs. Even as electoral democracies became the international norm, attention shifted to 'electoral authoritarianism'. Andreas Schedler, a member of the International Forum for Democratic Studies at the NED,[5] writes,

> Electoral authoritarian regimes practice authoritarianism behind the institutional facades of representative democracy. They hold regular multiparty elections at the national level, yet violate liberal–democratic minimum standards in systematic and profound ways. Since the end of the Cold War, they have turned into the most common form of non-democratic rule in the world.[6]

According to Schedler, monitoring elections is only one part of democratisation; the other is institutional reform.[7] International actors should put 'reluctant rulers under pressure',[8] counter 'electoral market restrictions' by hooking up with protests for greater inclusion in the electoral process, 'sweeten their pressures by appealing to the long-term rationality of rulers' and concentrate their 'subversive energies on: legislatures and media',[9] in other words, influence the domestic political process as far as possible. What if all the pressures and sweeteners fail to unseat an IEM certified government that wishes to steer its own national course? Power is not power without the authority to punish.

The right to punish political leaders and public officials presupposes a relationship of 'authority of the punisher over the punished' and 'connotes relations of authority and subordination'.[10] In turn, authority presupposes an author and an actor. Harry Gould writes,

> When one person acts on behalf of another, the former is the actor, and the latter is the author – the author of the representative's actions. Acting on behalf of the author is to act with authority.[11]

Classical liberalism relies on the metaphor of contract to articulate citizen-state relations. Typically, contracts involve reciprocal rights and duties between the parties to a contract. Contracts must be *performed* by both parties and contracts provide for penalties when one party fails to perform their part. The social contract metaphor requires reciprocity in citizen-state relations. In return for conceding to the state the monopoly to punish citizens, social contract theory saves reciprocity in citizen-state relations by conferring on citizens, in theory at least, the right to penalise public officials through the court system and the elected representatives by revoking their authority to govern. The theoretical reciprocity notwithstanding, the meaning and scope of representation in political practices, the asymmetrical power relations between the citizens and states, and states' monopoly of violence against citizens have been problematic in democratic theories. Accountability removes the very notion of reciprocal relations between citizens and states based on mutual rights and obligations and replaces it with account giving to an account-holder. Mark Bovens observes,

> As a concept, however, 'public accountability' is rather elusive. It is a hurrah-word, like 'learning,' 'responsibility,' or 'solidarity' – nobody can be against it. ... The concept has become a rhetorical device; it serves as a synonym for many loosely defined political desiderata, such as transparency, equity, democracy, efficiency, and integrity ... .[12]

Furthermore,

> 'Public accountability' is not just another political catchword, it also refers to institutionalized practices of account giving. ... Accountability involves two central questions therefore – accountable to whom and for what?[13]

Who is the account-holder? Social movements imagine it is the citizens. The architecture of power in the epoch of imperialism suggests otherwise. The concept of authorisation as a *political* idea with its ideological basis in social contract and the idea of accountability as an *economic* concept with its ideological basis in accounting has important connotations for democracy and social movements. Third World social movements emphasise the erosion of sovereignty but continue to demand *accountability* from political leaders and public officials as if the horizontal and vertical relations between citizens-states, economy-state-civil society and philosophy-politics-law remain unaffected by the unravelling of sovereignty. Not surprisingly, re-scripting rights, democracy and political accountability in the epoch of imperialism occurred not in the fields of political philosophy, as it did in the seventeenth and eighteenth centuries, but rather from the pragmatic concerns of states in international law. The imprint of the principles of colonial governance marks the re-scripted rights, democracy and accountability.

RE-SCRIPTING POLITICAL AUTHORISATION

Anne-Marie Slaughter's re-theorisation, more than any other, sets up the context within which to understand the recognition of victim rights and political accountability in international law. Slaughter, formerly a board member of the NED and director of policy planning for the US State Department between 2009 and 2011, was named by the influential US magazine *Foreign Policy* as one of the Top 100 Global Thinkers for four years in a row.[14] Responding to perceptions of US unilateralism after Reagan and Bush administrations, Slaughter reworks international law and institutions to the possibilities created by the end of the Cold War for the US. Globalisation has transformed the institution of the state and their modes of operating according to Slaughter. Governments, 'like terrorists, arms dealers, money launderers, drug dealers', and other criminals, operate through 'networks of officials, police investigators, financial regulators, judges and legislators, finance ministers, central bankers, environmental officials'.[15] Each network has a specific aim but generally they expand 'regulatory reach', 'build trust', 'establish relationships' and create incentives to establish good reputations and avoid bad ones, and develop best practices.[16] These government networks must be accountable. To who? We know that the terrorists, arms dealers and criminals are subject to the authority of states. It is not possible to escape the vexed question of sovereignty in public accountability.

One way to resolve the persistent issue of sovereignty, Slaughter argues, is to redefine it. According to Slaughter, the concept of sovereignty must be disaggregated.[17]

> ... If states are acting in the international system through their own component government institutions – regulatory agencies, ministries, courts, legislatures – why shouldn't each of these institutions exercise a measure of sovereignty – sovereignty specifically defined and tailored to their functions and capability?[18]

Slaughter justifies disaggregated sovereignty as the means to bring democracy, greater efficiency and accountability for the people of the Third World. A disaggregated state must be governed without a government according to Slaughter.[19] Disaggregated states are underpinned by an *international* regime of rights which act as the normative standard of our times. National governance is part of a *global* responsibility that states owe to the international community of states. Disaggregated sovereignty is operationalised in global governance theories by the doctrine of subsidiarity. Subsidiarity, according to Slaughter, is the normative principle required to structure the global process of disaggregated sovereignty and supranational institutions.[20] The subsidiarity principle ensures that national government officials will undertake tasks of global governance within their states.[21] Political leaders and public officials, according to Slaughter, have dual functions.[22] They are responsible to their domestic constituencies for their domestic *and* transnational activities. They are 'participants in structures of global governance' and

> … must have, *a basic operating code* that takes account of the rights and interests of *all peoples*. …, they should ultimately be *directly subject to the international legal obligations* that currently apply to their nations as unitary states.[23] (Italics added)

NGOs and social movements must also reconstitute citizen-state relations as networks within specific market segments that mirror the global markets. Mirroring the disaggregated state, NGOs must also operate as disaggregated international networks. US and G7 NGOs and social movements *also* have an international role to play in ensuring their own public officials remain accountable for their *international* activities.

> This concept of dual function would make it far easier for organisa-tions like Public Citizen [a US advocacy group] to mobilize ordinary Americans to understand that their government officials may well be playing on a larger global or regional playing field and to monitor their activities. These officials may have two faces, internal and external, but they still have only one audience.[24]

Presumably, that audience for organisations like Public Citizen is the domestic US audience. Civil society groups must ensure that all three branches of the state, the executive, judiciary and the legislature, are *properly linked to their global counterparts.*[25] Government networks must be used as the 'spines of larger policy networks'.[26] NGOs, in Slaughter's view, mediate between 'interest groups' and 'ordinary citizens' on the one hand and 'branches of legislators' on the other and play a pivotal role in accountability.[27] The rights discourse is the vehicle that draws social movements into the new global governance model, even if that was not their intention.

The implications of dual accountability for Third World states are different however. Whereas, public officials in G7 states are accountable to domestic 'civil society' for their international conduct, public officials in Third World states must embed unequal international relations within their national constitutions and remain accountable to the 'international community', law and institutions. Third World NGOs and social movements must hold their political leaders and public officials accountable for failure to effectively incorporate international norms within their states and thereby aid international actors to police their public officials and political leaders. State crimes, victim rights and accountability are located within these larger economic, political, ideological, legal and institutional developments in the post-WWII era.

What is most interesting about Slaughter's re-theorisation of governance and accountability is that it resonates with principles of colonial governance in colonies and protectorates under Indirect Rule in the British Empire. Sir Henry Maine (1822–1888), a British jurist, legal historian and law member of the governing council for India from 1862 to 1869, was the first to develop a revisionist theory of Westphalian sovereignty: the idea that sovereignty was absolute and indivisible. Like Slaughter, Maine tailored the idea of sovereignty to meet the needs of colonial governance by simply redefining absolute sovereignty of the Westphalian type as shared sovereignty between a superior European state (the paramount power) and inferior native states (the subsidiary power). Disaggregated sovereignty may be seen as the further development of Maine's shared sovereignty. Maine was also the first to theorise the principle of paramountcy/subsidiarity in relations between native rulers and the British state and provide theoretical justifications for the Office of the Resident, which exercised the authority for 'regime change' when native rulers acted against the laws of the Empire.[28] The shift from authorisation to accountability and the resonances of principles of global governance with colonial governance provide the context within which to evaluate the internationalisation of victim rights and the crime of 'abuse of power' in the epoch of imperialism.

PANAMA: THE US 'WAR ON DRUGS', MILITARISM AND VICTIM PROTECTION

An international accountability regime for political leaders and public officials presupposes the existence of an 'international community' against which the offence is committed. In a world of 'disaggregated sovereignty' and subsidiarity, it is questionable whether an international community of states is really a 'community' as commonly understood. In the absence of universal citizenship, it cannot be assumed that 'international community' comprises all people everywhere at all times. In the absence of a public domain in international affairs with rights and entitlements for all the world's citizens the extent to which principles of classical liberalism can be zoomed out to the international plane is also questionable. The expansion of international criminal jurisdiction is located within this ambiguity of meaning about who and what constitutes the international community. General Manuel Noriega's trial was a turning point in the script for a new regime of international trials and punishment of political leaders and public officials in the name of 'victim justice'.

General Noriega, the former President of Panama, was the first head of state in the post-WWII era to be sentenced by a foreign government, the US, and imprisoned there for thirty years. Panama was invaded by the US in 1989 in a military operation code-named Operation Just Cause to arrest General Noriega and abduct him to the US to stand trial before a Florida court.[29] The Noriega trial came at an opportune moment when the fate of deposed communist leaders emerged as an important political question for G7 states. In that context, the trial of Slobodan Milošević by the International Criminal Tribunal for the former Yugoslavia (ICTY), a specially constituted tribunal by the UNSC in 1993, marked the first international trial of a head of state after the Nuremberg and Tokyo trials in 1946.[30] The Milošević indictment followed NATO bombings of Serbia. Since the Noriega and Milošević trials international indictments and trials of heads of states and political leaders have become a familiar feature of contemporary international law and politics.[31] The arrest, detention, trial and imprisonment of the former President of Panama reveals the limitations of covert actions for regime changes, the impulse for institutionalisation of mechanisms to punish political leaders and public officials, and the processes and logics that led eventually to the legalisation, internationalisation and institutionalisation of the rights of victims and accountability in the post-WWII era.

Sovereignty of Panama was always an inflammatory issue in US-Panama relations.[32] In 1964 tensions with the US reached a flashpoint and Panama broke diplomatic ties with the US following anti-US riots in the country.[33] Noriega had worked for the US military and intelligence establishment and been on the CIA payroll since the early 1960s.[34] He helped re-establish US ties with Panama, posed no threat to US military bases in the country or its economic interests in the Panama Canal.[35] Noriega aided US efforts to arm and train 'contra' rebels to oust the government of Nicaragua (see Chapter 4).[36] His pivotal role in safeguarding US interests in Panama also emboldened him. Noriega used his proximity to the CIA to sell intelligence services to different states including Cuba and for drug trafficking.[37] In the 1970s he was nearly indicted for gunrunning and drug trafficking but saved by his friends in the US military and intelligence establishment.[38] By 1987 there was popular opposition to Noriega's rule and differences emerged within the military establishments in Panama and the US about his role.[39] The US administration imposed economic sanctions against the *people* of Panama in 1987 to weaken Noriega's rule, but the US administration was still reluctant to cut ties with Noriega.[40] The economic hardships caused by the sanctions intensified popular opposition to Noriega's presidency and amplified the demands to end his rule.

In line with the democracy promotion policy of doing overtly what the US had, hitherto, done covertly, the US attempted to depose Noriega through the election process. One of the earliest 'field trials' of NED strategy was in Panama. Electoral opposition to Noriega was funded by the US state through the CIA.[41] Business groups played a key role in organising elections in Panama.[42] IEM was led by former US presidents, President Jimmy Carter of the Democratic Party and President Gerald Ford of the Republican Party, and the team included former Joint Chiefs of Staff of the US and a British MP amongst others.[43] About the same time, curiously, a Florida court began to consider criminal proceedings against Noriega in 1988.[44] Noriega attempted, unsuccessfully, to negotiate an exit strategy, offering to step down on the condition of immunity from criminal prosecution in the US.[45] Denied the possibilities of an exit strategy Noriega became defiant. Noriega challenged the independence of election monitors.[46] Attempts to depose Noriega 'democratically' failed and the US attempted to organise a coup from within Panama's military establishment. Those attempts also failed.[47] Given his long-standing relationship with the US military intelligence services and the CIA it is possible to speculate that it was difficult if not impossible for the US to grant him immunity from prosecution.

The OAS declined the US request to derecognise the Noriega government.[48] The US launched Operation Just Cause and sent 9500 additional troops to support the 12,000 troops already stationed there to militarily invade Panama, arrest its president and bring him to trial in Florida in the US.[49] The US gave four reasons for the military invasion of Panama: i) to safeguard American lives; ii) to restore democracy; iii) to preserve Panama Canal treaties; and iv) to secure General Noriega to face federal drug charges in the US.[50] From these reasons, it is possible to see how the mission to promote democracy is inextricably tangled with US economic interests, ideological justifications, national security interests, demonisation of leaders and criminal justice.

Each one of these issues raised controversial questions about the legality of US military intervention under the UN Charter. Britain was quick to support the invasion and Margaret Thatcher declared 'the rule of democracy should be upheld'.[51] The majority of the 15 UNSC members supported a UNGA resolution condemning the invasion but it was vetoed by the US, UK and France.[52] If the objective of the exercise was to promote democracy in Panama, then swearing in the opposition candidate, Guillermo Endara, declared elected by the IEM team led by two former US presidents, at a US military base in Panama at the same time as the launch of Operation Just Cause, did not help the legitimacy of democracy promotion policies underway.[53] Estimates of the numbers of people who died in the military operation vary from 314 to 8000.[54]

The Noriega case raised four main legal questions that were addressed initially in the US courts and later amplified internationally. The first question concerned the legal status of Noriega: was he a prisoner of war under the Geneva Conventions? Was he a head of state with state and/ or diplomatic immunities or was he simply a criminal, a drug trafficker, money launderer and racketeer? The second question concerned the extraterritorial jurisdiction of US courts to punish criminal acts committed outside the US. The third question was whether armed invasion of Panama to abduct and arrest Noriega to bring him to trial breached procedural requirements of a fair trial. The fourth issue concerned his extradition to France *after* he had served his sentence in the US.[55] The Florida court ruled in favour of the US on all four questions. US prosecutors attempted unsuccessfully to depoliticise the case by limiting the indictment against Noriega to drug trafficking charges. Obviously, he could not be charged with the real reasons for US displeasure with him: double-crossing the CIA. The Florida court affirmed extraterritorial jurisdiction of US courts and held that the US had the authority to bring anyone who had committed a crime anywhere in the world to justice in the US if the crime affected the security of the state and US citizens.

In the post-WWII era of national independence and decolonisation, the arrest and trial of Noriega challenged the legitimacy of unilateral US action against the legally recognised president of another sovereign state. There were too many big elephants in the court-room during the trial: Operation Just Cause, the Geneva Conventions, diplomatic immunity for heads of states in international law, universal jurisdiction of US courts. The verdict compromised the prestige of the US judicial system. Many saw the ruling as most likely because of the 'deference afforded to the President of the United States and his administration in the area of foreign affairs'.[56] Noriega's lawyer told the *New York Times* after the verdict that

... the United States will now trample across the entire world, imposing its will upon so-called independent, sovereign nations. Unless leaders of foreign governments are willing to kneel once a day and face Washington and give grace to George Bush, they, too, may be in the same posture as General Noriega.[57]

His sentiment was shared by many in the Third World. It did not help matters that soon after the invasion of Panama President Bush had pre-warned that Noriega's arrest would send 'a clear signal that the U.S. [was] serious in its determination that those charged with promoting the distribution of drugs cannot escape the scrutiny of justice'.[58] The Noriega trial created divisions within the US with some calling for the establishment of an international forum for the indictment of foreign nationals for the sake of greater credibility and others opposing it.[59] Doing overtly what the US, UK and other US allies had hitherto done covertly required much more than an effective and invasive intelligence and military apparatus. It required a legal order that allows hitherto illegal actions to be done legally. More importantly, it required establishing the underlying grammar for the new right: its subject, substance, the basis for entitlement and the social purpose.

When President Bush signed the warrant to arrest General Noriega *'and any other persons in Panama* currently under indictment *in the United States* for drug-related offences' (italics added) he relied on the newly enhanced overseas law enforcement powers to wage 'war on drugs'.[60] The National Defense Authorization Act (NDAA) adopted in 1989 designated the Department of Defense as 'the single lead agency' of the federal government for detecting and monitoring maritime and aerial shipments of illicit drugs into the US.[61] The US Southern Command (SOUTHCOM) based in Panama was the first to take on the new 'war on drugs'.[62] The US 'war on drugs' was a real war, not a metaphorical one. From its inception, the 'war on drugs' was international in scope. Martin Jelsma writes,

> In hindsight, the war on drugs can be seen as a transition between the Cold War and the War on Terror, in terms of legitimising military operations, bases and interventions abroad.[63]

The 'war on drugs', conducted initially in Latin America, included components that were in every sense militaristic: deployment of troops, arrest and detention, logistical support, training and equipment, advice, intelligence sharing, close relationships with the military and defence establishments of the target countries, in short an active and aggressive involvement in the very heart of Latin American states.[64] General Wesley K. Clark, the then Commander in Chief of SOUTHCOM, testified to the Senate Armed Services Committee in March 1997 that closer ties with Latin American forces help to encourage

> … subordination to civilian authorities, defense transparency, peaceful resolution of disputes, *and protection of human rights* … .[65] (Italics added)

As a national security issue, the 'war on drugs' intersected with the more conventional geopolitical wars. Panama became the regional base for waging 'war on drugs' in the other Latin American countries.[66] In contrast, in Afghanistan the US and its NATO allies refrained from aerial spraying of poppy fields fearing that the peasants who relied on poppy cultivation for their living might be driven to the Taliban.[67] In Columbia where there was a left-wing insurgency, the 'war on drugs' became a counterinsurgency strategy against a political movement.[68]

The moral justification for the 'war on drugs' was victim protection. Mafia violence, state violence, armed revolutionary movements, political violence, vigilante violence, all produced victims. The rights of victims of all forms of violence needed protection. Victim rights blurred the boundaries between inter- and intra-national wars, insurgency and counterinsurgency, and economic crimes and political crimes. Victim rights, as justification for 'war on drugs', shifted attention away from the social causes of drug production in the Third World such as poverty, wars, the expropriation by transnational corporations, displacement and dispossession by development projects, debt crises, structural adjustment programmes and periodic financial crises, issues that social movements campaign against regularly. The 'war on drugs' turned to suppliers, transit routes and aerial spraying of coca crops and similar intrusive policing by US military in the target countries. What's wrong with fighting drug traffickers one might ask? Victim rights shifted the focus from the central question at the heart of liberal democracy: who has the authority to punish wrongdoings and who authorises the US to police drug traffickers around the world?

The legal justifications for unilaterally internationalising and militarising the supposedly domestic 'war on drugs' was more problematic. The centrality of state sovereignty principle in international law meant the US still needed the consent of the states, by whatever means, to intervene. Internally, in the post-Watergate environment, military operations under executive orders, like Operation Blast Furnace to combat drug crimes in Bolivia for example,[69] came under Congress scrutiny. The US Congress enacted Anti-Drug Abuse Acts in 1986 and 1988, both domestic statutes with international reach. The statutes may have given the US president the authority to conduct 'war on drugs' beyond its borders but did not change existing international law on state sovereignty or non-intervention in the internal affairs of another state or diplomatic immunities. The Noriega case questioned the legitimacy of the international scope of US domestic law and the Universal Jurisdiction principle (see below). Without an international source of authority for the extraterritorial 'war on drugs' it was difficult to replicate the Panama example in systemic ways. From the mid 1980s, alongside pursuing the 'war on drugs' on the ground, US initiatives in the UN pursued the development of international instruments to wage 'war on drugs' in the name of victim rights and accountability.

VICTIM PROTECTION: INTERNATIONALISING AND LEGALISING THE 'WAR ON DRUGS'

The US 'war on drugs' was the context for the United Nations Convention against Illicit Traffic in Narcotic Drugs and Psychotropic Substances 1988. The US took a lead role in drafting the 1988 Convention and appointed a multi-agency negotiating team.[70] Drug trafficking and control in international law is as old as imperialism going back to opium wars between China, Britain and the US under the British Empire. The International Opium Commission was established in 1909 to regulate opium trade.[71]

The main goals for the US in the treaty negotiations were 'compulsory obligations and guidelines for procedures which would improve the ability of law enforcement agencies'.[72] Extradition of individuals charged with drug trafficking was at the top of the US list of priorities as bilateral extradition treaties and cooperation agreements were 'cumbersome and limited in scope of application'.[73] The other priorities were 'asset tracing and forfeiture', 'mutual legal assistance', requiring states to include *in their statute books* provisions to transfer persons in custody to give evidence and freeze assets; 'maritime anti-drug enforcement procedures' to search vessels and carriers anywhere; powers to eradicate illicit crops and 'controlled delivery' to police drug trafficking routes leading to arrest and recovery.[74] The 1988 Convention would oblige states to comply with internationally recognised enforcement procedures. As the negotiating team reported to the US Senate caucus on International Narcotics Control,

> Moreover, many countries which may be reluctant to participate directly with the United States on a bilateral basis may find a multilateral agreement against drug trafficking more palatable.[75]

US negotiating positions were approved in the UN 'with less controversy than expected'.[76] These changes include a broader definition of carriers to include public and private carriers, inclusion of money laundering as a crime, recognition of all offences in the Convention as extraditable offences where there are no bilateral extradition treaties between states, 'de-politicisation' of drug offences, i.e. exclude social questions, funding requests from states to implement the provisions and attempts to attribute responsibilities to the consuming countries for the drug problem. The US got its way on most issues in the 1988 Convention. In the words of the negotiating team,

> [t]he U.S. negotiators should be commended for these efforts, and should continue to block any attempts to blame unilaterally so-called consuming countries for the international narcotics trafficking and abuse problem.[77]

The 1988 Convention goes beyond previous anti-drug trafficking conventions which set standards, identified narcotic substances and provided norms that states could adopt and seeks to establish international enforcement mechanisms. Ms Ellen Warlow of the US State Department explains that multilateral treaties were needed to standardise, harmonise and internationalise transnational crimes as they help US diplomacy to firm up the implementation of those laws through bilateral treaties on extradition, evidence gathering, and above all prosecution of foreign nationals in *US courts* for transnational crimes,[78] in other words, to do overtly what the US had done covertly in Noriega's case.

Roger S. Clark notes that after the Cold War, Western states 'would prefer to concentrate on transnational crime'.[79] Expansion in the scope of international criminal jurisdiction in the name of accountability and victim rights continued throughout the 1980s.[80] The United Nations Convention against Transnational Organized Crime of 2000[81] most comprehensively expands the scope of international criminal jurisdiction beyond drugs and includes every type of criminal activity committed by three or more people involving *any* association or link with another country.[82] It includes money laundering,[83] corruption,[84] prosecution, adjudication and seizure,[85] extradition,[86] mutual legal assistance for prosecuting crimes[87] and requires states to introduce or modify laws to meet the 2000 Convention standards.[88] Third World political leaders and public officials are now required to legislate into existence their own Damocles Swords to hang above their heads cheered on by NSMs, NGOs and INGOs. Who are they accountable to however? At the same time, who can argue against the need to combat drug mafias, corrupt politicians and officials, insurgents and so many other 'baddies' in the world who victimise innocent victims without rights?

The 'war on drugs', the first strand in establishing rights of victims, regularised and routinised an international criminal jurisdiction far beyond the more exceptional war crimes established by the Nuremberg principles. The 'war on drugs' established the substance of the new victim rights: international criminal justice. It established the moral justification for the new right, i.e. victim protection. The subject of rights and the basis of entitlement proved more challenging and developed in the second and third strands on international criminal justice.

'RIGHTS OF VICTIMS':
FROM CIVIL LIBERTIES TO VICTIMOLOGY

Rights of Victims and Neoliberal Reforms in 'Mature Democracies'

Classical liberalism does not recognise rights of victims; it cannot. Having ceded monopoly on violence to the state, the power to punish citizens for wrongdoing remains the sole prerogative of the state, which the state undertakes in the name of citizens and their security. That *was* the social contract. Until the middle of the twentieth century public citizens were more concerned about encroachment of state powers on freedoms of citizens, in other words, the anxiety was about civil liberties and authoritarianism. The world wars transformed the liberal state into what David Edgerton calls the 'warfare state' by integrating bureaucracy, military, economic, media and civil society organisations as wartime necessity.[89] The 'warfare state' was never dismantled after WWII. As wartime anxieties receded so did the support for the insensitive, alienating, administrative, police and corporate bureaucracies that had come to occupy social and democratic spaces in Euro-American societies. In the 1960s, social movements in the US, concerned about rising crime rates, alienation of minorities, disproportionate numbers of African-American and indigenous people in prisons, demanded better prison conditions and fairer trials, i.e. classical civil liberties.[90] Women's movements in the US were at the vanguard of the demands for a more responsive state demanding concrete assistance for counselling services, refuge and financial assistance for rape victims.[91]

Neoliberal reforms introduced by Ronald Reagan in the US and Margaret Thatcher in the UK turned the demands for administrative reforms on its head. Crime control became an important ideological tool for neoliberal reforms.[92] The language of rights was central to flipping the calls for administrative reforms into crime control.[93] Law reforms articulated the demands for a responsive state as 'rights of victims'. Victimology emerged as a sub-field of criminology rivalling conventional penology.[94] Social movements picked up the language of rights without recognising what was entailed by it. Movements for victim rights began initially in the US and the UK in the 1960s and spread to New Zealand, Canada and other European states.[95] When the UNGA considered legalising the 'rights of victims' in the mid 1980s victim rights was well established in the 'mature democracies'.

Victim rights enable neoliberal states to remain 'neutral' to prisoners and victims alike and allow 'competition' between retribution and recidivism to play out in society frequently with a quiet nudge from the invisible hand of the market. It enables states to trade-off rights of victim rights and prisoner rights by 'balancing' them 'fairly'. Whereas prisoner rights focused on crime prevention and programmes to prevent recidivism the new emphasis on victims diverted attention from the social causes of crime to individual compensation. Policies of inclusion and exclusion, funding, and positivist definitions of entitlements to services, i.e. 'the fine print' of the law, mired victim rights further in the unresponsive state that victims had set out to challenge. Victim rights enhanced the authority of the state over victims and offenders alike.

Rights and 'Abuse of Power' in the UN

The UN mandate to promote progressive penal reform was turned on its head in the 1980s. Campaigns of professional groups like the International Penal and Penitentiary Commission (IPPC) to improve prison conditions in the US and Europe since 1872[96] were recognised by the League of Nations in 1930[97] at the instance of UK advocacy groups at a time when state sovereignty was the 'holy cow' in international affairs. In retrospect, the work of these groups prefigures the type of liberal internationalism we see today where social movements, imperialist states, NGOs, IOs work in concert to internationalise social issues in ways that reinforce imperial power. The 1920s was a decade of 'unstable equilibrium' for the British Empire[98] beleaguered by the economic and social costs of WWI, unrest in the colonies and the crisis of capitalism. Led by the liberal British elite, e.g. the Fabian Society, supported by the

British Foreign Office, organisations like the Association for Moral and Social Hygiene (AMSH) and the International Bureau for the Suppression of Traffic in Women and Children (IBSTWC) worked initially to rescue European women from trafficking and later expanded their work to the colonies.[99] Britain used the moral authority of the NGOs to incorporate social and humanitarian clauses in the Treaty of Versailles which set up the League of Nations.[100] The UN Charter incorporated and expanded the social, humanitarian, cultural role for the organisation. The work of British NGOs during the interwar years helped Britain to 'internationalize imperialism'.[101] Under the UN, the Economic and Social Council (ECOSOC) took over the social work of the IPPC.[102] Under the ECOSOC's Commission on Crime Prevention and Control (CCPC) the IPPC's conventional concerns about crime like treatment of prisoners, recidivism, parole and social causes of crime gave way to 'rights of victims' and 'abuse of power'.[103]

The recognition of 'abuse of power' is the other side of the recognition of 'rights of victims' and directly targets political leaders and public officials. At the insistence of Third World states interested in sanctioning corporate crimes[104] the CCPC in July 1976, put 'gilded criminality' on its agenda.[105] 'Gilded criminality' underwent interesting 'linguistic compromises' thereafter. In 1978 the CCPC included 'abuse of power' on the agenda of the forthcoming Sixth Congress of the United Nations Prevention of Crimes and Treatment of Offenders which was to be held in 1980.[106] The Sixth Congress resolved that alongside treatment of offenders 'attention should *also* be given to the problems of victims of crime …'[107] (italics added). For the Third World states 'abuse of power' was about abuse of *economic power* by corporations and victim rights, about support for victims of corporate crimes.[108] For the First World states abuse of power was about abuse of *political power* by political leaders and public officials. Canada, Spain, Sweden, Switzerland, the US and Venezuela sponsored the draft resolution on abuse of power giving the resolution a distinct political orientation.[109] Drawing on the Additional Protocol to the Geneva Convention on rules of armed conflicts, the resolution urged states to end extrajudicial executions of political opponents by 'armed forces, law enforcement or other governmental agencies or by paramilitary or political groups' in intrastate wars and civil conflicts, arguing that from the victims' standpoint it matters little whether the war is international or national.

On 29 November 1985, the UNGA adopted the *Declaration of Basic Principles of Justice for Victims of Crime and Abuse of Power*. The Declaration defines victim rights as rights of victims of 'abuse of power'. The 'linguistic compromises' turned 'gilded criminality' by corporations into international accountability of political leaders and public officials. The linguistic trade-offs notwithstanding the fact remains that whereas Western states with veto powers are able to pursue political 'abuse of power', Third World states are hardly in a position to pursue corporate abuses of power, more so as the most powerful corporations are nationals of G7 states.

INGOs and social movements contributed to flipping 'gilded criminality' of corporations into the broader 'abuse of power' by political leaders and public officials. The World Society of Victimology, a scientific society which had campaigned for recognition of victim rights in the 'mature democracies', lobbied the UN to adopt their draft code on international victim rights. Initially, their draft code did not include 'abuse of power'.[110] On the suggestion of Irene Melup, a US national working as the Senior Social Affairs Officer of the United Nations Crime Prevention and Criminal Justice Branch at the time, the Society redrafted their Code to include victims of abuse of powers to bring it within the remit of the pre-existing CCPC's resolutions. Melup enlisted other academics to draft proposals on victim rights for the UN secretariat.[111] The Declaration invites states to negotiate multilateral treaties on victim rights.[112]

International recognition of victim rights legitimises international interventions against abuse of power and provides the legal grounds for stronger states to pursue and prosecute other wars in other UN forums such as the 'war on drugs' and the 'war on terror' in the name of victims and accountability. In other words, it brings back principles of paramountcy and subsidiarity of the colonial era, re-theorised by public scholars like Slaughter, and embeds them in international law. What does this do to the original idea of representative democracy as political empowerment of citizens to take action against wrongdoing by political leaders and public officials, an idea that is deeply embedded in liberal imaginations? The point here is not whether victim rights and abuse of power should or should not be internationalised and legalised – but rather what does the legalisation and internationalisation do to our ideas of political authorisation, political power and us as agents of political change? What does it do to classical liberalism?

THE INTERNATIONAL CRIMINAL COURT:
'AN INTERNATIONAL COURT TO TRY AFRICAN LEADERS'?

Nuremberg Principles

The International Criminal Court (ICC), established in 2002 and operational since 2005, directly subjects political leaders and public officials to international criminal jurisdiction. The ICC *is* about victims. Under the aegis of the UNOHCHR international criminal law, crime prevention and 'human' rights were integrated into a comprehensive international regime of public accountability and 'abuse of power'. The legal recognition of 'rights of victims' was the conceptual tool and organising device to establish an international regime for punishment of 'abuse of power'. If the trial of General Noriega was the turning point in re-scripting a new regime of accountability for political leaders and public officials, recognising the rights of victims in international law in *non-war contexts* is a condition precedent for the ICC. Typically, in the epoch of imperialism, the groundwork for re-scripting rights of citizens as rights of victims began after the end of WWII. The ICC formally institutionalises and universalises as a permanent feature of the international order a process that began with the Nuremberg trials.

The most significant idea formalised in the first Nuremberg principle was that *individuals* may be punished by *foreign states* for acts considered a crime in international law. Equally significant were the ideas that atrocities by a government against a section of its own people was an *international* crime, and that individuals were responsible for their actions to an *international community of states* beyond their own states and fellow citizens. After the Nuremberg decision, the US moved the UNGA to affirm the Nuremberg principles thereby making them a component of the body of international law.[113] The Nuremberg principles were limited to three categories of crimes: 'crimes against peace', 'war crimes' and 'crimes against humanity' occurring within a narrow context of international wars.

The Nuremberg and Tokyo trials were seen by many as 'victor's justice' because acts committed by the Nazis were punished whereas similar acts of the Allies were not.[114] Historically, victor's justice was a *political* act directed at securing the subordination of political leaders and the citizens in the vanquished territories.[115] Until WWI victorious states could claim war reparations as remedy. The burden of war reparation on Germany after WWI fuelled WWII.[116] WWII separated economic and political issues in war settlements. The prize for WWII was not reparations but the integration of the Axis economies and militaries into emerging global TMF capitalism. The integration established groupings of dominant capitalist states like the OECD in 1948 and G6 in 1975 (later G7). Nuremberg and Tokyo tribunals tried and punished individual political figures and public officials. The Nuremberg trials did more than securing victor's justice however. They wrote victor's justice into the body of international law as an enduring principle applicable to all states beyond WWII. The tools for meting out victor's justice were readily available, therefore, after the victory of the G7 states in the Cold War.[117]

ICC: Rationale and Scope

The Nuremberg principles remained in suspended animation until the end of the Cold War.[118] In the interim the expansion of international criminal jurisdiction occurred outside contexts of war, as discussed above. By the early 1990s influential voices in the US began calling for a more interventionist role in bringing political leaders around the world to justice.[119] Samantha Power, formerly a US journalist, and the US ambassador to the UN under the Obama administration, states in her Pulitzer Prize winning book, 'A Problem From Hell', that by 1992 US diplomats in Bosnia became eager to see a Western military intervention.[120] Her description of the role for social movements and NGOs in the military intervention is revealing. Power writes,

> But internal appeals alone were unlikely to make a dent in the con-sciousness of senior policymakers so firmly opposed to intervening. The State Department dissenters *needed help from American reporters, editorial boards, and advocacy groups*. Initially, they did not really get it [Journalists were unfamiliar with Bosnia] and compensated for their ignorance with *an effort to be 'even-handed' and 'neutral'* ... .
> In early August 1992, however, *the proponents of intervention within the U.S. government gained a weapon in their struggle*: The Western media finally won access to Serb concentration camps. ... Journalists not only began challenging U.S. policy, but *they supplied photographic images and refugee sagas that galvanized heretofore silent elite opinion*. Crucially, the advocates of humanitarian intervention began to win the support *of both liberals committed to advancing human rights as*

well as staunch Republican Cold Warriors, who believed the U.S. had the responsibility and the power to stop Serb aggression in Europe. The Bush administration's chosen policy of nonintervention suddenly came to feel politically untenable.[121] (Italics added)

In 1992, on a motion by the US, the UNSC commissioned two *private* US organisations, the Soros Foundation and the MacArthur Foundation, to investigate allegations of genocide in the former Yugoslavia following reports by the US-based Human Rights Watch and Roy Gutman, an American journalist. Both foundations provided financial support to the UN's work.[122] The model of 'contracting out' public functions at the highest levels of UN administration has since become a trend in many UN operations. The US Secretary of State Lawrence Eagleburger called for the establishment of a war crimes tribunal for the former Yugoslavia at a conference in London in late 1992.[123] In early 1993 the UNSC established the ICTY. The US role in the ICTY was controversial.[124] The ICTY was followed by the International Criminal Tribunal for Rwanda (ICTR). Experimentation with mixed tribunals (combining domestic and international law and judges) ensued in East Timor, Sierra Leone, Bosnia, Cambodia and Lebanon and other states.[125] The stage was set for a permanent criminal court.

The ICC has jurisdiction to try three types of crimes: genocide, crimes against humanity, war crimes if the states consent to its jurisdiction.[126] Negotiations for the Rome statutes were contentious.[127] The main concern for the US was to protect its servicepersons deployed around the world. US anxiety to protect her servicemen generated an opinion that the ICC should remain independent of the UNSC.[128] For Third World states the creation of a series of ad hoc international criminal trials by the UNSC modelled on ICTY generated new fears about US unilateralism. Yet the idea of an independent ICC resonates with liberal ideas of judicial independence within states. The analogy is false. The UNSC-states relationship in the international domain is not comparable to the citizen-state relationship in the national domain.

The ICC establishes institutional mechanisms to bring justice to victims of political crimes. The political rationale for the ICC is that political crimes against people threaten peace and security, a central concern for the UN.[129] The institutional rationale is to make it obligatory for states to incorporate international standards in their domestic law for accountability of public officials and political leaders. The ethical rationale for the ICC is that 'unimaginable atrocities' against millions 'deeply shock the conscience of humanity'.[130] Conceptualised in this way, the systemic causes of atrocities become irrelevant. Individual punishment for 'abuse of power' reduces international crimes to individual deviance and delinks it from the economic causes for civil wars and conflicts that manifest as ethnic or sectarian or class conflicts in intra-national wars in the Third World.

The procedural provisions in the Rome statutes, the 'fine print' of the law, wrote-in ways to protect citizens of the 'established democracies' from international trials and punishment. The ICC became, as William Schabas argues, a carefully crafted institution where principles of complementarity require the ICC to proceed with investigations only if the state responsible can be shown as 'unwilling or unable' to proceed.[131] The UNSC continues to have powers to refer and defer complaints. Any investigation can be effectively blocked by the UNSC. The prosecutor exercises wide discretion to decline or investigate crimes on his or her own motion or based on complaints by states and/or NGOs. Selectivity and opacity in the prosecutor's decision-making has called into question the impartiality of the prosecutor's office.[132] Resourcing issues for the ICC means only a small number of cases can be brought to trial. International legal standards are modelled on European civil law and Anglo-American Common Law systems. There is an in-built bias therefore in favour of Euro-American legal systems when assessing the capacities of states to prosecute their own offenders and the complementarity principle.

ICC, Africa and the Third World

The ICC's work so far has focused almost entirely on indicting African leaders.[133] The campaigns for indictment of African leaders and officials sound much like the colonial characterisation of natives as corrupt, incompetent men without respect for law or humanity. The arrest warrant issued by the ICC against the President of Sudan, Omar al-Bashir, in 2008 alarmed African states. The referral of a sitting head of state to the ICC came from the UNSC and perceived to be at the insistence of the US. It followed a controversial campaign on Darfur funded and supported by influential US NGOs.[134] The African Union called on the UNSC to defer the ICC proceeding.[135] In an act of open defiance, in June 2015, the South African government allowed al-Bashir to attend a meeting of the African National Congress in South Africa and return to Sudan without arrest.[136]

Outside the ICC atrocities by the US and the UK in well-known cases like Abu Ghraib, Guantanamo, Bagram, Falluja, Basra, extraordinary renditions for torture, contamination of civilians from depleted uranium in Iraq,[137] use of the white phosphorous by Israel in Palestine,[138] use of Daisy bombs in Afghanistan[139] continue to scandalise the conscience of the world. Regime changes by the Office of the Resident during the colonial era look harmless in retrospect.

African and Latin American states were most enthusiastic about the ICC. Both continents were theatres where the military and economic aspects of the Cold War were played out with devastating consequences for the people, environment, economy and, above all, democratic institutions on which rights rest. More powerful states and states at war like China, Israel, the US, India, Iran, Japan, Turkey, Iraq, Libya, Qatar, Yemen, Pakistan, Saudi Arabia, Sudan, Syria are not signatories to the ICC statutes. The end of the Cold War created new expectations within the UN. UN inspector Maurice Bertrand writes that between 1987 and 1992 Third World states were under the illusion that with the end of the Cold War they would be liberated from 'the shackles of the East-West divide', that 'the veto would be no more than a bad memory' and the public opinion generated by many governments and the media 'helped to instil a belief in the rebirth of the UN' which would occupy the security vacuum.[140] Further, he writes, '… in fact, they [the illusions] were shared to only a very limited extent by those responsible for foreign policy in the United States and other major Western powers'.[141]

The NGOs and the ICC

International NGOs were instrumental in getting Third World states to ratify the Rome statutes, providing them with legal advice and support, including guidance on domestic legislation. Their campaigns and formation of wide networks within countries created a political environment in favour of the ICC.[142] Like with the IEMs, the ICC agenda brought together a coalition of powerful 'human' rights organisations funded and supported by the North American and European states amplifying and legitimising the elite voices that were calling for overtly interventionist policies around the world.[143] After the ILC submitted draft ICC statutes to the UNGA in 1994 twenty-five human rights organisations met in New York in February 1995 to form a

coalition 'to advocate the establishment of an effective and just international criminal court' and set up an informal steering committee.[144]
Prominent members of the steering committee for the Coalition for an
International Criminal Court (CICC), which is a key player in setting
up the ICC, include Amnesty International – an influential British NGO
with an annual income of nearly £58.5 million in 2012[145] and criticised
for proximity to British and US governments,[146] Human Rights Watch
– the US organisation criticised for having a 'revolving door' to US
administration,[147] Parliamentarians for Global Action – a European
NGO funded by European governments and the EU,[148] the Canadian
International Centre for Human Rights and Democratic Development
(ICHRDD) – a statutory organisation set up in 1988 to promote human
rights overseas, with 78 per cent of its budget coming from the Canadian
government and reporting to the Canadian parliament,[149] No Peace
Without Justice – an NGO founded by prominent libertarian Italian
politician Emma Bonino, formerly Italy's foreign minister and member
of the EU parliament.[150] The CICC included the United States Faith and
Ethics Network for the International Criminal Court (US FENICC), a
coalition of religious, interfaith ethical and humanist NGOs and linked
to faith networks within the UN and the World Economic Forum.[151]

By 1998, when the UN convened the diplomatic conference to adopt
the Rome statutes, the CICC comprised a network of eight hundred
organisations and had four hundred and fifty individuals represented
at the Rome diplomatic conference. The larger NGOs sent delegations
larger than many government delegations.[152] After the ICC became
operational, the CICC has played an instrumental role in bringing cases
to the ICC and building pressure on Third World states to incorporate
crimes in the ICC statutes into domestic law. Much of ICC's work has
been in Africa and Latin America. Social movements that distanced
themselves from the methods of the CICC and their funding sources
nevertheless supported the idea of accountability and victim justice
against abuse of power. Their aims are indeed far from objectionable –
the question remains: who has the authority to punish abusers of power?
Classical liberalism says the people alone have that authority. In the
epoch of imperialism that authority passes to the largest economic and
military powers. This passing is not a matter of semantics or ethics. It is
about grasping how some states subjugate others, legally and militarily,
which is the essence of imperialism.

UNIVERSAL JURISDICTION

A note on Universal Jurisdiction is in order before concluding this chapter on victim rights and abuse of power. The Noriega decision was a radical departure from the general principle of law that a state's criminal jurisdiction is limited to crimes committed within their states or by their nationals. The doctrine of Universal Jurisdiction delinks the crime and the prosecuting state. Any state can, in theory, prosecute any crime anywhere.[153] Belgium and Spain, drawing on Enlightenment scholars like Hugo Grotius and Emer de Vattel, incorporated the principle into domestic laws.[154] In 2003 seven Iraqi families filed cases against former President G.W. Bush Sr, Vice President Dick Cheney, US Secretary of State Colin Powell and General Norman Schwarzkopf the American Commander of the first Gulf War in a Belgian court alleging that they were responsible for the 1991 bombing of a civilian air raid shelter in Baghdad that caused the deaths of the family members. Lutz and Reiger write,

> In response, the United States reportedly threatened to pull NATO headquarters out of Brussels unless the law was changed. This pressure was too much even for progressive Belgium, which regards itself as a small country with a special moral role. A bill already before parliament that repealed the universal jurisdiction statute was quickly pushed through and adopted into law in April 2003.[155]

In 2009 Spain was forced to amend its laws to limit Universal Jurisdiction when the victims of state violence in Guantanamo Bay prison and Gaza initiated proceedings against the US and Israel.[156] In 2014 Spanish courts issued arrest warrants against China's former President Jiang Zemin and former Prime Minister Li Peng in proceedings initiated by Tibetan victims of 'human' rights abuses living in Spain. The Spanish parliament fast-tracked law to further curtail extraterritorial jurisdiction of Spanish courts.[157] Luc Reydems writes,

> [the Universal Jurisdiction cases] raise policy and ideological issues concerning ... Western judicial imperialism. ... In view of their lack of resources, of institutional capacity, and, it must be said, of military and political power, the latter [the developing countries] are unlikely

to take an active role in these legal developments. The 'universal' in 'universal jurisdiction' may remain wishful thinking for a long time.[158]

In the liberal imaginations of refugee and migrant justice movements victim rights carry the capacity to bring perpetrators to justice if only they invoked their rights.

CONCLUSION

Richard Mulgan highlights two uses of the term accountability. *External accountability* is often vertical and hierarchical and implies responsibility to and scrutiny by another external and/or higher authority. *Internal accountability* is the *inner* sense of moral obligation.[159] It is possible to see how internationalisation and legalisation of rights of victims organises both dimensions of accountability. On the one hand, it establishes external vertical accountability to an 'international authority of states' as an objective function. On the other hand, it establishes internal accountability by recognising moral culpability of individual political leaders and public officials as the subjective grounds for international prosecutions. Vertical accountability in the epoch of imperialism requires Third World leaders and officials to give 'account to' those who manage global governance. 'Abuse of power' hangs like Damocles' sword on them.

Melvin J. Dubnick argues that the word 'accountability' has acquired a cultural keyword status, and transfigured from 'an instrument of governing' to 'an end in itself' within the context of governing.[160] It is 'an indicator and measure of the unsettled nature of governance in this tumultuous and transitional time'.[161] The epoch of imperialism de-politicises society and shrinks the political sphere and the political agency of people. The primacy of politics is replaced with the primacy of 'rule of law' and political agency is confined to different market segments. Bereft of visions for nation or society or humanity, social movements must compete with each other to keep the state's attention. The political concept of 'authorisation' is transformed into the economic idea of 'accountability'. The hat-trick is performed by the rights of victims.

6

Intangible Property Rights: The IMF as Underwriters

For at least another hundred years we must pretend to ourselves and to everyone that fair is foul and foul is fair; for foul is useful and fair is not. Avarice and usury and precaution must be our gods for a little longer still. For only they can lead us out of the tunnel of economic necessity into daylight. (John Maynard Keynes, Economic Possibilities for Our Grandchildren, 1930, p. 372)[1]

An important premise of this book is that property and 'human' rights are contingent and constitute a comprehensive regime of rights. Another premise is that real changes in real relations in the real world precede formal legal rights and their institutionalisation. If first generation rights like representative democracy and popular sovereignty were re-scripted as 'right to free and fair elections' and 'rights of victims', as Chapters 4 and 5 argued, what were the drivers of those changes? If capitalism is the generative mechanism for modern societies, how did TMF capitalism reconfigure a new regime of property and 'human' rights?

The preconditions for TMF capitalism are necessarily *international* in scope: international property rights, contract laws, trade and exchange mechanisms, disputes settlement, regulatory institutions and so on as well as international 'human' rights. It is easy to forget that nineteenth-century rights were limited within nation-states and the colonies were outside the liberal order for the most part. This chapter examines new property rights under TMF capitalism. The new intangible property rights were forged on the anvil of Third World debt crises in the 1970s and 1980s, the manifestations of which, from *Caracazo* in Venezuela to Boko Haram in Nigeria were discussed in Chapter 2. The internationalisation and legalisation of property rights was preceded by real changes in real property relations between Third World states, the US-led G7 states, transnational corporations, banks and financial institutions mediated by IEOs like the World Bank and IMF. This chapter examines how the

IMF emerged as the underwriter for new forms of intangible property innovated by transnational banks and investors after WWII.

INTANGIBLE PROPERTY AND USURERS' NEW DILEMMA

Property is a legal relation. It is the *settlement* by the state about exclusive access to resources, about who gets what and how much.

> Property is a legal fiction. It is a synthesis word for all laws against trespass. Through this process, the government renders highly probable that we can enjoy real dominion over that which we claim as our own. ... But property itself is nothing more than a residuum of all the things that the state does to permit me to call something my own and to have a reasonable probability of making it stick. 'The market' comes after the risk of property ownership itself has been close to eliminated.[2]

As a legal construct, what is or is not property can change. The revolutionary development during early mercantile capitalism was the idea that one's own labour could be alienable private property to be bought and sold because the law recognised it as one's personal 'property'. A related revolutionary idea was land as alienable property. Together, the two legal constructs reorganised relations between nature and people and tore up feudatory property relations. Alienability is the defining attribute of private property in capitalist relations based on commodity production. By the turn of the twentieth century property rights to labour and nature had become so entrenched they appeared fundamental to any constitutional order. In their external relations capitalist nation-states during the mercantile era focused on securing favourable terms of trade for goods and commodities for national traders. Later, they colonised nations to secure raw materials and markets for their industries. As capitalism expanded in scale, banks and investors began exporting surplus capital to other states and colonies. Capitalist nation-states turned attention to securing favourable terms and conditions for foreign investments for their national corporations from other states. The national legal and institutional frameworks of NCI capitalism no longer 'fitted' the expanding transnational activities of industries and investors.

Trading in money as a commodity in its own right, entailed in capital exports, led to innovations in new forms of property. Recall that John

Maynard Keynes floated the idea of government bonds as the route to economic recovery, a move that created international bond markets based on no other security than the authority of the state. The innovation of new forms of property accelerated especially after the economic crises beginning in the late 1960s and early 1970s. Currencies, debts, securities, innovations in insurance, hedge funds, futures trading, risks and other financial 'products', in the language of finance capitalism, became tradable property. These new forms of property established by fiat of law were, unlike land, forests, minerals and such, intangible or 'virtual' property. They were not backed by real assets comparable to currencies backed by gold reserves. These were free-floating monetary instruments that worked because the lawyers invented them and regulatory authorities like the Securities and Exchange Commission recognised them. Financial 'products' no longer represent value embodied in commodities. These new *securities* trade in *insecurities*. In the 1970s trading in derivatives was considered too small for statistics. By 1987 the derivatives market was US$ 273 trillion.[3]

Historically, the establishment of new property rights has always been violent and socially disruptive. Seventeenth- and eighteenth-century property rights caused displacement, dispossession and widespread social upheavals in European societies. Those upheavals led to recognition of poor laws and demands that the state takes some responsibility for displaced and dispossessed citizens, in other words, for 'human' rights. International property rights brought with them dispossession and displacement on a global scale during the debt crises and demands of 'human' rights and the rights resurgence discussed in Chapter 2. The actors and context for the new international rights regime were worlds apart from those in the nineteenth century however. When the possibility of debt-default by Mexico triggered the debt crises in the early 1980s, 'free markets' of the nineteenth-century type had *de facto* disappeared in the G7 states. The structure of the banking industry had undergone radical transformations during and after the world wars.[4] Banking activities had branched into conventional banking and the financial sectors. Banks, which traditionally shared the risks and benefits of trade and manufacturing, became poor second cousins to the expanding financial sector trading in new financial 'products'. In turn, the financial sector distanced itself from manufacturing or trading.[5] Their interest in financing projects was solely for the purposes of earning interest, i.e. usury in the classical sense. During the sovereign debt crises in the 1980s, like classical usurers, modern financial banks faced what I shall call the *usurer's dilemma* portrayed so wonderfully by Shakespeare in *The Merchant of Venice*. For money lending to be profitable business, usurers must extract everything of value from the debtors. At the same time, usurers must ensure the debtor does not die. Dead debtors do not borrow or pay interest on loans. The *usurer's dilemma* is a useful metaphor to understand the incorporation of 'human' rights by G7 states and IEOs in the wake of the violence and social disruption that the new property rights brought across the Third World.

THE DEBT CRISIS: A BRIEF TIMELINE

The establishment of intangible properties and their recognition as substantive rights in the 1980s had been a project in the making since WWI. The institutional and legal frameworks for reconstructing capitalism were forged during the world wars and after WWII, as discussed in Chapter 3. Reconstruction included reconstruction of physical infrastructures destroyed by the world wars, institutional infrastructures including markets, states, and property rights, contracts and dispute resolution as well as reconstructing colonial relations disrupted by the imploding empires of the NCI era. Until around 1965 reconstruction of capitalism was state-led through administrative and diplomatic interventions. Many institutions were established during the world wars to support emerging TMF capitalism in the capitalist states. For example, in 1934 during the height of the recession in the US, the government set up the Export Import Bank (EXIM Bank), which was later institutionalised as an independent agency of the US state in 1945 after WWII ended. In the UK, the government established the UK's Export Credits Guarantee Department (ECGD) in 1919 during the economic recession. After WWI investments in Britain's colonies to export manufactured goods became a way out of Britain's own domestic recession.[6] These domestic institutions in capitalist states are aligned to IOs in ways that Third World states are not.

Until the mid 1960s capitalist states secured favourable conditions for the overseas activities of their corporations through administrative, state, diplomacy and military initiatives. For example, Third World states received bilateral 'tied-aid' which came with conditions that included purchase of goods and services from corporations of the creditor states.[7] Transnational Corporations (TNC) expanded rapidly by manufacturing cheap goods for consumption in the US and Europe using cheap labour and natural resources in the Third World and importing high value goods from their home states in the US and EU into Third World states to set up industries to manufacture tradable goods. They received guarantees against losses in Foreign Direct Investments from domestic institutions like the EXIM Bank and ECGD. These administrative, state and diplomacy-led initiatives transformed *real relations* between Third World states, IEOs and the G7. They could not, however, establish legally recognised international property rights with the entire gamut of contracts, dispute resolution and regulatory mechanisms.

By the late 1960s there was economic turmoil in the belly of post-WWII capitalism, the US. The severe recession around 1968 ended the post-WWII expansion of US manufacturing, banking and investments. Several factors contributed to the economic turmoil such as the plateauing of demand for US goods after post-war reconstruction of Europe under the Marshall Plan, the oil embargo by OPEC countries in 1973, the Yom Kippur War, the Iranian Revolution, the Iran-Iraq War, US deficits and the fall in the value of the US dollar.[8] So severe was the crisis that President Nixon unilaterally ended the fixed parity between the US dollar and gold and between the US dollar and other currencies in August 1971 following extreme volatility in the value of the US dollar.[9] France threatened to end its own currency's exchange rates linked to the US dollar.[10] The unilateral decision by the US led to the collapse of the post-WWII Bretton Woods monetary system and ended the supremacy of the US dollar.[11]

Transnationalisation of investments and manufacturing brought new freedoms for TNCs that altered their relations to nation and state in qualitative ways. US TNCs responded to the crisis by relocating their manufacturing in the Third World where manufacturing costs were cheaper.[12] US banks, which dominated global banking, responded to the crisis in the US economy by banking their overseas earnings in European, predominantly London, banks, outside the regulatory oversight of US authorities. Sovereign borrowers absorbed the plentiful petrodollars from the oil trade, the loans came with large commissions on loan placements and the size and length of development projects held out the promise of being in business for a long time. The profitability of lending to Third World states can be gauged from the fact that international lending of thirteen US banks was 34.2 per cent of their total profits in 1973 and 47.7 per cent in 1975, and an estimated 75 per cent of the profits of US banks in 1976 came from their foreign operations.[13] Relocation of labour and manufacturing drove a spatial/geographical wedge between manufacturing and financial sectors. A different kind of spatial/geographic wedge emerged in the regulatory frameworks for transnational finance. Banking and finance were concentrated in a few major centres in the US (mainly New York) and the UK (mainly the City of London) polarising financial capitals from the rest of the country. The crises transformed the relations between states and corporations in ways that are qualitatively different from the relations between state and economy under the nation-states of nineteenth-century capitalism. The legal and institutional infrastructures changed slowly if at all, and in an ad hoc fashion when they did.

Newly independent Third World states, flush with the elan of new-found sovereignty, concerned that TNCs exploited their natures and peoples and unequal trading system,[14] saw borrowing from private banks as a way out of 'state oppression' of the G7. Private banks were more interested in interest repayments than their state's policies.[15] Between 1972 and 1975, in just three years, the debt owed by Third World states to private financial institutions increased by more than 200 per cent. Private debt as share of poor countries' debt increased from 2 per cent in 1971 to 6 per cent in 1980; for middle-income countries the proportion increased from 14 to 30 per cent in 1980 and for industrialised countries it increased from 38 to 65 per cent.[16] In 1979 the US Federal Reserve dramatically increased interest rates from 9 per cent to 12 per cent to a further 16 per cent. The new monetary policy, which lasted until 1985, was disastrous for the Third World states. Trapped into long-term loans on floating interest rates, their interest burden soared. Debt servicing burdens for Third World states also increased. The proportion of new loans going to service old debt rose from 37 per cent between 1970 and 1976 to a whopping 88 per cent in 1980. A large proportion of the gross national product of the countries went to private banks to service old debts. Sue Branford and Bernardo Kucinski write with reference to Latin America,

During the whole history of capitalism, there is no other case of such intense income appropriation by strictly banking methods.[17]

Unlike TNCs, lending institutions could simply withdraw their money and leave or refuse to lend. Banks had no commitment to the country beyond the repayment of their interests and principal. Third World states could not unilaterally readjust their service obligations by exercising sovereign powers as they could do with TNCs in manufacturing.[18] States could not reschedule debts to private banks by bilateral negotiations as with the bilateral and multilateral loans. Many Third World states were on the brink of bankruptcy and several declared they were unable to repay the debts owed to private banks and financial institutions.

The sovereignty principle ruled the liberal imaginations of economic actors like banks and lending institutions as much as social movements and Third World states. 'Countries don't go bankrupt', John Reed of Citicorp told the shareholders.[19] By the early 1980s it seemed that countries could indeed go bankrupt. The stark reality of large investment destinations like Mexico, Argentina, Chile, Philippines, Nigeria, Costa Rica, Jamaica, amongst others defaulting on sovereign debts, stared hard at the banking industry dominated by US banks. Mr Graeme F. Rea, the Deputy General Counsel of the IMF, told the special panel on Restructuring Sovereign Debt at the American Association of International Law's annual conference on 15 April 1983,

By the end of 1981, of the total outstanding external debt of nonoil developing countries of some $600 billion, almost 60 percent was owed to commercial banks, and nearly 90 percent of the commercial banks' claims were concentrated in only 20 countries. Last summer it became clear that three of the largest borrowers, Mexico, Brazil, and Argentina, were in serious payments difficulties. The sheer size of the amounts threatened to induce a potential debt and liquidity crisis that could undermine the stability of the international banking system and the monetary system itself. There was serious concern whether the system would be able to cope with a crisis of this magnitude.[20]

Creditors knew their rights against private debtors, they could file for receivership. Receivership for sovereign states was unthinkable.

SOVEREIGN BANKRUPTCY: 'NO COURT TO GO TO'

Sovereign bankruptcy suddenly made the need for debt recovery mechanisms for sovereign debts a matter of urgency. Debt recovery presupposes established property rights recognised by creditors and lenders alike and sovereign debt recovery presupposes *international* property rights which were unsettled at the time. Sovereign bankruptcy presented new types of legal questions. When three publicly owned banks in Costa Rica defaulted on their debts in 1981 thirty-eight out of thirty-nine creditors accepted a debt restructuring package. One creditor declined to accept the package and instead sued Costa Rica before the US courts for settlement of the debt. In *Allied Bank International v. Banco Credito Agricola de Cartago*, the US courts initially upheld the doctrine of Acts of State. Acts of State doctrine presumes that acts of foreign sovereigns are valid and non-justiciable, and recognises sovereign immunities.[21] Effectively, the decision meant US banks could not recover the money lent to Costa Rican banks. The US government joined the appeal proceedings by Allied Bank as amicus curiae. The appeal court reversed the decision on different grounds. The appeal court relied on the location test. As the debts were contracted in Costa Rica but payable in New York, the court held that US courts had jurisdiction to hear the case.[22] The decision in *Allied Bank* left many unresolved issues about recovery proceedings against foreign sovereigns. Besides, in financial transactions involving global consortia where is the location of the transaction for jurisdictional purposes? In a later case *A.I. Credit Corp. v. Government of Jamaica* decided by the Southern District Court of New York,[23] amidst complex debt restructuring negotiations involving the US administration, the IMF, the lending consortia and the Jamaican government, a lone bank decided to break ranks with the consortia and file summary proceedings for recovery of debts. The court acknowledged that the claim could be devastating for Jamaica and that the involvement of the US administration could give the debt rescheduling agreements an 'Acts of State' character. Nevertheless, the court found that those considerations were extraneous to the issue before the court which was, in the court's view, quite straightforward. A debt was a debt for all that, and if a creditor came before a court with a contract for payment the court had no option but to grant summary judgment. The Jamaican case raised the prospect of a single rogue bank breaking ranks with the rest of the banking 'pack' and torpedo the entire sovereign debt recovery programme by driving a country to default, the usurer's nightmare. In large consortia lending rogue banks needed disciplining as much as defaulting sovereigns.

In the colonial era neither location nor sovereign immunity presented a problem as the host and home states had a shared legal identity. Instead 'gunboat diplomacy' enabled forced recovery of the host states' goods to realise debts. For example, German, British and Italian naval ships jointly intervened in Venezuela in 1902, the British navy in Guatemala in 1913 to realise the debts owed to their home creditors. The US took over the customs system of Santa Domingo to assure debt repayment.[24] In the post-WWII context, 'gunboat diplomacy' to recover debts was out of question under the UN system. The need for certainty and for an international legal framework to protect property rights was articulated by David Suratgar, Director of Morgan, Grenfell & Co., Ltd, London in the following words,

> Demonstrably, what has been lacking is an agreed framework for 'working out' a sovereign debt crisis. There is no international procedure comparable to chapter 11 of the Federal Bankruptcy Act. There is no forum to make sure that any settlement reached is equitable to all creditors and provides a real opportunity for an LDC [Less Developed Country] to work its way out of its particular problems and pay back its debts on a basis consistent with good economic and external debt management.[25]

Several proposals for a legal and institutional framework for sovereign debt recovery were discussed at the 1983 annual conference of the American Association of International Law (ASIL). Mr Brower of the District of Columbia Bar and chair of the panel on Restructuring Sovereign Debt at that conference summed up the proceedings in the following words,

> There was, however, no court to go to, there was no agency and no body of law. In a way, it was the law of the jungle in the strictest sense. ... The real question, which had not really been publicly addressed, was the development of regularized procedures and institutions. ... No existing institution was either willing or designed by present mission to fill the gap, and *it was not really in the province of commercial banks to establish an appropriate public international institution*. Since no debtor ever thought he would become bankrupt, it was not possible to call upon the putative bankrupts of the future to arrange their own funerals. *As a result, who would do it, and how would it be done?* That was the fundamental question that needed to be addressed. (Italics added)[26]

Sovereign defaults and debt recovery became the single biggest challenge for international lawyers, their clients, the private banks and the US administration in the 1970s and early 1980s.[27] Chapter 11 of the US Federal Bankruptcy Act turns on the concept of debtor-in-possession. A debtor on the verge of default may approach bankruptcy courts with a restructuring plan to save the enterprise. If the plan is approved the debtor continues to manage the enterprise but does so in the capacity of a trustee for the creditors. The restructuring plan must be put to the creditors and approved by them and the implementation of the restructuring plan is supervised by the courts.[28] In most jurisdictions the shift from individual debtors of the mercantile era to corporate debtors of the TMF era has brought about radical shifts in ideas of receivership to recover debts. The concept of 'corporate rescue' in bankruptcy laws provide for Company Voluntary Rescue (CVR) arrangements to save the enterprise as a going, profit-making concern so as to save the value of the enterprise for the creditors.[29] The main legal challenge in the case of sovereign debtors was to find an authority that will take the place of the bankruptcy courts and a restructuring plan over which the creditors, the international banks and corporations can have control. Solutions to these challenges presuppose the existence of settled property rights. The Mexican debt crisis provided the lever to install *international* property rights.

MEXICO'S SOVEREIGN DEBT AND INTERNATIONAL PROPERTY RIGHTS

If Nicaragua was the milestone in rewriting the script for representative democracy and Panama for political authorisation, Mexico was the milestone in re-scripting international property rights for transient, intangible property under TMF capitalism: the rights of private international creditors. In 1982 Mexico declared it was unable to meet its debt repayment obligations to the private banks, which threatened a global debt crisis. By that stage twenty countries had had their debts rescheduled.[30] It was during the course of the negotiations over successive bail-out packages for Mexico, however, that the contours for an international property rights regime emerged. Mexico has faced major financial crises throughout the post-WWII era in the 1960s, 1976, 1982, 1986, 1994 and 2009. The solution to each crisis created the conditions for the next one. Each solution proposed a set of wide-ranging reforms of the Mexican economy, state and society that 'remade' the Mexican economy.[31] Restructuring sovereign debts was the lever that allowed the Mexican economy to be 'remade'. In turn, 'remaking' the Mexican economy, state and society became a model for other Third World states.

Mexico has been the neo-colonial 'backyard' of the US where asymmetrical relations between two legally independent states are entrenched systemically over a long period.[32] Mexico is nominally sovereign but every fifty years or so forced by economic and political circumstances to renegotiate a set of treaties with the US. The US-Mexico treaties, beginning with the Treaty of Guadalupe-Hindalgo in 1848 to the more recent North American Free Trade Agreement (NAFTA) in 1994, negotiated against the backdrop of the looming peso crisis, include commercial and trade concessions and clauses about rights of Mexican people linked to the concessions.[33] Mexican history demonstrates the ways in which post-WWII imperialism is characterised by a coalescence of formal sovereignty, imperial economic interests and discourse of rights and freedoms for working people.

During and immediately after the world wars, after the treaties of the 1940s renewed the terms of the interstate relations, Mexico became an attractive destination for US TNCs and FDIs in heavy industries including the petroleum industry. Mexico became the 'miracle economy' with consistently high levels of 'growth' measured as expansion of manufacturing, trade and investments using economic indicators developed by investors and their economists. The miracle growth came with deep polarisation within Mexican society. The claims for state resources in the form of subsidies, spending on health, education and housing by the poor-majority and the claims of the rich-but influential minority for tax concessions, investments in infrastructures and industries and freedom to move capital overseas introduced a deep rift in democratic politics that played out in particular ways during the series of debt crises.[34] After WWII the government prioritised development of national industries to reduce reliance on TNCs making Mexico less attractive to TNCs in the mid 1960s. Mexico's attempts to expand national industry to pay for the loans through export earnings failed because the increased export earnings were wiped out by the high cost of imported capital goods producing a balance of payment deficit.[35] From 1965 to 1970 whereas loans increased at an annual rate of 34 per cent, FDIs increased only by 5.5 per cent. Interest payments rose four times and debt servicing grew from 35 to 95 per cent of new loans.[36] In other words, Mexico had all the signs of classical usury where Mexico was borrowing to repay previous loans. The Mexican government turned to the IMF for a stabilisation loan that came with conditions for macroeconomic reforms to control inflation and maintain a stable currency.

The restrictive conditions by the IMF and official aid agencies of the G7 states drove Mexico away from bilateral and multilateral donors to private financial lenders in the 1970s.[37] However, the floating interest rates and the rise of US Federal Reserve's prime rates that followed increased Mexico's debt repayment burden. By 1981 Mexico topped the list of the ten most indebted countries.[38] Mexico's debt increased from US$ 55 billion to US$ 80 billion, over 60 per cent of which was owed to US banks. Alarmed by the levels of Mexico's debt, US banks reduced the length of the loans, requiring repayments within a year. Whereas only 5 per cent of Mexico's debts were repayable within one year in the first half of 1981, by the end of the year the proportion increased to 22 per cent and most of the new loans were due in six months. Panic responses by banks exacerbated a fragile situation. The announcement in 1982 that Mexico could not meet its debt repayment obligations to US banks triggered the possibility of collapse of the US banking system. A collapse of the US banking system in turn had the potential to trigger a global financial collapse. Not surprisingly, the Mexican government approached the US administration for a rescue plan that would pacify the US banks.

The US banks too turned to their government to be rescued. Ironically, the clamour by the banks to be rescued came at a time when the Reagan administration promoted free-market laissez-faire in the US.[39] Departing from core free-market principles, Paul A. Volcker, an ideological neoliberal and the Chairman of the Federal Reserve Board under the Reagan administration, told the House Committee on Banking, Finance and Urban Affairs,

> The international financial system is not separable *from our domestic banking and credit system*. The same institutions are involved in both markets. A shock to one would be a shock to the other. In that very real sense, we are not considering esoteric matters of international finance, or primarily what is in the interest of heavily indebted developing countries, although that is involved. *We are talking about dealing with a threat to the recovery, the jobs, and the prosperity of our own country, a threat essentially without parallel in the postwar period.*[40] (Italics added)

Volcker reminded US legislators that for every US$ 1 billion of lost exports US workers lost 25,000 jobs and that the decline in Mexico's imports of US goods would cost as many as 250,000 US jobs.[41] The US government responded to requests by the Mexican government *and* the US banks by agreeing to buy Mexican oil at prices below market value to boost its oil reserves and to pay Mexico in advance for the oil, payment that Mexico could use to pay back the US and G7 banks.[42] What was the source of legal authority for the US administration to intervene swiftly to stave off a global financial crisis? The answer invites grasping the compatibilities between domestic US institutions and the IEOs under TMF capitalism.

The US was able to bail-out its banks by providing urgent cash assistance to Mexico because of a special type of fund called the Emergency Stabilization Fund (ESF) which authorises the executive to access discretionary funds without legislative oversight and very little documentation, provided the loan is repaid with interest within six months. The ESF, set up between the world war years in 1934 under the Gold Reserve Act 1934 as wartime necessity, was never dismantled after WWII ended.[43] The ESF has been described variously as 'slush funds', 'war chest'[44] and as an 'international firebrigade'.[45] It is possible to argue that the ESF is to the US economy what the CIA is to US national security. The 'international firebrigade' had intervened in several sovereign debt crises before the Mexican debt crisis in August 1982, most of them to stabilise economies in Latin America and the Caribbean.[46] ESF loans are advanced on the condition that the debtor country applies simultaneously for an IMF stabilisation loan. Thus, the IMF lends money to the debtor states so they can repay private banks.

How can the US be so certain that the IMF, a legally autonomous multilateral IEO, will comply with the debtor country's request for a long-term stabilisation loan to bail-out US banks? The ESF-IMF system was, for all that, a state-driven administrative initiative which fell short of establishing legal rights and obligations between sovereign debtors and private lenders. The system was indeed an 'international firebrigade' that rushed to put out one fire after another. As the debt crisis spiralled to global proportions something more than an international firebrigade was needed. An internationally recognised property rights regime with all its underlying grammar: the subject (international property rights), the substance (sovereign debtors and private creditors), the basis for entitlement (debt servicing contracts and dispute resolution) and social purpose of entitlements (development and growth) were needed.

IMF AS UNDERWRITERS OF
INTERNATIONAL PROPERTY RIGHTS

Between 1955 and 1968 the IMF had little relevance for the economies of Third World states.[47] In the course of addressing the sovereign debt crisis, the G7 states re-scripted the IMF's Articles of Agreement and reinvented a new role for the IMF.[48] The new role effectively transformed the IMF into an underwriter for sovereign debts as property. The Oxford English Dictionary defines 'to underwrite' as 'undertake to finance or otherwise support or guarantee (something) ...' . Underwriters insure people, corporations and other legal entities against risks in return for payments. The OED defines the verb to insure as 'secure or protect someone against a possible contingency'. The need for underwriting arises from the insecurities and risks inherent in market economies driven by competition and profits. The insurance industry for example *markets* insecurity for a profit by taking on the risks that people, corporations and legal entities face in a world of uncertainties. 'Profit is a fundamental underwriting objective [and] underwriting decisions are made in search for basis on which to accept risk at a profit.'[49]

Three major amendments to the IMF's Articles of Association after 1968 are important for re-scripting its new role as underwriter. The first amendment in 1969, coming close on the heels of the US economic crisis in 1968, allowed the IMF to create Special Drawing Rights (SDR), a special type of drawing facility authorised by the IMF that states could use for a 'wide range of transactions and operations'.[50] The drawing rights were calculated on the basis of quotas for each state based on their subscriptions. The SDRs functioned as a new type of money (international property as subject of rights) that states could use to buy goods and services from G7 states.

The first amendment enabled the IMF to play a role analogous to that of reserve banks within states – i.e. a global reserve bank for Third World reserve banks.[51] It also enabled the IMF to set macroeconomic conditions attached to the stabilisation loans, the substance of international property rights. The IMF thus emerged as the lynchpin of stabilisation agreements that managed the rights and obligations of sovereign debtors and private lenders. A second important feature of the first amendment is that it introduced a special majority of 85 per cent of voting strength for decisions concerning adjustments or increases in state quotas. The amendment gave the US authority to veto decisions on quotas of states so long as the US was able to maintain a voting power that was just above 15 per cent of the quota.[52] The US institutional clout comes on the heels of eroding economic power.[53]

The first amendment established the subject of international property rights (sovereign debts and SDRs) but the substance of rights was at best partially established without rights and remedies for contracting parties. The creditors, private banks, could not force sovereign states to reorganise their economies, or insist on austerity conditions or force states to cutbacks on social spending and subsidies to repay debts to G7 banks. Above all, they could not sue defaulting sovereign debtors. As the sovereign debt crisis ballooned in the 1970s, G7 banks demanded increased collaterals including real estate and payment guarantees for their loans.[54] The banks insisted that states request IMF stabilisation loans concurrently with requests for rescheduling debts owed to private banks.[55] As a result, the IMF was 'placed more and more in the position of appearing to guarantee private capital'.[56] The IMF's proximity to the private banks became controversial.[57]

The need for common strategies in debt renegotiations led to informal associations of bankers like the Paris Club formed in the course of the debt negotiations with Argentina in 1956 and the London Club in the course of debt negotiations with Zaire. The consortia for the Mexican debt for example involved 1,600 banks acting collectively. As Glasberg puts it: 'Their size all but guaranteed the large banks a federal bailout, since the U.S. government has always feared the economic and political repercussions of bankruptcies among major banks.'[58] Notwithstanding their collective power, banks did not have *legal* legs to stand on in an international system founded on state sovereignty principle. The IMF too had limitations. The IMF's remit under the Articles were limited to balance of payments and macroeconomic policies. The IMF could not 'micromanage' the borrowing states by insisting on how the states should adjust their manufacturing, trade, agriculture or social policies to deliver on the macroeconomic stabilisation that the IMF packages provided for. Without a legal framework, sovereign debt negotiations could not be embedded in the international legal order in systemic ways. Each sovereign debt had to be negotiated and renegotiated on a case by case basis. Sovereign debt negotiations lurched from one crisis to the next with all the uncertainties entailed in the process.

The second set of amendments to the Articles of Association in 1978 established new legal basis for the IMF's underwriting activities.[59] The Jamaica Agreement of 1976 established the principles of the changes that were formalised in the 1978 amendments. The amendments introduced six new measures. First, the amendments ended the obligation of states to use gold in transactions with the IMF and the IMF's authority to accept gold in its transactions with states. Second, the official price of gold was abolished allowing market forces to determine gold prices. Third, floating exchange rates were legalised. Fourth, one-sixth of the IMF's gold reserves were returned to the member states proportionate to their quotas. Fifth, a trust-fund for the benefit of indebted Third World states was set up from the proceeds of sale of one-sixth of the IMF's gold reserves. Sixth, the amendments gave the IMF wide-ranging surveillance powers over a state's economic policies.[60] The second amendments accepted as fait accompli the unilateral end to the gold standard by the US and the unilateral floating of currencies by European states in 1958. The SDRs created new liquidity making increased loan transactions possible. The enhanced surveillance powers gave the IMF the legal authority to adopt intrusive policies probing the economic and social policy of debtor states from food programmes to primary health care to banking, trade and agriculture. The trust-funds signalled arrangements for sovereign debt restructuring to become a systemic feature of the international system.

The banks had at last found their guarantor for sovereign debts but not without paying a price. Using the 'moral hazard' and the 'free riders' arguments (see Chapter 7) the IMF insisted that all participating banks must pay 7 per cent of their exposure to Mexican debt as a condition for the bail-out. The smaller US banks in the consortium with smaller exposures were unhappy about being forced to take on the same burden as the big banks. The European and Japanese banks were unhappy with the 'seven percent solution' as it came to be known arguing they were made to contribute to what was essentially a bail-out of the big US banks. The big US banks prevailed upon the smaller ones and non-US banks to stay with the 'pack' to survive.[61] The US could use its dominant position in the IMF to bring the other G7 states on board as the failure of US banks could lead on to a failure of other G7 banks, being as they were, part of a 'pack' in consortium lending. The bail-out package negotiated between the US, private banks, Mexico and the IMF was the first major IMF intervention in a sovereign bankruptcy after the second amendments. The IMF emerged as the underwriter in bail-out packages which included austerity packages, cuts to social spending, disciplining trade unions to keep wages down, cutbacks on subsidies to agriculture and such. The Mexican bail-out package became the precursor for the unpopular Structural Adjustment Programme (SAPs). The big US banks became bigger as a result of the bail-out. Their capacity to inflict harm on the global financial system increased their bargaining leverage with the states and the IEOs.[62] William S. Ogden, Vice Chairman of Chase Manhattan Bank, N.A., deposing before the US Congress in 1982 noted,

With one out of five U.S. jobs export related, and with over one third of U.S. exports going to LDCs [Less Developed Countries], it is an inescapable fact that this country's wellbeing is vitally affected by the debt problem and by our ability and *willingness* to solve it.[63] (Italics added)

The SAPs did not resolve the debt problem however. The SAPs were not designed to end indebtedness of Third World states; rather they were designed to bail-out the global banking industry led by large US banks. Nevertheless, from the standpoint of development of international property rights the 'seven percent solution' is significant in that it established the legal principle of equality of all creditors and equal rights of all parties in sovereign debts restructuring.[64] These equality clauses were to become a regular feature in later debt restructuring agreements. Equality clauses paved the way for 'human' rights of other social groups beyond bankers, investors, IEOs and G7 states in debt restructuring, arguments considered in the next chapter. Suffice to note here that debt negotiations established equal property rights in international law first before recognising the 'human' right claims of other social actors.

The third amendment had a punitive ring and provided for suspension of voting rights of member states that did not repay their debts as agreed in the bail-out contracts. Given their low weighting in the voting power within the IMF, the effect of suspension on indebted states was less about their votes in decision-making and more about lowering their credit ratings with investors.[65] The third amendment to the IMF Articles effectively blacklisted indebted states from access to funds, trade, goods and services and resources from private and public sectors. It was the final noose that could bring about the demise of an indebted state, the 'failed state' phenomenon. The three amendments blurred the boundaries between 'private' and 'public' and 'national' and 'international' domains in law. The amendments to the Articles transformed the role of the IMF from an international 'currency exchange' manager to an underwriter for private debts.

Amendments to the IMF's Articles formalised two classes of states in the post-WWII order. This divide, uncritically referred to as the 'North-South' divide, became a feature of the international legal and institutional order. The first class of states, also the 'first class' states, are those that no longer need the IMF, states that David Bradlow calls the 'supplier states'.[66] The 'supplier states' regained their monetary sovereignty from the IMF after the collapse of the Bretton Woods system in 1971 and set up new forums such as the Financial Stability Forum and turned to other existing forums such as the G7, OECD, the Bank for International Settlement and the organisations of industry regulators such as the Basel Committee of Bank Regulators and the International Organization of Securities Commissions to coordinate and manage the regulatory aspects of TMF capitalism. The second class of states, also the 'second class' states, are what Bradlow calls the 'consumer states'.[67] The 'consumer states' need the IMF without which they could lose access to credits, markets, goods and services and face economic collapse.[68] The US economic crises and the debt crises that followed turned the IMF into a regulator and overseer of the 'second class states'. The amendments instituted the subject of property rights, left its substance inconclusive and stopped short of addressing the justifications and purpose of international property rights that transformed sovereign states into debtors like any other.

IN SEARCH OF SOVEREIGN BANKRUPTCY PROCEDURES

To recap, the aim of civil recovery proceedings in bankruptcy proceedings is to provide a procedure for orderly recovery of as much money as possible for the creditors and to ensure fair distribution of the monies recovered amongst creditors. The aim is not to punish the debtors but to save the enterprise as a going concern which still had value for the creditors. Recognition of settled property rights by creditors and debtors is a necessary precondition for enforcement of contractual obligations between debtors and creditors. IMF as underwriter transformed Third World sovereign states into borrowers like any other corporate entity borrowing from capital markets to engage in profitable activities using its entrepreneurial talent and taking attendant risks. Sovereign debt became subject to contracts and adjudication like any other private debt.

The 'Washington Consensus' (WC) may be seen as an underwriting arrangement whereby the IMF agrees to underwrite the risks of private bankers and financiers in their transactions with sovereign borrowers, the Third World states. As the 'chief negotiator' between banks, corporations, G7 states, Third World debtor states and other IOs, the IMF through SAPs imposes contractual obligations on Third World states to repay *public* debts to *private* lenders. The 'Washington Consensus' is a term coined by John Williamson of the Institute of International Economics, a US think tank set up in 1989 whose Board of Directors include former treasury and trade officials in the US government, former IMF and WB officials, journalists from leading financial newspapers and partners and directors of hedge-funds, leading US banks, corporations and foundations.[69] Williamson argued that by 1989 there was already a *de facto* consensus amongst the Washington institutions on ten policy instruments for Third World states. Williamson explained,

> The Washington [in the 'Washington Consensus'] is both the political Washington of Congress and senior members of the administration and the technocratic Washington of the international financial institutions, the economic agencies of the U.S. government, the Federal Reserve Board, and the think tanks. The Institute for International Economics made a contribution to codifying and propagating several aspects of the Washington consensus in its publication Toward Renewed Economic Growth in Latin America ... .[70]

The ten policy instruments included i) fiscal discipline; ii) reordering public expenditure priorities; iii) tax reforms; iv) liberalising interest rates; v) a competitive exchange rate; vi) trade liberalisation; vii) liberalisation of inward foreign direct investment; viii) privatisation; ix) deregulation; and more importantly for the subject matter of this book x) property rights.[71] The ten policy instruments constitute a complete package of investment and property rights that 'roll back the state' from the economy and 'roll in' the IEOs and G7 institutions as 'regulators' of Third World economies. The SAPs allowed private investors and corporations to redeem their debts by entering into arrangements like the debt swaps or buy assets of state-owned enterprises at low costs in exchange for debt repayments. The debt-swap agreements used for sovereign debtors were comparable to legal instruments used in corporate rescue plans and CVR arrangements in bankruptcy procedures by private companies.[72] The SAPs took on the legal form of contracts between states, private lenders and the IEOs. As contracts, they had the appearance of a voluntary transaction. The levels of 'coercion' in any agreement depended on the circumstances of the parties, the failures and successes of their transactions and their relative bargaining power.

The IMF led the debate on extending ideas of 'corporate rescue' to sovereign debtors canvassing for legal framework to deal with sovereign bankruptcies. The debate involved IEOs, think tanks, states, media and academics.[73] In the discussions, Chapter 11 of the US Federal Bankruptcy Act continued to provide the model for an international regime of property rights. Anne Krueger, First Deputy Managing Director of the IMF in a speech to the American Enterprise Institute in Washington, DC on 26 November 2001 said,

> Our model is one of a domestic bankruptcy court, ... As I have emphasized already, our primary objective in creating a formal mechanism of this type would be to create incentives for debtors and creditors to reach agreement of their own accord, so the mechanism would rarely need to be used. There is an analogy here with domestic insolvency regimes like the US bankruptcy court. When they are well-developed and predictable in their operation, *the bulk of domestic corporate restructuring takes place 'in the shadow of the law' rather than in court.* This approach would benefit creditors as well as debtors.[74] (Italics added)

Jeffery Sachs, a US economist named twice in the *Time 100* list of most influential leaders, architect of the UN Millennium Development Goals and advisor to the UN Secretary General on Third World development, voiced his concerns about the risks entailed in market-based solutions and the scramble for liquidating Third World assets,

> Preventing such a destructive race to liquidate assets is one of the major purposes of a bankruptcy code, which restricts the ability of individual creditors to act against the group interest. Unfortunately, countries cannot file for Chapter 11 protection.[75]

The WC reconfigured nationalism and internationalism in the post-war interstate system. Charles Gore argues that post-WWII international order combined 'normative economic nationalism' associated with policies like import-substitution, national self-sufficiency and nationalist ideology with 'methodological internationalism' associated with European modernisation and Third World development. The WC reversed this combination of nationalism and internationalism. Internationalism became the normative economic domain through which national economic performances would be evaluated.[76] Recalling Anne-Marie Slaughter (Chapter 5), in the reversed combination the new nationalism of states was to become efficient managers of a segment of the global economy.

SOVEREIGN DEBTS IN THE UN

For Third World states reeling under the 'market fundamentalism' of WC-SAPs on the one hand and domestic opposition to austerity on the other, the UNGA was the only international forum available to act against '[u]nilateral economic measures as a means of political and economic coercion against developing countries'.[77] In February 1979 the Group of 77 voted for the establishment of an independent International Debt Commission that debtor states could approach to restructure their debts in ways that would not throttle their economic development. The UNGA initiated a parallel process alongside the IEOs, G7 states and private banks and financial institutions to develop a mechanism for sovereign debt restructuring by debtor nations.[78] Creditor states did not support the proposal. The US led the opposition arguing that debt restructuring was beyond the expertise of the UNGA and that the IEOs were better placed to monitor mechanisms for sovereign debt recovery.[79] The proposal to link debt to development was considered to be in the debtors' favour whereas the proposals of the IMF were considered to be in favour of creditors.[80] The UN Human Rights Council canvassed for the principle that 'human' rights issues should be considered in debt restructuring. On 9 September 2014, the Group of 77 plus China moved a resolution in the UNGA to

> ... elaborate and adopt ..., a multilateral legal framework for the sovereign debt restructuring processes with a view to, inter alia, increasing efficiency, stability and predictability of the international

financial system as well as achieving sustained, inclusive and equitable economic growth and sustainable development, in accordance with national circumstances and priorities.[81]

One hundred and twenty-four countries voted in favour of the resolution, eleven countries voted against and forty-one countries abstained. The EU, which normally votes as a bloc, voted separately as individual states. This strategy allowed the UK and Germany to vote against the resolution with the US, Japan, Canada, Australia and New Zealand. Most of the other EU states abstained.[82]

When UNGA adopted the resolution in 2014 three and half decades of SAPs had established the rights of private creditors, legalised LPG regimes under WTO, and numerous bilateral and multilateral investment agreements had established the rights of private investors to sue Third World states before Investor-State Dispute Settlement (ISID) tribunals, the WB's International Center for Settlement of Investment Disputes (ICSID) and NAFTA tribunals.[83] The UNGA resolution was too little too late. In any event, UNGA resolutions are recommendations whereas SAP contracts are binding legal instruments.

SOCIAL MOVEMENTS: FAITH, FORGIVENESS AND 'HUMAN' RIGHTS

The debt crisis is also the moment of the birth of NSMs and the rise of what NSMs call 'global civil society'. It was the moment when global alliances against SAPs campaigned against their devastating impacts on Third World societies. Above all, it was the moment of the 'Rights Way to Development', a movement spearheaded by INGOs to incorporate 'human' rights in economic development of Third World societies. The Jubilee 2000 campaign was amongst the most high-profile international campaigns. Jubilee 2000 demanded that IEOs and G7 states cancel Third World debt.

In the Third World, opposition to SAPs was first and foremost against their own governments for signing up to IMF's conditions, against their government's inability to find solutions to the problems that their countries faced, and against the widespread perception that the leadership of independence movements had failed to deliver. Throughout the 1970s, 1980s, 1990s and 2000s, opposition to economic policies led to wide-ranging political responses, debates and alliances in the Third

World.[84] In India, Nepal, Philippines, Indonesia, OSMs resurged to face new questions about the social and political changes. The crisis of Third World states was also a moment of political creativity in the Third World. The Jubilee 2000 campaign intervened at a critical juncture in the debates within Third World social movements on sovereign debts.

The largest aid organisations in the UK rallied to develop common responses to the debt crisis and protests against SAPs, LPG and austerity in the Third World. In the mid 1990s they established the Debt Crisis Network (DCN). The conceptual framing of Third World debt in the DCN came from the work of a retired academic in the UK, Martin Dent, who invoked the biblical idea of the Jubilee Year. Every fifty years, the idea of the Jubilee Year calls on Christians to forgive debts, free slaves and return lands to the rightful owners.[85] According to Ann Pettifor, one of the coordinators of the DCN, the reasons for the network of aid agencies to frame the debt issue on the biblical idea of the Jubilee year was

> ... the DCN believed that linking a campaign for debt cancellation to the Jubilee year, the year 2000, a 'kairos time' to use Dent's words, was likely to resonate with, and therefore mobilize, large numbers of people of faith in *Western creditor nations. But Martin Dent's big idea was brilliant for other reasons, best known to advertising and marketing agencies. Most successful communication comes from linking two ideas that may appear bizarrely different but that actually, in combination, have a terrific dynamic, or synchronicity.* In this case, Dent linked, first, a huge, almost global celebration of the passing of time, and second, an (apparently) *obscure* biblical mandate to periodically cancel debts, free slaves, and restore land to its rightful owners. The effect was to be electrifying.[86] (Italics added)

There is a conscious attempt to use advertising industry practices on branding and appeal for the campaign. The Jubilee Year concept drew support from the most high-profile politicians and public figures in the G7 states and beyond. 'Indeed, Michael Camdessus, the Managing Director of the IMF, the architect of the debt crisis, was apparently brought, "face to face with the hostility of world Catholic leaders toward the institution he led and its economic policies" by the Jubilee 2000 campaign according to Ann Pettifor.'[87] Apparently, when the Irish rock star Bono met US Senator Jesse Helms, who had earlier equated 'foreign aid with throwing money down "ratholes"', Helms wept on hearing

Bono's argument about the biblical origins of the Jubilee Year.[88] The
Jubilee campaign mobilised groups in the Third World and the First
World. The Jubilee campaign used empirical descriptions of the effects
of SAPs to demand debt cancellation as the way to enforce 'human' rights
of people in the Third World to basic conditions of life: food, water and
other socio-economic rights.

'Cancellation' morphed into 'forgiveness'. The campaign appealed
to the very people and institutions that created the crisis to show
forgiveness and compassion and appealed to the rioters and rebels
in the Third World to have faith in 'human' rights. The Jubilee 2000
campaign gathered 24.2 million signatures in one hundred and sixty-six
countries. At their Cologne summit in 1999 the G7 countries committed
US$ 100 billion to debt *relief* (not cancellation) for multilateral aid and
US$ 10 million (a small sum for the G7!) for bilateral debts.[89] The IMF
insisted that debt relief must be linked to LPG reforms. The international campaign petered out after the Jubilee Year in 2000 and debts and
periodic financial crises returned.

There are two points to note from this account of the Jubilee 2000
campaign. One is the materiality of the demand for debt cancellation.
Intervening in the debates about debt cancellations in the World Social
Forum (WSF), I wrote in 2004,

... the idea of cancellation is based on forgiveness and compassion.
It overlooks a small detail, namely, that what is called debt is in fact
expropriation of the Third World and a means of continued appropriation of their land, labour and natural resources in a new form
euphemistically termed 'development' in the post-war era. In that
sense it is not a 'debt' at all. Not surprisingly, the Churches throughout
the Jubilee year were most vocal in advocating cancellation of Third
World debt based on the Christian idea of plenary indulgence and
absolution so that the slate is cleaned and the old ties resumed. *Every
good banker too knows that periodically bad debts must be written off
for banking to continue to be business as usual.*[90] (Italics added)

What is interesting about the way the biblical concept of the Jubilee Year
was invoked by the campaign is that the biblical idea calls for forgiving
debts, freeing slaves and returning lands to lawful owners. There was
no Jubilee 2000 campaign to shut down sweat shops around the Third
World where workers slaved to provide cheap goods and services to the

citizens of the G7 states. Far from returning lands to the lawful owners – the indigenous people and Third World peasants – land acquisitions for WB-funded projects remains the single biggest reason for widespread poverty, large-scale internal displacements and ethnic conflicts in Third World countries, as discussed in Chapter 1.

The second point concerns erasing historical memories about socialist interventions on debts owed to foreign investors. During and after the world wars socialist movements demanded debt *repudiation* not cancellation or forgiveness. In 1917, the former USSR repudiated debts accrued by the Tsarist government on the grounds that the debts were not incurred for the benefit of the Russian people.[91] The Costa Rican government repudiated debts owed to the US in 1919 arguing the US did not recognise the Costa Rican government, so it could not claim debt repayment.[92] China repudiated debts after the successful revolution in 1949 on the same grounds, as did Cuba in 1961 and several other countries. In retrospect, the economies of the countries that repudiated debts, not surprisingly, recovered and became more productive. In the 1980s, at the height of the debt crisis, Cuba called on the Latin American states to form a debtors' cartel and repudiate debts.[93] The option of repudiating debts appeared attractive to many Latin American states and peoples. The mere threat of a debtors' cartel improved the bargaining positions of the Latin American countries negotiating their national debts.[94]

Framing the debt crises as a 'human' rights issue diverted attention from the real reasons for the debt crises and the reality that national debts were the new mechanisms for expropriation of Third World labours and natures in the epoch of imperialism. Samuel Moyn suggests,

> … only the ideological dissociation of liberalism and empire, after more than a century of long and deep connection, paved the way for the rise of human rights. Scholars still debate whether liberalism has a genetic or only contingent relationship to imperialism, but what does seem clear is that only when formal empire ended did in fact (and perhaps could in theory) a powerful internationalism based on rights come to the fore.[95]

The process of ideological dissociation of liberalism and Empire is contingent on loss of historical memories of struggles and interventions, a hiatus between past and present, a loss of knowledge learned from collective experiences in the past as guides to actions in the present to bring about a better future.

CONCLUSION

This chapter shows how sovereign indebtedness, caused by manipulating interest rate, was a means to off-load the economic crisis of capitalism on the Third World. It highlights how the subjugation of Third World states occurs through public contracts between indebted sovereigns, private banks and financial institutions and G7 states underwritten by the IMF. Establishing international property rights in sovereign debts is a necessary condition for subjugation through contracts. In the nineteenth century capitalist states used *political power* derived from nationalism, constitutionalism and republicanism, and principles of state sovereignty to defend their own national corporations and economies. The debt crises demonstrates how the power balance between states and corporations is altered in the era of TMF capitalism. In the twentieth century, corporations and banks use their *economic powers* to intervene and restructure states through a process that is best described as 'state-capture'. Successive financial crises have increased the domination of banks and financial institutions located in the G7 states and subjugated them to the will of banks and financial institutions.

Classical liberalism conceptualised 'free markets' as the spontaneous interactions of individuals engaged in exchange transactions in the market place. According to Adam Smith, those transactions were the 'the invisible hand of the market'. The spontaneous transactions created a self-reproducing social order according to Smith. TMF capitalism, with its reliance on the IMF to keep the global currencies 'pegged' to the US dollar, with its extraordinary power to manipulate economies of states through monetary interventions in favour of a small group of G7 states, is very far away from classical ideas of free markets. Property rights in the post-WWII order were instituted not by individuals engaged in spontaneous buying and selling as in early capitalism but by monopolistic transnational corporations, banks and financial institutions acting as syndicates, engaged as consortia 'packs' in state-capture to alter the legal and institutional order in their favour. TMF capitalism reverses the logic of classical liberalism. Monopolistic corporations and banks minimise competition within states internally and externally, as we saw with consortium lending. G7 states and IEOs impose an illiberal 'right-less' order that is the very antithesis of liberal rights. In the words of Razeen Sally, classical liberalism was 'liberalism from below' whereas neoliberal internationalism is 'liberalism from above'.[96]

'Liberalism from above' is a contradiction in terms. Liberalism from above resembles the economic and political architecture of fascist states founded on the unity of states, economies and civil societies. The prevalence of fascist type states as the general model of states everywhere in the post-WWII era makes the 'bourgeois democratic' states of classical liberalism a thing of the past. 'Liberalism from above' introduces societal changes through law reforms introduced by a small coterie of powerful institutions, in this case the G7 states and IEOs. Elsewhere I have called this type of social change 'mobilisation from the top'.[97] 'Liberalism from below' in the eighteenth and nineteenth centuries was produced by mass uprisings and economic revolutions in which European property owners were forced to seek the support of property-less classes and grant concessions to the whole of society in order to inscribe the right to property in a new legal order as an inalienable right. Liberalism from below involves 'mobilisation from below'. These differences between the social processes through which property rights were inscribed in the legal order in the seventeenth and eighteenth centuries and in the twentieth and twenty-first centuries are at two opposite ends of the democracy pole, the first one coming from below against an established feudal order, the second imposed from above by powerful economic actors against the gains of struggles for freedom by working people during and after the world wars.

7

Rights in International Neoliberal Risk-governance Regime

Englishmen are as great fanatics in politics as Mohamedans in religion. They suppose no country can be saved without English institutions. (Thomas Munro (1761–1827), Governor of Madras Presidency in India under the English East India Company, in C. Ramachandran, *East India Company and South Indian Economy*, p. 171)[1]

The Narmada Bachao Andolan (Save Narmada Movement, or the NBA) is perhaps amongst the more well-known and written about movements. It is an early example of an INGO networking model of organising.[2] Mobilising 'bottom-up' for over a decade since the late 1970s, the NBA worked tirelessly to hold the state accountable for rehabilitation and resettlement of people displaced by the World Bank (WB)-funded Narmada dam project, a vast complex of projects straddling four states in India. As a neo-Gandhian movement, the NBA was committed to non-violence and constitutionalism. The NBA knocked on the doors of the government and the WB for over a decade, presenting evidence of human impacts and appealing to the conscience of government and WB officials. Project-displaced people claiming socio-economic rights in national development was hardly anything new in India or indeed the Third World. But, something short of a miracle happened in October 1989. The US House of Representatives invited the NBA activists to testify before the Senate on the human impacts of the WB's investments. Why did the US Senate become interested enough in the 'human' rights of dam-displaced people in India to invite the NBA activists to testify, and against the WB at that? Had moral arguments finally triumphed the conscience of political representatives? Answers to such questions require us to go beyond the normative discourses about 'human' rights in development and interrogate more closely the deeper undercurrents that drive the normative discourse. This chapter examines how 'human' rights claims by movements grounded in popular resistance like the

NBA, and many others, provided the handle for setting up a comprehensive global governance regime for the first time in history. Any apparatus of governance includes, must include, governance of propertied and property-less, *both*. This chapter examines the establishment of the *international neoliberal risk-governance regime* led by the WB. The pivot of the global risk-governance regime rests on the entwinement of property rights and 'human' rights in the epoch of imperialism. The entwinement called for radical revisions of the theoretical premises of rights and democracy in classical liberalism.

THE WORLD BANK'S ABOUT-TURN ON 'HUMAN' RIGHTS

Until the 1990s, the WB was adamant that it could not take into account the 'human' rights impacts of its lending decisions, arguing that its Articles of Association prohibited consideration of political matters, and 'human' rights were political matters.[3] The WB defended its position before the United Nations General Assembly (UNGA) in 1967 when it was called upon to explain its decision not to comply with UNGA's 1965 resolution directing Specialised Agencies to deny economic and technical assistance to South Africa for apartheid and to Portugal for its colonial policies.[4] In 1990, the WB, under the leadership of its legal counsel Ibrahim Shihata, made an about-turn on its long-held interpretation of the Articles of Agreement. The allegation that the WB is insensitive to 'human' rights was misplaced, Shihata argued.[5] What the WB had been doing all along since the inception of its activities was to give effect to socio-economic rights in international law such as the UN Declaration on the Right to Development adopted in 1986, the right to adequate living standards, education, nutrition and health in the International Convention on Economic, Social and Cultural Rights (UNCESCR), the UN Declaration on Social Progress and Development adopted in 1969, amongst others.[6] Shihata declared,

> The right to development as defined in this Declaration is one human right which the World Bank has been promoting throughout its history.[7]

To clarify doubts, Shihata added,

> ... the Bank *transforms many ideals of the UN* declarations and covenants regarding economic, social and cultural human rights

through its lending operations, its policy dialogue with its borrowing members, and through its research, publications and cooperation with governments and other agencies into realities.[8] (Italics added)

What brought about this about-turn? The NBA activists were invited to testify before the US Senate in the course of the hearings on the International Development and Finance Bill which was pending approval. The Bill proposed to provide comprehensive Congress oversight of multilateral and regional financial institutions including the WB and IMF and to include environmental and 'human' rights standards as part of debt restructuring initiatives.[9] The International Development and Finance Act 1989 was passed in December 1989 soon after the NBA testimonies. The 1989 Act required the US Treasury to use US votes and influence in multilateral banks including the WB to promote environmental and social impact assessments and, further, to make the impact assessment report available 120 days ahead of the WB's vote on the project. The US Treasury was to direct its executive directors in the WB to abstain from voting if the environmental and social conditions were not met.[10] The Act complements the earlier Foreign Assistance Act 1961 which was substantially revised in 1972 and again in 1975 to link 'human' rights to US foreign aid and give Congress reporting and investigating powers, including the power to veto executive actions.[11] The WB is legally independent of the US administration.[12] The Act of 1989 gave the US Congress the powers to do overtly what the executive had done covertly: direct the US nominees in the IEOs and other regional development banks to advance US national interests.[13] The International Development and Finance Bill ought to have raised alarm bells for Third World activists. Instead liberal imaginations invisibilised the politics of rights and the Senate's interest in 'human' rights of displaced people.

In 1989, about the same time as the US Senate invited the NBA activists to testify before it, the WB appointed an independent review of the Narmada project headed by Bradford Morse, former member of the US House of Representatives and the head of the United Nations Development Programme (UNDP), and Thomas Berger, former Canadian Member of Parliament, Supreme Court Judge and commissioner of inquiries on indigenous issues in Canada. The report of the Independent Review caused a stir when it found that the WB had indeed breached environmental standards and the 'human' rights of indigenous peoples, and its own internal guidelines on resettlement of displaced people.[14] Following the review, the WB developed operational guidelines incorporating 'human', environmental and indigenous people's rights to guide funding decisions.[15] To the NBA activists, and anti-dam activists around the world, it appeared that their campaign was working and that the WB was, at long last, becoming sensitised to 'human' rights issues in the projects it funded.

Until the early 1980s resettlement and rehabilitation policies were the responsibilities of national governments. The pressure for Congress oversight over US executive's nominees on the WB's executive, prompted the WB to develop its own internal policies on resettlement. In 1982 the WB began the process of internal change when it appointed Thayer Scudder, a leading anthropologist and critic of large dams, to report on resettlement and rehabilitation policies.[16] The 'independent' review by the Morse committee was the second. The WB's voluntary actions at self-reform could not, however, ward off scrutiny altogether. Congressional oversight over the WB's activities raises fundamental questions about the independence of IEOs.

Something changed too in the way the INGOs operated in the late 1980s. Voluntary humanitarian organisations like ARCH, providing health services to the communities in the areas covered by the Narmada dam project began to take interest in the NBA, a social justice movement, in ways they had not done previously. ARCH brought the conditions of project-affected people to the attention of UK-based INGO OXFAM.[17] In turn, OXFAM's interventions drew the attention of environmental movements against large dams in the US.[18] The involvement of US environmental movements shifted the locus of the international campaign from the UK to the US where the political culture of lobbying congressmen and senators was well entrenched and where the International Rivers Network leadership was well connected to the political establishment. For the US anti-dam movements, the NBA presented an opportunity to universalise their cause beyond the US. In 1985 US environmental movements formed the International Rivers Network (IRN). The opposition to the Narmada dam was one of IRN's first high-profile international campaigns against the environmental impacts of WB-funded dam projects, an issue which was largely limited to the US. The IRN is a US organisation funded by a web of private foundations, corporations and individuals, so characteristic of the INGOs that emerged in the 1980s,[19] discussed in Chapter 2. The IRN is administered by US nationals with a small international advisory team which includes members of the NBA.[20]

It can be seen from the above that each actor had their own reasons for canvassing the 'human' rights of project-displaced people in the Narmada valley. The Senate's reasons for hearing the NBA activists were very different from the NBA's reasons for testifying before it and the IRN's reasons for lobbying the NBA cause. For the US legislators the connections between economic and political, debt, banking crisis and human and environmental rights, US national interests and the international order were always entwined. 'Human' rights were always in relation to property rights. The activists did not make that connection however. The involvement of US environmental movements introduced a hiatus between the national and international focus of the anti-dam movement. Within India the focus of the NBA was and remains displacement and rehabilitation, i.e. 'human' rights, whereas for the IRN, and the Euro-American environmental movements more generally, the focus was and remains on the environmental impacts of large dams. The hiatus introduce cleavages within India between the NBA and movements in other sectors struggling against the IEO-G7-imposed developmental models. The cleavages thwarted the development of national political alliances for alternatives to the WB-G7 models of development.[21]

It is pertinent to note here that early 'human' rights discourse in the Third World grew in *opposition* to the development discourse of the post-WWII era.[22] By the 1990s INGOs transformed the complexion of 'human' rights. INGOs took the critique of development and its social impacts from Third World social movements and brought it within a rights framework under the slogan 'rights way to development'.[23] 'Human' rights went from standing in opposition to the IEO-supported development model to becoming the vehicle for neoliberal restructuring. These developments did not occur in an economic and political vacuum; rather they occurred in the context of the economic crises in capitalist countries, the debt crises, the development crises, anxieties about the state of the environment in the G7 states and the establishment of the NED.

FROM MARKET FUNDAMENTALISM TO GOVERNANCE FUNDAMENTALISM

Having made the about-turn on 'human' rights, the WB led the way out of the impasse created by monetary approaches to the debt crises by steering the way out of the IMF's 'market fundamentalism' to 'governance fundamentalism'. The Washington Consensus (WC) unravelled due to internal contradictions between different actors: banks and financial institutions, the manufacturing TNCs, Third World investors and manufacturers, First and Third World states, the small banks and large banks in the global consortia, the US and other G7 states and IOs like the United Nations International Children's Fund (UNICEF).[24] Joseph Stiglitz, Chair of the Council of Economic Advisors in the Clinton administration from 1995 to 1997 and Senior Vice President and Chief Economist of the World Bank from 1997 to 2000, at the very centre of the Washington establishment, was amongst the prominent opponents of the WC-SAPs. The Consensus turned into a cacophony of arguments. The WB's opposition was not about the principles of WC as such, but rather that macroeconomic instruments and monetary policies could not sustain a productive infrastructure that could keep the sovereign debtor sufficiently alive and productive to be able to continue repaying the sovereign usurer. Corporate Voluntary Rescue (CVR) schemes, after all, are micro-managed, something the IMF could not do under its Articles of Agreement. Property rights are not rights properly speaking without enforcement mechanisms like bankruptcy proceedings, dispute resolution, contract laws and allocation of entitlements to different claimants when there is a dispute or bankruptcy. Besides corporate bankruptcy procedures require CVR plans to include all stakeholders interested in the company, including workers, trade unions and consumer organisations, to 'stake their claims' in the CVR. The WB's solution was what scholars have called the 'post-Washington Consensus'.

The crux of the post-Washington Consensus (post-WC) is governance. In addition to the SAPs of the 1980s, post-WC added ten additional conditions relating to law reforms aimed at setting up legal frameworks for i) corporate governance; ii) anti-corruption; iii) labour rights facilitative of flexible labour markets (read hiring and firing laws); iv) compliance with WTO agreements; v) financial codes and standards; vi) 'prudent' capital-account opening; vii) non-intermediate exchange rate regimes; viii) independent central bank/inflation targeting; ix) social safety nets (read socio-economic rights); and x) targeted poverty reduction (read 'human' rights).[25] Together, the law reforms put international property rights centre-stage and included 'human' rights as an integral component of the international neoliberal risk-governance regime discussed below.

Rights governance entails allocating who is entitled to what and how much. WB's 'Good Governance Programmes' (GGPs), discussed below, give effect to the post-WC by establishing the substance and subject of rights of international creditors and national citizens, rich and poor, natural and legal persons. 'Human' rights go hand in hand with WTO agreements, flexible labour markets and reforms of national institutions. If restructuring Third World states was implicit in the WC, it was made an explicit goal in the post-WC.[26] The 'governance turn' drew the WB into micro-management of Third World economies and politics.[27] The 'governance turn' under the aegis of the WB included governance of sovereign debtors *as well as private creditors.*

The Baker Plan, launched by the US Treasury Secretary James Baker at the annual meeting of the WB in Seoul in October 1985 before a gathering of one hundred and forty-nine countries, urged the WB to play a larger role in reviving debt-ridden economies.[28] Conceptually, the Baker Plan takes inspiration from CVR schemes in bankruptcy proceedings.[29] The Baker Plan introduced the idea of a 'growth-oriented' debt adjustment plan. Third World states must transform their countries into manufacturing platforms for TNCs[30] and keep production lines running to repay debts. The states act as trustees of international creditors and must, therefore, manage national economies to meet debt obligations to private international creditors. The Baker Plan signalled a shift from 'market fundamentalism' of the IMF to a new 'governance fundamentalism' of the WB and from macro-management and monetary solutions of the IMF to micro-management and governance solutions by the WB. The most significant component of the new 'governance fundamentalism' under the WB for the purposes of internationalisation of rights was the inclusion of social and political actors, i.e. 'civil society' actors, in debt restructuring and economic governance. The Baker Plan for the first time involved Mexican trade unions in debt negotiations.[31] The pact with the unions led to a particular way of speaking about democracy where all sections of society accepted the property rights of international banks and financial institutions and the obligations of states to treat creditors' claims on an equal footing with citizens' claims. After trade unions, including 'civil society' groups like NGOs, social movements, experts, academics, think tanks and others in debt negotiations was a short second step. Export-oriented growth as a component of debt restructuring resembles CVR plans in sovereign debt restructuring.

RE-SCRIPTING THE STATE IN GLOBAL GOVERNANCE

The extensive re-theorisation of rights under classical liberalism that becomes necessary for entwining property rights and 'human' rights in a new *international* governance regime is provided by the rise to prominence of a school of thought known as New Institutional Economics (NIE). Rights and Law are the bedrock of NIE. The kernel of the post-WC is the idea that institutions are essential for markets to work efficiently.[32] Institutions, according to Douglass North, a pioneer of NIE, are

> ... rules of the game of a society, or more formally, are the humanly devised constraints that structure human interaction. They are composed of formal rules (statute law, common law, regulations), informal constraints (conventions, norms of behaviour and self-imposed codes of conduct), and the enforcement characteristics of both. Organisations are the players: groups of individuals bound by a common purpose to achieve objectives. They include political bodies (political parties, the senate, a city council, a regulatory agency): economic bodies (firms, trade unions, family, farms, cooperatives); social bodies (schools, colleges, vocational training centres).[33]

The distinction between institutions and organisations in NIE is conceptually important for three reasons. *First*, if institutions are rules of the game and organisations the players then international economy becomes amenable to game theories and Third and Second World societies a board game. Clear rules make it possible for the players to 'play the game by the rules'. By including a number of different types of right-bearing players, e.g. social movements, indigenous peoples, minorities, political parties, women's groups, the game gives the players greater choices. Rights establish rules of the game for the players. All players must know each other's and their own rights clearly so that they can play the game by the rules. *Second*, rights scripted for the game save the game while allowing players to compete as winners and losers. Trade unions may lose their moves to save public sector enterprises but women may gain greater social and political participation. By playing the game by the rules, the players save the game even when one or more right-bearers lose. *Third*, and more importantly, the distinction highlights two classes of organisations: those that set the rules and those who play the game. It mirrors on the normative plane, the objective emergence of two classes of states, supplier/consumer states and creditor/debtor states, discussed in Chapter 6.

The distinction between institutions and organisations in NIE gives all organisational actors, international and national, the flexibility to develop a wide array of policy choices tailored to each country and local authority without watering down the substance of LPG-SAP principles.[34] It has the appeal of 'public choices', to use a neoliberal phrase, that states and organisations can make to adapt to the international order. Rights allocate resources amongst players and set rules for each player about permissible 'rational choices' (another neoliberal phrase) for the players. The international institutions, in contrast, the IEOs, TNCs and financial institutions, the G7 states set the rules of the game and leave the local political and social configurations, i.e. the specificities of organisational models to the states, local authorities, regulatory authorities and different segments of society organised 'democratically' as labour, indigenous peoples, students, environmental, rural, urban organisations. The institutions-organisations distinction gives globalisation, liberalisation, privatisation an appearance of historical inevitability for the players who may not question who designed the game and set its rules if they wish to play the game at all. Everyone, including social movements, NGOs, experts, professionals can participate in the game and indeed play it differently so long as they follow the rules and the goals that the designers of the game have set for each player. The reasons for the proliferation of rights discussed in Chapter 1 become clear.

Rights in classical liberalism *established* the state-market dualism. Rights in the epoch of imperialism *transcend* the state-market dualism. NIE thinkers sought to transcend the state/market dualism and open the theoretical pathway to re-script a new role for the state in the economy, a role that had developed in state practices since the end of WWII but remained on ad hoc theoretical footings. States are transformed by NIE from sovereigns authorised by citizens to act as referee between competing civil society actors in classical liberalism (see Chapter 5) into risk managers of a branch of an internationalised economy (see below). Post-WC is a different board game. Rights in this new game acquire a different meaning for the players. In this new game, when social movements advance rights to this or that thing they are either claiming their 'fair share' or seeking to increase and/or realise their 'share' of the sovereign wealth/debt. As players in the sovereign debt game, social movements like other players must 'do their bit' to mitigate risks to investments and save the game even if they sometimes win or lose individual plays. Rights in the NIE-informed post-WC, divert attention from the reality that the 'assets' of the enterprise of the state, i.e. the national economy, are the natures, labours and cultures of people in the state, and do not 'belong' to anyone as property to be bought and sold.

'INSURANCE AS GOVERNANCE': THE INTERNATIONAL NEOLIBERAL RISK-GOVERNANCE REGIME

In 1996 US activists formed BankTrack, a coalition of NGOs and social movements to monitor private financial institutions investing in development projects.[35] Similar initiatives in Europe led to an international coalition of large INGOs like Greenpeace, World Wildlife Fund, Friends of the Earth in Europe and the Sierra Club. In 2002 BankTrack adopted the Collevecchio Declaration on Financial Institutions. The Declaration demanded that International Financial Institutions commit to six principles voluntarily: sustainability, no-harm, responsibility, accountability, transparency and sustainable markets and governance. The Collevecchio Declaration, adopted by over one hundred NGOs around the world, seeks to embed 'human' rights in the governance of insurance and financial markets. The WB responded by convening through International Finance Corporation (IFC) a meeting of bankers in October 2002 to persuade them to voluntarily adopt a set of environmental and social risk management practices knows as the Equator Principles.[36] Adopted in 2003, by 2008 sixty banks and financial institutions covering 85 per cent of the global project finance market had signed up to the Equator Principles.[37] 'Human' rights as risk management is an idea that is central in the entwinement of property rights and 'human' rights in the international neoliberal risk management regime that the WB led the way in establishing after the perspectival switch in its reinterpretation of its Articles of Agreement.

Alongside incorporating 'human' rights within its constitutional remit by reinterpreting its Articles, the WB launched a new multilateral initiative, the Multilateral Investment Guarantee Agreement (MIGA) in 1985 to provide insurance to creditors and investors against *non-commercial risks*. Insurance, following Richard Ericson et al., *is* governance. In their seminal work on the sociology of the insurance industry in Canada and the US, Ericson et al. argue that insurance is a technology of governance beyond the state. The state is sovereign within geographical boundaries and corporations within institutional boundaries, and both are entwined in the insurance industry. Insurance also governs other industries through its 'powers of transferring and distributing risks'.[38] As an apparatus of governance it matters little whether insurance is organised through the state or private industry schemes or combinations of both.[39]

In the early twentieth century the insurance industry transformed risk into intangible tradable property in the financial markets. Throughout the post-WWII era innovations in new insurance 'products' as intangible property spread the risks of TMF capitalism across capitalist societies. In a sense, the welfare state made all of society subject to governance by insurance. The sovereign debt crises exacerbated anxieties about risk on a global scale. Indeed the transnational scale and societal scope of risks have prompted some scholars to describe post-WWII societies as risk societies.[40]

MIGA was prompted by concerns that erosion of creditor confidence was leading to reverse outflow of wealth from Third World countries, reducing their capacities to repay anything, a creditor's worst nightmare. Ibrahim E.L. Shihata, the architect of the Good Governance Programme which incorporated 'human' rights into debt restructuring,[41] told the ASIL annual meeting that not only had commercial lending and foreign direct investments to Third World states declined, '[w]orse still, investment flows have begun to take a perverse direction, from the poor to the rich countries'.[42] MIGA governs risks in sovereign debts. Non-commercial risks include direct and indirect threats to foreign investments, including currency transfer risks arising from delays or restrictions by host governments;[43] nationalisation and expropriation risks including confiscation, sequestration, seizure, attachment and freezing of assets';[44] breach of contract, including situations where the creditor is unable to enforce awards in their favour or where there is unreasonable delay in settling the claim;[45] and political risks arising from wars, civil wars, revolutions, insurrections, *coups d'état* and other political events.[46] MIGA provides for protection of property rights by setting up mechanisms for risk management and governance in three ways.

First, it makes the incorporation of investment dispute resolution clauses in Bilateral Investment Treaties (BIT) between states a condition for insurance.[47] Since it began operations, the absence of investor dispute resolution mechanisms impelled the WB to act as mediator and arbitrator. In 1961 the WB initiated the process to establish the

International Center for Settlement of Investment Disputes (ICSID), which culminated in 1966 with the Convention on the Settlement of Investment Disputes between States and Nationals of Other States (ICSID Convention) adopted by twenty states. Although ICSID was established as an autonomous institution it is part of the WB Group and its governance structures are tied to the WB.[48]

Second, it offers insurance for risks of expropriation of foreign property by Third World states.[49] With formal independence, the sovereignty principle gave colonies the political and legal authority to nationalise or expropriate assets of foreigners with or without compensation.[50] 'Diplomatic protection' was seen as inadequate by investors as it, 'eventually became an institutionalized legal technique justified by appeals to treaties, state practice, and legal commentators'.[51] BITs and ICSID establish two key attributes of international property rights: recognition of entitlements and dispute resolution mechanisms. The *third strand* in MIGA is important for 'human' rights and concerns *moral hazard*. Moral hazard is the reverse side of risk-taking and pivotal to the insurance industry in liberal societies for over two hundred years.[52] Moral hazard is a practical industry concept used to define, produce, take and manage the assessment of risk-takers and likely harms.[53] Market mechanisms transform risk into an extrinsic factor where the moral foundation of risk management is 'relentlessly utilitarian'.[54] In such a regime the distinctions between 'the guilty and the innocent or the culpable and the blameless' are no longer useful and the 'objective of controlling risk as effectively as possible prevails over all else'.[55]

'Human' rights violations could be sources of investment risks, and therefore 'non-commercial' risk for insurance purposes.[56] When social movements organise protests against displacement by infrastructure projects, when indigenous people claim ancestral lands, or industries run sweatshops causing accidents, or land acquisitions create social conflicts between groups of people, when states intervene militarily, or civil wars prevail, profitability of investments is adversely affected.[57] Social movements could, potentially, hold up projects, reduce profits, or introduce uncertainties in business with their protests and campaigns. Non-commercial risks include situations when states refuse to abide by arbitration awards by multilateral institutions like ICSID and/or other international arbitration bodies or cave into popular demands. Industries and investors must act 'responsibly' by paying for insurance against political and non-commercial risks. To qualify for political risk insurance investors must demonstrate they have taken steps to mitigate 'human' rights violations in the same way as someone purchasing occupational health insurance must install safety equipment to qualify. The requirement presupposes an *objective* 'human' right standard that can be statistically classified and categorised and scientifically predicted. In other words, it requires a measurable 'human' rights standard. The need to measure 'human' rights has, in turn, led to social science techniques of indicators, a set of 'tick-boxes' that have little to do with the conditions of real persons in the real world.[58] Instead objectified 'human' rights indicators operate as a component of actuarial techniques adopted by the WB and private insurers to insure international investment risks.

The WB uses actuarial techniques to identify, categorise and classify risks. States may be classified based on political conditions, national and per capita income by gathering information on economic and institutional infrastructures and other criteria. Everything from sustainable development, climate change to poverty eradication is governed by indicators, objectified, and subject to contracts and insurance. A recent report published by the Cambridge Institute for Sustainability and Leadership (CSIL) finds,

> Effective insurance regulation supports human rights by enabling financial inclusion, incentivising risk reduction behaviours and facilitating economic recovery after a disaster. Disruptive insurance regulation, or no regulation at all, deprives the poorest people in our world from protecting their own lives and assets.[59]

Information is the key to probability predictions. Accurate information presupposes administrative transparency in the Third World and must be corruption-free as corruption distorts information, warps the quality of data and affects the reliability of indicators and future predictions. Risk governance necessitates full-blown public sector reforms, rule of law, accountability, transparency and access to information, all of which invite new rights discussed below under GGPs.

Until the end of the nineteenth century the responsibility for risks rested with the risk-takers: 'you make your bed, you lie on it' type of approach.[60] The locus of moral wrongdoing shifted from the risk-taker to the *sources* of risk and the regulation of risks that posed danger to the public.[61] From the 1940s onwards general liability of decision-makers to the public in tort law replaced compensation payments based on insurance contracts.[62] These shifts have profound implications for the establishment of general liability for compensation of 'human' rights violations in the international property regime. Rights are no longer entitlements to economic and political liberties free from state interventions as in classical liberalism. Instead rights are the right to be free from certain consequences identified in regulatory standards set collaboratively by states, industries and 'civil societies'. Theodore Lowi writes, '[r]isk is a name we give to unwanted outcomes, and probability is a number we assign to risk'.[63] Risk is a deeply ideological construct and risk as property even more so. The *subjective* clamour for 'human' rights by social movements as a normative standard obscures its *objective* function in the international neoliberal risk-governance regime.

Voluntary codes like the Equator Principles leave the 'choice' of risk management to the industry actors just as insurance companies make home insurance available if I choose to buy it.[64] The property belongs to the investors in the same way as my home belongs to me. The Collevecchio Declaration holds out the promise to people that society will be free from the risks specified if the investors complied with the principles. NGOs and social movements also play their part in risk governance by participating in setting standards and monitoring them when standards established to govern risk as private property fail. NGOs like BankTrack may claim 'my code is better than the WB's', but the argument does little to disrupt the international neoliberal risk-governance regime for property rights.

GOOD GOVERNANCE AND 'HUMAN' RIGHTS IN RISK-GOVERNANCE REGIME

The WB's Good Governance Programmes (GGPs) operationalise post-WC rights. GGPs are reform packages that states must agree to in order to qualify for WB loans. GGPs comprise institutional reforms in four interrelated areas: i) public administration; ii) rule of law; iii) accountability; iv) transparency. All four components are about reformulations of traditional liberal rights and law. Not surprisingly, since the 1990s Third World states have crowded their statute books with law reforms. The WB defines governance as 'the manner in which power is exercised in the management of a country's economic and social resources for development'.[65] Bad governance is 'personalisation of power, lack of human rights, endemic corruption and un-elected and unaccountable governments'.[66] The WB's definition is modified and adapted by different IOs and G7's overseas aid agencies.[67] Nevertheless, UN definitions complement the WB definitions of governance.

Public Sector Reforms

New Public Administration (NAP), a pivotal component of GGPs, is a set of public sector reforms that encompass eight sectors where the state must reform itself to be eligible for financing. Public sector reforms give effect to the new right to democratic governance. The right to democratic governance extends to property owners and property-less people. Public sector reforms include public expenditure analysis and management,[68] administrative and civil service reforms including retraining civil servants,[69] revenue policy and administration,[70] stringent anti-corruption rules, decentralisation,[71] legal and judicial reform, sectoral institution building[72] and public sector enterprise reform.[73] In 1983 the WB for the first time flagged public sector reforms as a key area of reform in its report *Management in Development*.[74] Between 1990 and 1996 public sector reforms became more directly about restructuring Third World states in four areas: public sector management, accountability, the legal framework for development and information and transparency.[75] By 2006 one-sixth of WB loans were given to central governments' public sector reforms and 47 per cent of loans from the WB and 74 per cent from the International Development Association (IDA) had one or more projects with components in at least one of the four areas identified in GGPs and public sector reforms.[76]

Traditional liberalism considered public administration to be responsible for public governance. The WB's GGPs reverse the order of responsibility. 'Good governance' is now held responsible for the NPA. NPA adopts corporate management techniques in public administration.[77] Governments are necessary because only governments can provide two types of 'public goods': 'rules to make markets work efficiently' and 'corrective interventions when there are market failures'.[78] This view of law-making as a 'public good' is far, far away from the idea in classical liberalism that legislators make laws to give effect to their electoral mandates (see Chapter 5). NPA sees redistribution of power within the apparatus of the state as essential for governments to develop capacities to govern. The vehicle for redistribution of power is a clear recognition of rights of different 'stakeholders'. Rights for Enlightenment liberals were synonymous with maximum freedom from state interference in economic and social life. Rights established under the GGPs in contrast are about discipline, command and control of states and citizens.

Rule of Law

Rule of Law (RoL) reforms focus on institutional design of legal and justice systems. The meaning of RoL in GGPs is much the same as in traditional liberalism: that law must be publicly known, that law must be clear in meaning and predictable, that law must apply equally to everyone and, lastly, that disputes about rights and entitlements must be settled by an independent judicial authority. Establishing new rights are central to RoL reforms. RoL reforms include changes to substantive laws (civil and criminal) to harmonise them with international standards as well as institutional reforms.[79] Substantive laws include new civil and political rights (e.g. rights of homosexuals, indigenous peoples), socio-economic rights and cultural rights, amongst others.[80] RoL reforms focus on delivery of justice by introducing rights and entitlements as well as supporting education and training for legal profession-als, establishing codes of conduct, strengthening tax administration, reforming legislatures, training legislators, establishing independent regulatory authorities, training local governments and linking all of these professions, personnel and bodies to similar international networks. RoL reforms include government's own compliance with law by accepting judicial independence, accountability and transparency principles for civil servants.

Under classical liberalism *states established* a constitutional order based on separation of powers between the three limbs of the state: the executive, legislature and judiciary, to ensure RoL prevailed. In the epoch of imperialism, in contrast, Third World states are subject to rule of law established by international institutions under *real contractual obligations* in loans and debt bail-out agreements. This is no small difference in the meaning of RoL and the place of rights within it. The post-WC makes an about-turn from the WC on politics. The WC-SAPs took the 'markets know best' approach. In contrast, the post-WC-GGPs lending policies, in line with the NIE distinction between institutions and organisations discussed above, *create polities*. IEOs and G7 states *create polities* by setting the rules of the game. According to Douglass North, stable political institutions are essential for political and economic reforms. To create political institutions (not the same thing as engaging in politics) it is essential to change not only the institutions but also the 'belief systems for successful reforms since it is *the mental models of the actors that will shape choices*'[81] (italics added). Evolving norms of behaviour supportive of the new rules will take time. Regardless, the norms need to be reinforced for the *behaviour of polities* to stabilise.[82] Economic growth can occur under autocratic rule but they are inherently unstable. Long-term growth needs protection of civil and political freedoms. Formal constraints to behaviour through codes of conduct, laws and conventions are necessary but not sufficient for continued economic performance. The *belief systems* of people need to change for economic performance to stabilise.[83] 'Non-market' institutions in the post-WC speak are therefore necessary for economic growth and performance. 'Non-market' institutions include property rights, contracts and enforcement, political rights and parties, trade unions and labour rights, organisations of indigenous peoples and their rights and women's rights and non-discrimination laws, rights of minorities and representation for them and rights of other segments of society (homosexuals, disabled people, the elderly), each as bearers of rights in their own sectors.[84]

The WB is estimated to have supported three hundred and thirty RoL projects dealing with legal and judicial reforms in over one hundred countries by 2001, and spent US$ 3.8 billion since 1993.[85] Unlike the seventeenth- and eighteenth-century rights which emerged in opposition to feudalism, Church and state, twentieth- and twenty-first-century rights are instituted, funded and financed from the very top, by imperialist institutions seeking to expand and intensify appropriation of natures, labours and cultures. It becomes possible to see how delinking 'human' from property rights is necessary for institutional reforms to create new polities, behaviours and mental models conducive to imperialism. RoL reforms change the institutional backbones of states. They turn critique of institutions by activists and critical scholars on its head. For example, the WB sees colonialism as one of the reasons why institutions do not function in the Third World and the reason why GGPs are necessary.[86] GGPs, however, operate in the same way as colonial administrative reforms did in that the economic logics of external/international actors transform political institutions. The irony of WB acting as self-proclaimed decoloniser is not difficult to see.

Accountability and Socio-economic Rights

Accountability in GGPs actualises socio-economic rights. The justification for accountability is corruption in the Third World. Different
'stakeholders' have different reasons to support accountability however.
TNCs support accountability against corruption as a safeguard against
'state-capture' by national companies who are proximate to public officials
and political leaders. Nancy Zucker Boswell, the Managing Director of
the US Chapter of Transparency International (TI) and member of the
Board of Directors of TI, writes, '[t]he transition from state-controlled to
market economies is jeopardized by corruption'.[87] Corruption impedes
the flow of international investments because 'the privatization process
has too frequently transferred the public assets to privileged insiders'.[88]
What is at stake is that

> Corruption has become a crosscutting issue with the potential *to
> dissipate the dividends of the end of the Cold War*: (1) the consolida-
> tion of democracy, political stability and respect for the rule of law;
> (2) effective development; and (3) *the expansion of open, competitive
> markets*.[89] (Italics added)

Engagement with the IEOs was part of the comprehensive international
push by the US to harmonise and criminalise corruption in international
law with a view to creating a 'level playing field' for US corporations. The
US led the criminalisation of corruption internationally (see Chapter 5)
with initiatives in the OECD for the OECD Convention on Combating
Bribery of Foreign Public Officials in International Business Transactions
in December 1997[90] and regional initiatives within the OAS led to the
Inter-American Convention against Corruption in 1996.[91] In December
1996 the US-sponsored resolution, the Declaration on Corruption
and Bribery in International Business Transaction, was adopted by
the UNGA.[92] For Thomas White, the Deputy Director at the Office of
Investment Affairs in the US State Department involved in internationalising US policy on corruption,

> Bribery distorts markets and hinders economic development. It
> undermines democratic accountability. *It disadvantages companies
> that refuse to engage in the practice.* Our goal is not only to level the
> playing field for U.S. firms but to strengthen the rules of the game so

that international economic competition will serve to foster economic development and the deepening of democratic institutions.[93] (Italics added)

For ordinary people in the Third World corruption is a scourge in everyday life. However, it was under the post-WC-inspired, NIE-supported GGPs that accountability against corruption became firmly lodged in the international neoliberal risk-governance regime linked to socio-economic rights and debt-workouts. In the GGPs, accountability is about giving effect to socio-economic rights to clean water, food, electricity, housing and other 'basic needs', in WB vocabulary. People in the Third World do not have 'basic needs' because their politicians and bureaucrats are unaccountable, not because TMF capitalism drains their wealth and resources. The question in Chapter 5 in the political domain returns in the economic domain: who are they accountable to?

Accountability in GGPs has a broader objective of ensuring public resources are 'efficiently' allocated and used and improving 'borrower performance' through stricter enforcement and penalties for non-compliance.[94] Accountability extends 'throughout the economic system'[95] beyond governments. Governments must ensure accountability in the private sector by putting in place 'company and security legislation, competitive policy, and regulatory oversight'.[96] This function becomes important in the wake of privatisation, 'as the state sheds many productive investments in developing countries'.[97] Public accountability extends to three groups: i) the general public who are the recipients of public services; ii) political leaders and administrators who must ensure private service providers remain accountable to them; and iii) the service providers themselves whose objectives must be profitability first and foremost.

At the macro level accountability involves i) '[a] properly functioning government accounting system for effective expenditure control and cash management'; ii) 'an external audit system'; and iii) mechanisms to review audits and follow-up actions.[98] More significantly, auditing of GGPs *must be* contracted out. Not surprisingly, since GGPs replaced SAPs there has been a marked increase in the role and influence of international accounting firms in public administration.[99] The Big Four in international accounting (Deloitte, Ernst & Young, KPMG and PricewaterhouseCoopers) play a prominent role as legal advisors in institutional reforms.[100] At the micro level accountability is about 'exit' and 'voice'.[101] People must have the right to exit a provider if they are dissatisfied with their services. State monopolies deny exit-rights and do not offer competitive prices.[102] Exit is possible when there is 'deregulation, contracting out of services to multiple private providers, and public-private or public-public competition'.[103]

'Voice' is about being responsive to people. Public participation is a keyword in GGPs[104] and the buzzword in social movements and critical scholarship. NPA must involve NGOs, social movements, community organisations as 'stakeholders' in decision-making. The WB recognises this can become a double-edged instrument as external funding for NGOs

> … carries with it a number of attendant risks, which include possibly shifting NGO accountability from their natural constituents to these agencies, and making NGOs vulnerable to subtle pressures from governments that must approve direct funding of them […].[105]

Therefore '[t]he rapidly changing relationship between the state and NGOs needs further research and reflection'.[106] The politics of funding divides social movements from NGOs more than anything else and the WB recognises this reality.[107] The emergence of Social Movement Studies as an interdisciplinary field in its own right in the academia parallels the need for 'further research and reflection' in the GGPs. Higher education research funding in the social sciences routinely tie funding to engagement with social movements and capacities to influence them in the governance apparatuses in different sectors.[108]

Transparency and the Right to Information

As a normative argument, the right to information sounds like a democratic right with potential to empower people to monitor public administration. What the right *does* suggests otherwise. The idea that information is an essential condition for market exchanges, and that market failures are attributable to lack of information is an old one in capitalism. The determination of price in classical liberal economics (a theory challenged most comprehensively by Karl Marx) depended on the capacity to predict what buyers were willing to pay and sellers willing to accept. A speculative probability element is inherent in the operations of markets therefore. In the public domain freedoms of speech and association were essential for people to assemble, form associations, exchange and share information. Trade unions, industry and community associations and political organisations provided the platforms for information exchanges. Information gathering relied on communitarian relationships between market actors. In the private domain, the right to privacy was necessary to limit the authority of the state. The right to information is not the same as the right to free speech and association however.

When classical liberal thinkers wrote about civil liberties, market exchanges occurred between a large number of small producers, firms and merchants within the nation-state. In contrast, market exchanges in the post-WWII world occur between large TNCs, global financial institutions and deep states with sophisticated security apparatuses for information gathering. Small manufacturers and investors providing ancillary services to the TNCs and investors are subsumed by the oligarchies as 'stakeholders'.[109] Personal and communitarian knowledge is an inadequate source of market information in the era of transnational monopolies. We saw that IMF's amended Articles of Agreement gave additional powers of surveillance over borrower states (see Chapter 6). The corollary to the right to information in the GGPs is not the right to privacy but rather the rights to surveillance, i.e. the right to gather data. Surveillance and data gathering, supported by advances in technology, transform a democratic communitarian activity into a totalitarian policing one.

NIE scholars also argue that market failures occur because of inadequate information. However, in NIE-GGPs information goes beyond communitarian knowledge about demand and supply. For Douglass North, incomplete information limits the 'mental capacity by which to process information', which in turn determines 'the cost of transacting which underlies the formation of institutions'.[110] Cognitive science is necessary to establish mental models and computing science for processing information. There is 'more to the issue of institutional adjustment' than the information revolution however.

That adjustment entails *a total societal transformation*. Impersonal exchange, minute specialisation and division of labour, a radical reduction in information costs, and world-wide interdependence entail

a complete transformation of every aspect of societal organisation.[111]
(Italics added)

For Robert Bates, if information is imperfect, social capital (e.g. education, social networks, political connections) become 'non-market' sources of information about choices and intentions of other actors.[112] More importantly, imperfect information could lead to '*the substitution of contractual relationships* for spot markets' (italics added) which could impede institutional developments.[113] The quality of information that reveals '*the capabilities or intentions of another*' is important. That type of information is 'often asymmetrically held; an agent may know his or her own type, even when others cannot', and '[i]n such a world, p*eople possess incentives to engage in behaviour that reveals private information*'[114] (italics added).

What better incentive to reveal one's private information than insurance!

For John Toye, another NIE scholar, insurance contracts are important models in NIE because they have developed advanced ways of addressing substantial information asymmetries between the parties. Insurance contracts have developed forms of contracts that address moral hazards to disincentivise behaviour that increase probabilities of risk, and contracts to address adverse selection that disincentivise reckless risk-taking.[115] SAPs encouraged moral hazards by 'offering loans which did not have adequate monitoring and policing provisions'.[116] The WB was 'tempting countries to be opportunistic' in the same way as insurance policies that tempt the insured to get a 'free ride' at the cost of the insurance company. The 'game' in SAPs was whether or not the borrowing country required the WB loan.[117] 'Where property rights are not legislated as common with land, air, common water' all users are 'free riders'. Therefore, it is important to establish socio-economic rights to land, air, water so that entitlements to the resources are established.[118]

Adverse selection requires accurate information about the risk so that risks can be apportioned between investors and debtors. The way to minimise moral hazards and adverse selection is to improve the structure of contracts and have surveillance systems to measure and forecast risks. Forecasting requires information. Probability analysis, forecasting and Futures Studies, which emerged in the post-WWII era are now established scientific fields of study with their own methodologies, journals and research programmes.[119] Collecting factual information and writing better contracts is only one part of the information asymmetries, however, and one that lies at the surface. Interventions by states to reform institutions are also 'plagued by information problems'.[120] The insurance contract model for GGPs, the links between property, 'human', socio-economic rights and information becomes clear in NIE-post-WC logics.

Re-scripting right to free speech as right to information is part of the initiatives that aim for 'a complete transformation of every aspect of societal organisation'. Protest movements flash the red-lights that signal impending market failures. Social movements are also one of several vehicles for full disclosure by states and corporations. Social movements support right to information on the one hand and at the same time oppose state and corporate surveillance of society as if the two were antithetical. The public-private dichotomy that underpins the right to free speech and the right to privacy in the old liberalism continues to pervade liberal imaginations. Unable to connect the dots, social movements join in the 'total social transformation' initiated by NIE ideology, funded and instituted by GGPs to make risks 'subject to contracts and adjudication' in property rights while at the same time opposing its adverse impacts on society as breaches of 'human' rights. The information age makes buying and selling information itself an important commodity and a 'public good' necessary for market transactions. British media reported that the UK tax authority Her Majesty's Revenue and Customs (HMRC) and the National Health Service (NHS) plan to sell their vast databases to private firms.[121] Why not, one might ask? When society is subsumed by the economy, unsold data that does not yield return on investment is a 'wasted resource'. Why not, that is, so long as social movements do not join the dots between the right to information and surveillance.

GGPS, RIGHTS AND THE ANTI-CORRUPTION MOVEMENT IN INDIA

How did social movements respond to the macro-level changes discussed above? The 'India Against Corruption' protest movement led by Arvind Kejriwal, considered by *Time Magazine* as the top ten news of 2011 alongside the Arab Spring in Egypt, exemplifies the responses.[122] It throws light on the way in which NIE and GGP ideas operate as an invisible trope that holds a coalescence of diverse developments. Kejriwal, a bureaucrat in the Indian Revenue Service, formed the NGO Parivartan

(Change) in 2000 while in service and began work in a Delhi slum helping slum-dwellers secure electricity connections, settle billing disputes and intervening in corruption disputes with local Public Distribution System (for food aid) and water services.[123] Kejriwal had earlier joined the National Campaign for People's Right to Information (NCPRI) to demand statutory rights to information in which many civil servants had also participated at a time when the WB and Asian Development Bank were organising 'good governance' training programmes for civil servants. These 'good governance' training programmes followed the LPG reforms in India that came in the wake of near debt-default in the 1990s and political instability with three prime ministers in two years between 1996 and 1998.

In 2002 the coalition government led by the Bharatiya Janata Party (BJP), an extreme Hindu fundamentalist party, enacted the Freedom of Information Act 2002, but did not bring the statute into effect. In 2004 the Congress Party, in opposition at the time, incorporated right to information in its election programme. Several NCPRI campaigners were members of the party's National Advisory Committee (NAC) and well connected with international networks such as Joseph Stiglitz's initiative, the International Task Force on Transparency, the Commonwealth Human Rights Initiative, amongst others.[124] In 2004, with the Congress Party in power, the NCPRI members in the NAC made legislation on freedom of information their priority. In 2005 the Freedom of Information Act was reworked and passed by Parliament as the Right to Information Act (RTI) bringing information firmly under a rights framework. The purpose of the Act in the statute is, however, to give effect to the United Nations Convention Against Corruption ratified by India.[125]

After the government passed the RTI Act in 2005, Kejriwal resigned from the civil services and launched the 'Drive Against Bribe' campaign in the capital using the Act to highlight corruption. In 2006, he received the prestigious Magsaysay Award for Emergent Leadership.[126] The Magsaysay Foundation was endowed by the Rockefeller Brothers Fund in 1957 for 'honoring greatness of spirit in selfless service to the people of Asia'.[127] The award brings international recognition to new leaders. Kejriwal's solution to corruption was simple: more policing and harsher sentences.[128] That changed by 2007 and his anti-corruption campaign demanded a law establishing an ombudsman (the lokpal) against corruption. India had an Anti-Corruption Bureau (ACB), a Central

Vigilance Commissioner (CVC), and numerous laws against corruption which from time to time brought corrupt officials to justice. Typical of the statutes of the pre-LPG era, the onus of bringing the corrupt to account rested with the state.

In March 2011, the far right Hindu nationalists, the Rashtriya Swayamsevak Sangh (RSS) (National Volunteer Organisation) to which the BJP is affiliated launched a national campaign against corruption mainly targeting the ruling Congress Party.[129] In 2010 Kejriwal and Parivartan launched the 'India Against Corruption' campaign. Kejriwal was seen by many as 'ideology-free'. He inducted prominent godmen Baba Ramdev (mired in his own corruption scandals) and Shri Shri Ravishankar, founder of the Art of Living Foundation with consultative status in the ECOSOC and close ties to the World Economic Forum.[130] He involved Kiran Bedi, sympathetic to the far right Hindu fundamen-talists and former Police Commissioner in charge of Delhi's Tihar Jail (notorious for torture and abuse of prisoners and rampant corruption in the prison system) and 74-year-old Gandhian Anna Hazare. Whereas the RSS-affiliated Sangh parivar mobilised support on the ground, the Kejriwal team used social media to mobilise urban middle-class public opinion, methods already popularised by Tunisian and Egyptian movements. Tactical advice came from Avaaz, the global advocacy group discussed in Chapter 2, which was also involved in a similar anti-corruption campaign in Brazil.[131]

Liberal social movements like the NBA and its allies in the National Alliance of People's Movements were thrown into confusion. They supported Kejriwal's movement against corruption even when they were uncomfortable about the explicitly Hindu-fundamentalist character of the leadership. The educated urban middle classes, the beneficiaries of LPG reforms (as in the Philippines) enthusiastically supported the hunger-strikers. Kejriwal was against corruption but not against LPG reforms. 'India Against Corruption' never questioned the political-economy of systemic corruption in India. Corruption was bad because it came in the way of efficient delivery of public services. For Kejriwal, corruption transcended macroeconomic policies. According to him, '[w]hether a particular utility is in the government sector or the private sector is an irrelevant debate' and '[l]iberalization, globali-zation – these things will never work until you improve the governance of the country'.[132] This view of corruption is consistent with that of the GGPs. Having a Gandhian to lead the protest camouflaged Hindu fundamentalism as well as the international context and connections. For the international media, the movement was an example of non-violent political change in the world's largest democracy. For the national media, the movement demonstrated possibilities of non-violent social change (notwithstanding that the NBA and similar movements had not succeeded in addressing the plight of displaced people after three decades of struggle).

Kejriwal's anti-corruption movement changed tack from the demand to bring the corrupt to account to the demand for legislation to establish an office of the Ombudsman, or the Lokpal. The purpose of the Lokpal Act which followed the protests was, as stated in the statute, to give effect to the United Nations Convention Against Corruption ratified by India.[133] The ombudsman has jurisdiction to hear all corruption cases under the Prevention of Corruption Act 1988. The office of the CVC continues alongside the ombudsman. Cases reported to the ombudsman will be investigated by the existing Criminal Bureau of Investigation. What changed beyond aligning India's anti-corruption and information regimes with international standards one might ask?

Kejriwal's anti-corruption movement ended with acrimonious arguments amongst the leaders over future directions. Kejriwal formed a new political party in 2012, the Aam Aadmi Party (the Common Man's Party), which is now one of India's many parliamentary parties. Hazare opposed participation in parliamentary politics. The BJP came out against Kejriwal for forming a new political party.[134] In 2014 the BJP, the electoral wing of the RSS, won elections and for the first time formed a far right Hindu nationalist government that is openly against Muslims, minorities, rationalists, other nationalities, women's freedoms and marginalised castes, but firmly committed to TMF capital globally. The BJP's victory was supported by TNCs and Indian corporations and BJP Prime Minister Narendra Modi, welcomed in the US, UK and G7 states. President Obama wrote an article on Prime Minister Modi describing him as 'India's Reformer-in Chief'.[135] The ombudsman was established but corruption scandals continue to dominate newspaper headlines.[136]

CONCLUSION

Similar stories may be told of the Tunisian, Egyptian and other 'uprisings'. A new model of mobilisation for social change has emerged that we may call *network mobilisation*. If network governance is 'governance without government' (Chapter 5), network mobilisation is mobilisation for change without real change. Its methods are everywhere. Network mobilisation mobilises from the top. It rarely challenges the global power structures and institutions. Indeed, it relies on them to incorporate global policies into the country in the name of 'bottom-up' change, participation and inclusion. Network mobilisation mobilises nationally and internationally, uses normative arguments and human stories told without context or history and leaves institutional changes to TMF capitalism. International media generate excitement and catapult selected movements momentarily into the public limelight. Its leaders gain prominence receiving awards, recognition, funding and grants at important junctures. Network mobilisation picks up strands, discourses and norms from diverse types of movements and combines them in arbitrary ways without locating itself in any. Most importantly for the purposes of this book, network mobilisation is invariably about rights, rights-based solutions and law reforms.

The causal connections between the macro-level developments: the NPA reforms, RoL, accountability against corruption, and transparency and information components of GGPs, and at the micro level, the sudden receptivity of bureaucracy and government to certain types of mobilisations, the NCPRI, the 'India Against Corruption' campaign for example, the law reforms at national and local levels, the international linkages and the sudden international media attention to particular types of issues remain apparently invisible. The macro conditions generated by TMF capitalism, international laws and institutions, nevertheless, operate as a trope that holds the diverse networks, the trajectories of their developments and triggers their sudden and unexpected crossings in the international neoliberal risk-governance regime.

PART III

Concluding Reflections

8

Rights and Social Movements in the 'Epoch of Imperialism'

Too often has it happened that, when history has taken a sharp turn, even progressive parties have for some time been unable to adapt themselves to the new situation and have repeated slogans which had formerly been correct but had now lost all meaning – lost it as 'suddenly' as the sharp turn in history was 'sudden'. (V.I. Lenin, On Slogans, 1917, p. 185)[1]

This book opened with the paradox of rights resurgence walking hand in hand with LPG reforms. It ends with the reverse paradox: rights and democracy are rolled back as I write this conclusion and reversal of LPG reforms is in the air in the very birthplaces of Trumanism and Keynesianism, Reaganism and Thatcherism. Brexit has happened and Trumpism is triumphant. The Law Commission in the UK has recommended harsh punishments for whistleblowers,[2] and the UK Parliament has passed what activists have called the 'Snoopers Charter' authorising enhanced powers of state surveillance.[3] In the US, claims of 'fake news' is a Kafkaesque dance with exposés of real false news by leading newspapers like the *Washington Post* and trust in the mainstream media at its lowest ever. On the other hand, President Trump tweets falsehoods to the nation and the world in one hundred and forty characters and riles against 'fake news'. Technologies invented for command-communication-control during the world wars are now used for command-communication-control of entire polities.[4] Politics unfolds as a series of scandalous deviance from ideals of nineteenth-century democracy.

Not so long ago NSMs campaigned hard against 'corporate globalisation', against NAFTA, APEC, AFTA and WTO, describing them as forms of neoliberal capitalism that privileged TNCs. Only weeks and months before the US elections there were protests and opposition in Europe and elsewhere against the Transatlantic Trade and Investment Partnership (TTIP) negotiations. Donald Trump has announced he is against NAFTA, and all global trade agreements, and he has withdrawn the US from TTIP negotiations. Shouldn't the European Left be rejoicing that their demands are met one hundred per cent by none other than the leader of the 'Free World'? The withdrawal from TTIP comes hand in hand with virulent racism. Brexit and Trumpism came riding the high-tides of vitriolic hatred against immigrants. As children and women, old and young, wash up on their shores in overloaded boats, Europeans are terrified that the cosy post-WWII bubble they have lived in might burst. Their angst is real. In the 1960s and 1970s the British Left opposed the European project, describing it as a bastion of global capitalism spawned by the US.[5] Now that the US, which championed the European project to create a united opposition to the former USSR, wishes to dismantle the EU,[6] the British political Left is confused and divided. The traditional divisions between parliamentary parties, the Republicans and Democrats in the US, Labour and Conservatives in the UK, social democrats and Christian democrats in Europe no longer hold as deep internal divisions within the parties tear them apart.

There is astonishment about the 'surveillance' state and the 'deep' state among the G7 Left when in fact the architecture of the post-WWII world is founded on 'deep' surveillance states with revolving doors between Economy-State-Civil Society. What is intriguing about the G7 Left's present astonishment is that leading scholars and campaigners in the early post-WWII years, from the founders of post-WWII science like Albert Einstein and Nobert Weiner and leaders in social sciences like Charles Wright-Mills, expressed their alarm about the undemocratic character of TMF capitalism. None other than US President Eisenhower gave the world the phrase 'military-industrial-complex'. Stories of the CIA's misdeeds have never gone out of circulation at least since the civil war in Greece in the 1940s. This book has discussed how covert operations became overt operations after the Watergate scandals in the US. Does doing overtly what was done covertly make the politics 'democratic'? What is astonishing is that many in the Euro-American Left are astonished, that they see the recent developments as something new and call for the restoration of liberal democracy all over again, this time in the very heartlands of liberal democracy.

There is consternation in the Third World too about the rise of openly racist politics, war-mongering, Islamophobia, the anti-Hispanic hysteria, the encirclement of China, Russia-baiting and the so-called 'global war on terror'. For decades, a century even, Latin American countries protested about US domination, about CIA- and NED-led interference in their affairs, about US imperialism. Shouldn't the Latin American NSMs be celebrating that Trump wishes to pull the drawbridge between their countries? Shouldn't Mexicans be cheering that they have the US off their backs at long last? As I write there is real anxiety about the unravelling of the globalisation project in the Third World, the very project that Third World NSMs opposed at least since the debt crises discussed in the foregoing chapters. Third World movements which complained about Western imperialism throughout the post-WWII era follow Euro-American NSM leadership and blame local tyrants, the Assads, Saddams and Gaddafis. Shouldn't they ask how it comes to pass that the Mandate territories, the spoils of WWI, the arbitrary carving up of their territories that brought the Assads, Saddams and Gaddafis to power are once again engulfed by imperial wars? What new tyrants might replace the old ones?

Muslims are anxious about Islamophobia and demand that liberal rights and freedoms are extended to them without discrimination. They too appear to have forgotten the histories of the Middle East, how Britain and France manipulated genuine Arab desire for freedom from the Ottoman Empire to dismember Turkey, replaced the Arab world with puppet regimes, the machinations of Britain and France at the Cairo and Medina conferences in 1922 to install a 'friendly' sheriff in Mecca, the handing over of the holy cities of Mecca and Medina to the al Saud family against opposition from large sections of Muslims, the Khalifet movement in South and South-East Asia and the general perception of what is called 'Islamophobia' today, the idea that Western nations were against Muslims.[7] As Euro-American liberals turn to the texts of European Enlightenment scholars, Islamic scholars turn to the Holy Koran to protest their innocence. Both leave the history of capitalism and imperialism out of the accounts for their plight.

During the interwar years millions of people from the Third World, reeling under wars, collapse of agriculture and devastation of their economies, migrated to Europe and North America to survive. Then as now they were subjected to virulent racism and discrimination even as they built railroads and highways and waterways for TMF capitalism. Inspirational diaspora movements mobilised migrant communities to return home and fight for national liberation. The most powerful of these was the Ghadar movement in South Asia which organised and supported anti-colonial resistance throughout the British Empire.[8] The diaspora

NSMs too forget histories and demand 'fair' treatment of migrants, when in fact no one should have to leave their homeland to survive. George Santayana wrote at the turn of the century, 'those who cannot remember the past are condemned to repeat it'. The rest of this chapter addresses the historical sources of divisions in the main strands of Left politics today. Drawing on my own engagement with OSMs in South Asia and NSMs internationally, this chapter reflects on the opposition to liberalism in the early twentieth century and the water that has flowed under the bridge since then. The epoch of imperialism presents new questions for social movements and critical scholars. How those questions are answered holds the keys to the future of human emancipation or the absence of it.

THE COLLAPSE OF LIBERALISM AND THREE WORLDS OF MARXISMS

Neoliberalism is under attack from the political Left and the Right, the Brexiteers and Trumpeteers as well as the NSMs and OSMs. At the turn of the century classical liberalism was also under attack from the political Left and Right. In the hyphenated nation-state, traditional liberals emphasised a return to the ideals of the democratic state in European Enlightenment thought whereas fascists emphasised the centrality of the nation in the European Enlightenment. Historically, Marxism provided the most thoroughgoing critique of liberalism, the ideology of European capitalism. Marxist critique joined the dots between economy, polity, wars and ideology that liberalism severs in theory and fetishises in practice. Marxists argued that both nation and the liberal state were the institutional preconditions for NCI capitalism founded on class antagonisms and exploitation of working people. In his pamphlet *The State and Revolution: The Marxist Theory of the State*, written in 1917, Lenin mapped the Marxist debates on the character of the nation-state and argued that a successful revolution must grasp the 'nature of the beast' as it were, the class antagonisms that underpinned the NCI state and intervene *independently* as an organised political force in the crisis of NCI capitalism that was unfolding before their eyes. The state was a political, economic, ideological institution with tentacles that permeated all of society. That NCI state has been transformed by TMF capitalism as the chapters in this book show. If we take the European nation-state to be the institutional umbrella of NCI capitalism, what is the institutional umbrella that shelters TMF capitalism? How do those institutions reinforce and reify national oppression? Lenin wrote a hundred years ago,

> ... capitalism has now singled out a *handful* (less than one-tenth of the inhabitants of the globe; less than one-fifth at a most 'generous' and liberal calculation) of exceptionally rich and powerful states which plunder the whole world simply by 'clipping coupons'.[9]

The 'handful' of states is now just seven, the G7 and the algorithms for electronic transfers of virtual money make 'clipping coupons' a redundant activity. The oppression by a small group of states over the vast majority qua *states* is the hallmark of expropriation in the epoch of imperialism. How do the legal frameworks and institutional tentacles of TMF capitalism permeate transnationally between nations and within nations in the domains of economy, politics, ideology and culture in the epoch of imperialism? What are the class and sub-national underpinnings of juridical states in the epoch of imperialism? If liberalism fences-off the thought-world from the real world, if ideological developments mirror real developments in the real world, then surely liberal imaginations within social movements must mark their imprints on the theories and practices of Marxism as well. The rest of this chapter sketches three main trajectories in the Marxist theories and practices that mirror the three worlds in the post-WWII era and the theories and practices of NSMs. As the most influential anti-capitalist ideology, Marxism permeates social movement thought in all three worlds, but does so in different ways and different combinations of liberalism.

THE LEGACIES OF THE SECOND INTERNATIONAL

The first trajectory is traceable to European socialist movements. What is striking in retrospect is the extent to which the colonial question became a source of tensions, divisions, splits, vacillations and ambivalence within early European socialist movements. The colonial question divided European socialists over questions like: Should European socialists demand reform of colonial policies? Were there some positive aspects to colonialism? Should socialists condemn colonialism unequivocally?[10] Many expatriate nationalists from colonies like India, Egypt, Ireland, Algeria and elsewhere were engaged in organising solidarity activities in support of the anti-colonial struggles at home and lobbied

European socialists. For example, Madam Bhikaji Cama, an expatriate Indian nationalist, attended the Second Stuttgart International Congress of Socialists in 1907 and proposed resolutions on colonialism. Organisations like the Paris India Society, Berlin India Society, India House in Britain staged protests, mobilised public opinion and published journals. The persecution of nationalists from India, Egypt and other colonies occurred on European soil. For example, Madan Lal Dhingra, an Indian nationalist, was executed in London in 1909. What is interesting is that the anti-colonial movements and the socialist movements organised along parallel lines in Europe even as socialists continued to debate colonialism in the universal language of class-struggle and nationalism. The world wars split European socialist movements. The significance of the anti-colonial movements for the socialist movements was recognised programmatically two decades later at the Second Congress of the Third International in 1920.

The trajectory of the Second International produced two main strands in the development of European Marxism. The first is Social Democracy as a dominant ideology of post-WWII states. Social democracy developed modes of centralised governance apparatuses that integrated economy-state-civil society relations, and established the institutional precondition for TMF capitalism as the chapters in this book suggest. The second is what we may call Academic Marxism. Until the late nineteenth century Marxism developed its influential theoretical critique of capitalism outside the academia. While Marx and his comrades engaged with academic writings of their times, their responses were invariably grounded in the struggles for emancipation by ordinary men and women in Europe. In the early twentieth century, the theoretical problems for Marxism were thrown up by the crises of NCI capitalism and liberalism as practical questions for socialist movements. In the post-WWII era, the questions for Marxist theory were thrown up by problems of post-WWII governance at home and imperial governance abroad. Honed within numerous academic disciplines, Academic Marxism incorporated the methodological and epistemological orientations of TMF capitalism: empiricism, positivism, disciplinary views of the world, legalism and constitutionalism, instrumentalist knowledge geared to social policy, statistical reasoning in public policy, privileging epistemology over ontology and the marginalisation of philosophy more generally.[11]

The rise of Development Studies as a field of inquiry, the expansion of Human Geography, Marxist sociology's interest in micro-level studies of Third World societies, Marxist anthropology's interest in markets and institutions in the Third World, amongst other disciplines focused on the newly independent Third World and expanded exponentially. Academic Marxism permeates Left understandings of TMF capitalism and provides the inputs for overseas development strategies and Third World governance. Academic Marxism produced influential theories like Post-structuralism, Neo-Marxism, Frankfurt School, and much else which continue to be un-problematically extended to understandings of Third World societies. These developments in European Marxism blur the theoretical boundaries between the historical evolution of colonial and capitalist societies and the resistances to colonialism and capitalism. Academic Marxism has a profound influence on Euro-American social movements. Its influence is relatively less on the political struggles and anti-imperialist movements in the Third World.

THE LEGACIES OF THE THIRD INTERNATIONAL

The second strand in Marxism lies on the trajectory of the Third International, the breakaway Left fraction of the Second International that opposed colonialism unequivocally. The coming together of insurgent national liberation struggles around the world with the socialist movements in Europe including Russia during NCI capitalism's moment of crisis altered the outcomes of the world wars in unexpected ways. Their interventions left structural imprints on the institutional architecture for TMF capitalism when the war ended. The competing conception of rights of nations to self-determination was perhaps the single most important structural imprint.

In 1907, Woodrow Wilson, who was to become the US president in 1912, declared '[c]oncessions obtained by financiers must be safeguarded by ministers of state, even if the sovereignty of unwilling nations be outraged in the process'.[12] Wilson's Secretary of State William Jennings Bryan told a gathering of US financiers candidly,

I can say, not merely in courtesy – but as a fact – my department is your department; the ambassadors, the ministers, and the consuls are all yours. It is their business to look after your interests and to guard your rights.[13]

At the same time, Wilson was the foremost champion of rights of nations to self-determination before, during and after WWI. Wilson argued that the right of nations to self-determination was a *legal* right and that it must be recognised internationally as such. Wilson's position influenced the Paris Peace Conference at the end of WWI and established the mandate system under the League of Nations. The idea of self-determination as a legal right was later formalised in the Montevideo Convention on Rights and Duties of States, 1933 between the US and Latin American states. The right was extended to other states under the Atlantic Charter signed between the US and the UK at the height of WWII in 1941, and institutionalised in the UN Charter. Wilson canvassed the idea of legal rights in the name of freedom for colonised nations. For Wilson, the agents of freedom in the colonies were the financiers and investors who would through their investments bring modernisation to the colonies. Freedom was freedom for investors and financiers from the constraints of the Empire system which limited their market access to colonies under preferential trading systems within Empires. The purpose of self-determination as a legal right was to establish equal access to colonial markets between capitalist states.

In contrast, Lenin argued that self-determination could never be a legal right. Refuting Wilson's arguments, Lenin argued that self-determination was a political claim, something colonies had to wrest through political actions. In *Right of Nations to Self-determination*, Lenin argued against different currents within the socialist movements that subscribed to the Wilsonian idea of self-determination as a legal right.[14] The theoretical understanding moved many national liberation struggles away from demands for legal rights and channelled their energies into organising for political change. It brought the socialist and national liberation struggles closer, and extended moral and material support to anti-colonial movements. Above all, it offered the national liberation struggles a political alternative that was neither a reformed Empire (e.g. dominion status for colonies) nor the Wilsonian legal rights with its promise of freedom. National liberation struggles *declared* independence; they did not demand the 'human' right to self-determination. It opened up possibilities of new international alliances that limited the victory of the Allies. In turn, the partial victory of the Allies had profound influence on the architecture of the post-WWII world.

The Third International was wound up in 1943.[15] The emergence of states as a subject of TMF capitalism and the distinctly different institutional, legal, technological, scientific, ideological and political infrastructures presupposed by TMF capitalism presented Marxist theory with too many complex questions that made a common theoretical position that suited all socialist and Third World states difficult to sustain. Justifying the dissolution of the Third International Mao Tse-tung wrote,

[t]he forms of revolutionary organizations must be adapted to the necessities of the revolutionary struggle. If a form of organization is no longer adapted to the necessities of the struggle, then this form of organization must be abolished.[16]

Much before the rise of postmodernist pluralism and difference in the Euro-American Left, Marxism became, *de facto*, pluralist and culturalist, as Chinese, Indian, Russian, Kenyan, Ghanaian and other Marxisms.

If European Marxism produced the knowledge base for global governance, Third World Marxism, bearing the birth-marks of national liberation struggles, produced the knowledge base for national governance. The national liberation struggles shifted the sites for Marxist struggles against capitalism. Liberalism permeated Third World Marxism in very different ways however. A fundamental premise of Marxism is that liberalism mystifies the relations between politics, economics, ideology and culture which are entwined in capitalism. Third World Marxism believed that it was possible to have capitalist-style economic development without colonies. They held out or held on to the possibility in the face of the histories of colonialism in the development of capitalism. Third World Marxism's attempts to reconcile a capitalist model of economic development without its external dimension – colonial expansionism – distorted the relations between economics, politics, ideology and culture of national independence.

Socialist nationalism did the same in different ways. Socialists held out the possibility that it was possible to retain the scientific and technological potential of capitalist production for wealth creation and overcome the dehumanisation and social polarisation by political control of states and through redistributive justice. Lenin was an admirer of Taylorism and Fordism and industrialisation built on colonial resources and labours. China's Great Leap Forward and Cultural Revolutions were attempts to develop a capitalist-style economy without capitalist politics and culture. However, large-scale production presupposes large bureaucracies and large-scale mobilisation of natural resources and labours. Large dams require centralised states, global investments, large bureaucracies, acquisition of large tracks of land and large-scale displacement of people. So does militarism capable of competing with TMF capitalism's vast military-industrial complexes with global outreach. Over time the architectures of the political economies of TMF capitalist states and socialist states became look-alikes.[17] The primacy of politics over economics introduced another type of voluntarism.

State Marxism transformed it into a ruling ideology. Thus, in the post-WWII era Marxism became deflated from a theory of resistance to a theory of governance as social democracy, Academic Marxism, Third World nationalism and socialist nationalism. The rights resurgence simply reaffirmed the ontological reality that in the real world economics, politics, ideology and culture work in concert, they always did. In that sense the paradox of rights and democracy is not a paradox at all. In times of crisis the mystique of liberalism and the promises of rights are laid bare.

REVOLUTIONARY MARXISM

The third strand in the development of Marxism is sometimes referred to as Revolutionary Marxism to differentiate it from social democratic, academic and state Marxisms. Revolutionary Marxism does not advocate participation in the institutions of governance; get a 'seat at the table' as it were. Revolutionary Marxism remains wedded to the idea of structural and revolutionary change. On the one hand their rights scepticism, their refusal to embrace liberalism and refusal to denounce armed-struggle as a legitimate form of struggle has brought upon followers of Revolutionary Marxism extraordinary state repression and subjected them to the 'global war on terror'. It has united NSMs inspired by the New Left in common cause with First and Third World states. NSMs seldom speak out against state repression against revolutionary Marxists. On the other hand the continuing expropriation of land, natural resources, displacement and devastation unleashed by each crisis of TMF capitalism and each round of LPG reforms means ideas of revolutionary and structural change continue to attract people in the Third World, especially in rural areas. The failure of liberal democracy to deliver economic, social and political justice gives credibility to their claims that liberal democracy works only for capitalists and imperialists. Revolutionary Marxism is anchored to local histories and celebrates past struggles for freedom and emancipation. By keeping alive the memories of past resistances, Revolutionary Marxism refreshes historical consciousness of communities and the desires for emancipation and freedom. Pushed back by the reversals in Russia, China and elsewhere and the consequent loss of international support, overshadowed by the influence of European academic Marxism and social democracy, on the one hand, and state socialisms, on the other, followers of Revolutionary Marxism battle on against the odds in many parts of the Third World including the Philippines, India, Nepal, Indonesia, Peru, Columbia, Brazil and other countries with varying degrees of political influence.

Lenin wrote, '[w]ithout revolutionary theory there can be no revolutionary movement' and further that the economic, political and theoretical struggles were distinct types of struggles and they need to be waged in their own turfs on their own terms.[18] Revolutionary Marxists stayed their ground in politics. They prioritised organised political struggles and assumed that theoretical problems of the 'epoch of imperialism' were settled by the revolutionary leaders of the early twentieth century. In *Marxism and Revisionism*, Lenin argues that until the late 1890s the main theoretical struggles were between liberalism and Marxism but after that the struggle against liberalism appears in Marxist avatars as intra-Marxist struggles within socialist movements.[19] At the moment of Liberal Marxism's triumph first in the Euro-American states in the 1960s and later as a global phenomenon alongside globalisation in the 1990s, Revolutionary Marxism abandoned the theoretical and philosophical battlefield altogether. The different trends within Marxism in the epoch of imperialism and their ramifications for the struggle against TMF capitalism, expropriation of nature and the 'nationality question' on the ground went more or less unchallenged. As NSMs swept through the Third World with 'globalisation' and GGPs, the failure of Revolutionary Marxism to address new forms of liberalism in the avatar of Liberal/ New Left Marxism introduced two types of theory-practice disjuncture in Marxist theory.

The first type of theory-practice disjuncture is the spatial disconnect between theories about capitalism and imperialism and political practices of resistance. Marxist theories since the end of WWII have developed within Euro-American academic and other knowledge institutions and resistance to TMF capitalism occurs largely and consistently in the Third World. In this respect, Marxist theoretical development mirrors the wider epistemological problem of knowledge in the epoch of imperialism. Theories are developed in the Euro-American institutions and the 'data' is supplied by Third World experiences. Ranjan Ghosh argues that there is an 'institutional overpowering' by American universities such that it becomes necessary to conform to 'notions of plurality, dissensus and nonexceptionalism' which emanates from the very requirement for 'openness, the spirit of reaching out and listening to the voice of the "other"'.[20] The geographical hiatus in theory and practices of human emancipation is a new challenge for praxis-oriented theories in the epoch of imperialism.

The second is a temporal disjuncture in theory and practice within Revolutionary Marxism. The fear of lapsing into liberalism and revisionism has produced a tendency within Revolutionary Marxism to undermine the importance of theory and philosophy for emancipation and freedom. Consequently, slogans from the past filter the understandings of the present and leave the future open to uncertain opportunities. Theory remains fossilised in the past even as problems of struggles on the ground present new questions for theory. Against the dazzling innovations of Liberal Marxism, Revolutionary Marxism sounds clichéd and dogmatic. Yet their adherence to the inspirational moment of struggles in the early twentieth century gives Revolutionary Marxism an intuitive understanding of what is entailed in contemporary political, economic, ideological and cultural developments. Playing down the role of theory and philosophy in Revolutionary Marxism comes at a historical juncture when it is most needed. Indeed it will not be an over-statement to say that in the present juncture the absence of theoretical and philosophical developments creates a knowledge vacuum that is filled with liberalism in new and varied avatars. The unresolved theoretical and philosophical problems of human emancipation in the stage of late imperialism leaves the resistance of Revolutionary Marxism on the ground in a state of irresolution – neither moving ahead nor entirely defeated. In India and the Philippines for example the cycle of state repression – peace-talks-collapse of peace-talks and resumption of state violence has continued for many decades.[21] The philosophical and theoretical problems of our times in fairness are paradigmatic in scope.

Marxism remains the most influential theory for social movements with a history that spans the epoch of imperialism and the three typologies of states after WWII. It has produced the most comprehensive and unrelenting critique of liberal capitalism, and the conceptual and methodological tools for the critique of capitalism. Although colonialism was recognised as a constitutive element of European capitalist development in Marx's writings, its place in the socialist project and human emancipation was never directly addressed. The Second Internationalists were confounded by the colonial question; the Third Internationalists recognised the importance of the colonial question and put it on the agenda of revolutions where it remains waiting to be addressed. The epoch of imperialism puts the colonial question in whatever form at the top of history's agenda. The colonial question unravels the European Enlightenment, the foundations of liberalism and rights.

THE THEORIES AND PRACTICES OF NSMs

NSM Theories: The Rise of the New Left

The New Left remains the single most important influence on the theoretical orientations of NSMs. The New Left is a broad eclectic church and draws on a wide variety of theoretical strands from Sartre's existentialism to Maoism. The sheer diversity of sources and orientations means the New Left has not produced a unified body of social theory. What can be said about the New Left is that they infuse Marxism with liberalism. The permeation of liberalism into Marxism in turn makes the liberal-Left distinctions difficult in theory and leads to a variety of convergences between liberal and Left politics in practice. Rights are the nub where convergences between Marxism and Liberalism occur in the New Left. The New Left promotes what I shall call the 'politics of equidistance'. The politics of equidistance is based on disillusion- ment rather than optimism. Disillusionment with socialist austerity and consumer capitalism, with state repression in socialist states and market repression in capitalist states, with curtailment of cultural freedoms in the socialist states and the corruption of culture in the capitalist states, with party politics under centralised command-and-control-style communist parties and corporate-funded capitalist parties, with liberalisms and Marxisms of the past, in a nutshell disillusionment with capitalism and socialism. The burden of social transformation and social justice falls on ethical/moral arguments and voluntarism.

Liberal Marxists are sceptical of rights and defend it at the same time. Anne Orford for example states, correctly, that the 'link between

property and personality in the liberal philosophical tradition forms one
of the conceptual links between capitalism and modern liberal law'[22] and
more importantly,

> [the] rights discourse may not be capable of contributing to the
> political practice of marginalizing the Western economy, precisely
> because it is central to constituting the *subject* of that economy.[23]

Her prognosis however is,

> [h]uman rights law can and does operate to subvert rather than
> facilitate this commitment to economic liberalization at any cost.
> However, in order for human rights to act as a constraint on globaliza-
> tion, rather than as a handmaiden to it, it is necessary for human rights
> lawyers to consider the ways in which the knowledge they produce is
> located in global networks of power.[24]

The foregoing chapters discussed how their very efforts to produce
knowledge 'located in the global networks of power' mirror TMF
capitalism in 'network mobilisation'. To argue that rights scepticism
can constrain globalisation reifies liberalism's power of promise, the
possibility that rights *may* mitigate the effects of globalisation.

Contesting the idea popular in social movements that rights may
be used for strategic engagement with the WB, James Gathii, a critical
scholar from the TWAIL school (Third World Approaches to International Law), states, correctly,

> It is [the] strategic engagement of rights work that has a disem-
> powering effect on human rights activism: the fact that these rights
> claims have to be redefined or reconciled by finding complementa-
> rity and compatibility with the economic policies of the World Bank.
> Consequently, human rights activists who have sought to use human
> rights as a means of demanding the World Bank to adopt an approach
> to development that is more humane, are constantly disappointed
> by the continued redefinition of their rights claims with counter-
> vailing rights claims mediated through reference to the background
> assumptions of the classical interpretation of the Bank's mandate.[25]

In his prognosis he goes on to state,

Yet, paradoxically the liberties protected by the commitments to human rights and political democracy in the good governance agenda also give the politically disenfranchised citizenry liberties that it was often denied under the authoritarianism that accompanied the developmentalism of the 1970s and 1980s.[26]

Chapter 7 considered how 'human' rights are integral to the neoliberal international risk-governance regime. Critical rights scholarship is replete with similar writings that demolish rights only to reinstate it again. Demolishing rights only to reinstate it mirrors, at the ideological and theoretical level on the political Left, TINA arguments of Margaret Thatcher – There Is No Alternative – or 'end of history' declarations of liberal triumphalism on the Right.[27] Social movements in the Third World struggling against TMF capitalism, WB and IMF policies that destroy their communities, natures and cultures, are attracted by the diagnosis but the prognosis leads to grave divisions, factionalism, splits and fragmentation, examples of which were discussed in the foregoing chapters. Liberalism invites people to struggle for utopian visions. People seldom put their lives on the line to defend abstract principles however.

A close analysis of successful revolutionary struggles of the early twentieth century reveals that people put their lives on the line to defend the things they need to make life possible. The point may be exemplified by a closer examination of the Chinese Revolution that inspired millions of oppressed nations in Asia, Africa and Latin America. For Liberals, the Chinese Revolution succeeded because of the charismatic personality of Chairman Mao who unfortunately turned out to be a dictator. Marxism's first premise, in contrast to liberalism, is that individuals do not make history, not even the most charismatic ones. For some Liberal Marxists, the Chinese Communist Party (CPC) under Mao's leadership started out correctly but deviated subsequently. Deviance presupposes a normative ideal and deflects attention from context.

Confronted with Japanese invasion and a disintegrating political order in China, the CPC moved to the rural hinterlands where the state was less concentrated and commenced a programme of land redistribution, considered to be the single largest property redistribution in history.[28] The liberal-nationalist Kuomintang led by Chiang Kai-Sheik argued for putting land reforms on hold until the Japanese were defeated for fear that land reforms will sow divisions in national unity against Japanese aggression. The CPC insisted on implementing 'land to the tiller' alongside Japanese resistance.[29] Anyone who knows anything about peasants should know that peasants will put their lives on the line to defend their lands. The US, which invested heavily in Kuomintang and Chiang Kai-sheik, and believing the principle of recognition in rights to self-determination in international law will keep Kuomintang in power, even gave China a seat in the UNSC. The US never expected the Chinese Revolution to continue after WWII ended. The distinction between liberal and non-liberal approaches becomes apparent.

Land reform was also the principal programme in the alliance between radical peasant leader Emiliano Zapata and Left-liberal Venustiano Carranza in the Mexican revolution in the early twentieth century. In that case, Carranza won the argument that land reforms must wait until the revolutionaries took power and a new constitutional order was established. Liberal constitutionalism's promise never materialised. Peasants continue to struggle for land to this day and Mexico lurches from crisis to crisis, as the chapters in this book have shown.

The Practices of NSMs: The World Social Forum

Ideas, this book has argued, presuppose certain material conditions. NSMs too require money, intellectual and theoretical resources, social networks and connections ('social capital' to use Pierre Bourdieu's phrase) and the capacities to 'make things happen'. An analysis of the World Social Forum (WSF) demonstrates the ideology and the materiality of a model global NSM in contemporary times.

In the late 1980s the NED funded a comprehensive study on democracy in Third World countries. The project was led by the founding editor of NED's *Journal of Democracy* and produced four edited volumes on the state of democracy in Africa, Asia, Latin America and Eastern Europe.[30] The point of departure for the volumes is that the ideological battles about fascism, Marxism-Leninism, quasi-socialism and military rule were things of the past leaving democracy as the only viable model. In other words, the research fleshed out the Fukuyama thesis with an array of case studies by scholars around the world. Contributors to the study were provided a theoretical framework for national case studies. The research produced forty-nine propositions on the possibilities of stable democracies in the Third World.[31] These volumes together with the journal were to become reference points for the state of democracy, as it were, outside the G7 countries and permeate democracy research.

A similar point of departure, viz., fascism, Marxism-Leninism, quasi-socialism and military rule, are things of the past, formed the basis for another Left intellectual project on democracy in the late 1990s against the backdrop of gathering protests against the SAPs and the WTO agenda. In 1998 the McArthur Foundation, one of the largest private philanthropic foundation in the US set up, amongst other things, to 'generate new knowledge about critical issues,'[32] awarded a grant for an international project on 'Reinventing Social Emancipation: Toward a New Manifesto', led by Boaventura Sousa de Santos. The project involved sixty-one researchers analysing fifty-three national initiatives on alternate democracies with national coordinators in Brazil, India, Columbia and Mozambique.[33] The project produced five volumes on alternatives: alternate democracy, alternate production, alternate knowledge, global social movements and social emancipation. The studies privileged Third World social movements opposed to OSMs and brought them into a global alliance.

Theoretically, the manifesto for NSMs is framed in Manichean terms. Capitalist and corporate globalisation which is 'bad' is juxtaposed to 'good' globalisation where a global civil society speaks out against the injustices of corporate and capitalist globalisation. According to Santos, 'Western modernity' has created divisions between 'capitalists, socialists, liberals and Marxists, reformists and revolutionaries, nationalists and internationalists'.

> ... such divisions today seem *anachronistic* or incapable of accounting for the cleavages that traverse the world ... both liberalism and Marxism seem to be undergoing today a deep crisis as well. The same could be said of the cleavage between reformism and revolution. *On the one hand, the idea of social revolution seems to have been erased from the political agenda, even the agenda of those who still consider themselves revolutionaries*; on the other hand, reformism, that is to say, the idea of a gradual and legal improvement of the patterns of sociability, has been replaced by the concepts of governability and governance. Finally the opposition between nationalists and internationalists seem to have lost its meaning in a time that designates itself as a time of globalisation.[34] (Italics added)

For Santos, the alternative to globalisation is '*participatory* democracy', 'alternative production systems' based on social and communitarian ethics, 'new *labour internationalisms*' 'emancipatory *multiculturalism, cultural citizenship* and justice', 'the defence of *biodiversity* and the struggle for *recognition of rival knowledge*'[35] (italics added). The GGP's conceptual vocabulary is not difficult to see in the Alternative Democracy project.[36] The similarities in the points of departures for the NED's democracy project and the Alternatives project are also interesting. Santos' research project brought together a range of intellectuals from a number of countries and produced a body of work that provides the theoretical and conceptual foundations for the WSF, the most influential international NSM.[37]

The choice of the four countries for national coordinators is interesting in retrospect. In all four countries ideas of social revolutions were/are very much alive. The point here is not the correctness or otherwise of OSMs' politics or theories. Rather the point is that the voluminous studies about social movements in those countries do not engage with the arguments and political questions posed by the OSMs. Instead OSMs are assumed to be irrelevant and that assumption is the point of departure for the theoretical foundations of global NSMs. In striking contrast, the socialist and national-liberation movement literatures of the early twentieth century engaged with other political movements and trends within the Left on theories, strategies and tactical differences. Indeed the purpose of writing was to engage with their opponents. Early twentieth-century theory developed in the course of political engagement with other movements. Today polemics is frowned upon even in Left-leaning social movements. By refusing to acknowledge the continued influence of OSMs in many parts of the Third World, NSMs like the WSF conceal from the world the extraordinary levels of state repression against movements opposed to liberal solutions to globalisation often in collaboration with G7 states who claim to act against the so-called 'global war on terror'.

The WSF was established in February 2000 two years after anti-globalisation protests in Seattle in which Euro-American trade unions, INGOs and NGOs and global NSMs and globally networked national NSMs participated. The organisation was conceptualised as the reverse or the 'other' of the annual corporate event, the World Economic Forum in Davos, mirroring in practice its theoretical juxtapositioning of 'bad' and 'good' globalisations. The WSF was formed with the support of prominent European NGOs, the Brazilian Workers Party (PT) which was in power in one of the provinces at that time and several European governments.[38] It receives funding and support from European and American foundations, INGOs and European governments. In line with New Left ideology, the WSF Charter prohibits political parties from being part of the WSF. Yet the WSF was formed by one of the most prominent political parties in Brazil which later came to power at the national level. The WSF was supported by parliamentary, social democratic Left parties in India, Brazil and other Third World countries, and by several European governments, parties and parliamentarians.[39] Interestingly, the WSF Charter permits exclusion of countries like Cuba, organisations like FARC, even the Madres de Plaza de Mayo, an organisation of the mothers of those 'disappeared' by the Argentinian military dictatorship of 1976–83.[40] Organisations are of course free to include or exclude membership and participation and seek support from anyone sympathetic to their cause. The point here is the WSF Charter describes the organisation as 'an open meeting place for groups and movements of civil society that are opposed to neoliberalism and to domination of the world by capital and any form of imperialism'.[41] The theoretical basis for the exclusion is the New Left idea that political parties tend to be totalitarian, that vertical mobilisations of the OSM type tend to be bureaucratic, that all ideologies curtail freedom of thought (as if New Left is not an ideology). These are ideas that feed into models of 'network mobilisations'.

However, OSMs do not disappear in reality simply because the theoretical foundations of global NSMs are premised on assumptions about their irrelevance. In 2004 the WSF organised a global forum in Mumbai. The more radical OSMs in India organised a parallel international event, the Mumbai Resistance 2004 (MR 2004).[42] The two events were across the road from each other, and it took little more than a pause at the traffic lights to get to the other global forum. The contrast between the two forums could not be sharper. The WSF was attended by world leading academics, the former prime Minister of Ireland and former UN Commissioner for Human Rights, former president of India, former prime minister of India, former vice president of the World Bank, sitting MPs from different countries, judges, Nobel Prize winners, alternate Nobel Prize winners and many former civil servants-turned-NGO officials. MR 2004 in stark contrast was attended by intellectuals engaged in political organising at local and national levels, peasants, students and workers and regional organisations under tight state surveillance and visa restrictions. The chief minister of the state and several MPs attended the WSF meeting whereas permission to hold a public meeting was refused to MR 2004.[43]

NSMs like the WSF channel protests away from historically grounded movements rooted in traditions of struggles against colonialism and imperialism in different countries.[44] The WSF after the Seattle protests in 1999 diverted attention away from entrenched domestic OSMs struggling against TMF capitalism. Their unease with the vocabulary of rights within the NSMs on the one hand and the absence of a vocabulary that speaks to their historical experiences of anti-colonial struggles on the other leaves organisations of the dispossessed in the Third World, the workers, peasants, students, marginalised castes, nationalities and classes in a quandary. The defence of liberal rights as a serious political alternative by global NSMs does not speak to people's lived experiences of state violence, torture, extrajudicial killings and state expropriation of lands and livelihoods not least because many Third World states are already liberal democracies or becoming one. India has been a model for liberal democracy in the Third World for example since 1947 at least and yet state violence, torture, custodial deaths, political uses of death penalties, military occupation of entire regions and extrajudicial killings are well documented by organisations in India and internationally throughout its post-Independence history.

By putting the failures of capitalism with socialism on par, the NSMs throw out a whole body of political and historical experiences in the struggle for emancipation from capitalist tyranny and human freedoms in the Third World. NSMs like the WSF celebrate anti-colonial struggles yet refrain from learning lessons from their organisational experiences and theoretical developments. Important amongst the organisational experiences of anti-colonial movements are those that relate to forming broad-based alliances of diverse ethnic, religious and racial groups against colonial rule. The unity that anti-colonial movements forged were not based on formal equality and cultural rights that liberalism promises but real equality based on safeguarding the interests of groups oppressed by colonial rule.[45] For example the Chinese Revolution was based on the understanding that society comprised classes with specific interests and that it was possible to unite groups whose interests were opposed to imperialism by developing a minimum programme of action. The Chinese Communist Party's 'four class alliance' thesis was the basis for a political programme to unite those social forces that were oppressed by colonialism. During the Indian Independence movement the Congress Party negotiated the terms of the alliance with peasant, workers, nationalities and regional organisations. The histories of national liberation struggles are replete with stories of political alliance building against colonialism. If politics is war by other means the Cold War was war to break the alliances on which Third World states were founded. What kind of new alliances might be needed to resist TMF capitalism as the ghosts of the world wars return to haunt the world again? In the absence of historical memory answers to such questions about struggles against imperialism fall back to liberal imaginings as the default position and bring back a rights-based political programme that was rejected a century ago.

In the early twentieth century Marxism engaged questions of colonialism, race, migration, ethnic diversity under the political agenda of what was called the 'nationality question'. The 'nationality question' addressed a distinct form of oppression where nations are subjugated to capital *as nations*, not reducible to class-struggle or 'bourgeois nationalism'. The New Left gives a 'cultural turn' to questions of colonialism. Colonialism for the New Left is not a necessary and contingent relation of capitalism as its external dimension but a cultural phenomenon that the post-WWII state, acting ethically, must fix. These approaches to colonialism in the past and present under whatever name leave out the specific forms that national oppression takes in different epochs of capitalism. NSMs like the WSF leave Third World social movements no wiser about what slogans they should organise under and how they should connect the dots between TMF capitalism and its political, cultural and social manifestations as racism, migration, suppression of so-called 'minorities', wars and national subjugation. Even the term 'nationality' or the 'nationality question', still widely used in the Third World, confuses and confounds European social movements on the political Left. The nationality question and ethnic conflicts are the bane of social movements in the Third World today. WSF has little to offer in intrastate conflicts like Kashmir or Kurds or Somalia or Sudan that tear apart communities and peoples and open the way for imperialist 'humanitarian' interventions.

CONCLUSION

The source of resilience of rights in socialist imaginations stems from socialist history itself. European socialists in the nineteenth century gave qualified support to what they called 'bourgeois democracy'. For the first time in history, bourgeois democracy recognised ordinary working people, the workers, the peasants, the tenant farmers in Europe as political actors. Women, people of colour, indigenous peoples and people of different sexual orientations were added to the list. Liberal rights, European socialists argued, although limited in scope gave working people the opportunities and spaces to organise themselves for political and social change. In the epoch of imperialism, the entwinement of transnational corporations, financial institutions and a 'handful of states' in Lenin's words makes 'bourgeois democracy' an illusion even for the citizens of G7 states. In the epoch of imperialism rights lose any limited progressive potential they may have had in the nineteenth century. Instead 'network mobilisation' enables TMF capitalism to mobilise society for expansion of TMF capitalism using the vehicle of rights.

Socio-economic rights in the twentieth century were complicit in bringing about the entwinement of TMF capitalism and imperial states. It is pertinent to remind ourselves that socio-economic rights associated with 'welfare capitalism' in Europe were first and foremost a state building project. Early European socialists opposed welfare legislation, calling it a sham as it did not address real causes of poverty and inequalities under capitalism.[46] During the interwar period of economic depression, the moment when social support was most pressing, capitalist states introduced austerity and curtailed socio-economic rights. Labour and socialist movements demanded the restoration of laws they had earlier rejected. Socio-economic rights and austerity programmes have alternated ever since.

It is important also to recognise that colonial peoples were never considered in the nineteenth-century debates on 'bourgeois democracy'. The colonial state, in contrast to the 'bourgeois democratic' state, was never an abstraction devoid of social attributes as Marx argued in *On The Jewish Question*. On the contrary, the colonial state proclaimed the White Man as the natural ruler of all races, religions, tribes, forms of property, cultures, religions and so on. The colonial state never recognised the civil liberties of its subjects – in slavery it did not recognise even the elementary personhood of African people. In the epoch of imperialism, the colonial question, i.e. the subjugation of states, nations and peoples by a small group of states, is the central question for human emancipation and freedom for the entire world. Liberalism never addressed the colonial question. Liberalism's freedoms were limited, historically and at present, to a privileged group of citizens in a small number of states. Classical Marxism considered the colonial question but only as a corollary of or incidental to the class-struggles and class emancipation in capitalist countries. Imperialism, as Lenin said, buys-off the working people in the capitalist countries and mutes their struggles. What is consumerism if not 'throwing crumbs' at the citizens of the First World to buy acquiescence to the expropriation of natures, labours and cultures of the millions of desperate people struggling to survive the ravages of TMF capitalism? Should we be surprised at all by the rights resurgence in the 1980s during optimism about renewed expansion of TMF capitalism and the anti-immigration vitriol to defend privileges of G7 citizens at present during another pessimistic downturn?

Taking national oppression as the central question of our times calls for a different way of framing the questions about the problems of our times. For example, if capitalism has throughout its history off-loaded its crises periodically on the Third World, and this book has shown how this has happened in the twentieth century, should social movements not be asking: how will the present crisis be off-loaded on the Third World and what should their responses be? If the focus on Reagan and Thatcher in the earlier crises could not prevent the deepening of TMF capitalism should social movements not move beyond Trump and May and ask what is happening to TMF capitalism that is creating such deep rifts in the heart of 'the establishment', the institutions of governance? If capitalism has always relied on wars to resolve the periodic crises, should social movements not be asking what a perpetual state of war entailed in a political-economy founded on military-industrial complexes, with military-bases in most Third World states means for human freedoms around the world? If the questions for science since the twentieth century are presented by militarism and transnational governance of political economy, should social movements not be asking what questions a people's science might ask and how it might answer them? If the state socialisms of the twentieth century challenge us to think about 'cherry-picking' from capitalism its scientific and techno-logical achievements, its constitutionalism and state sovereignty and dismissing liberal democracy and legalism, should socialist movements not be asking how can political programmes be synced with economic, ideological and cultural components of social transformations? What kind of political programmes are possible in the 'epoch of imperialism' that gives people a chance to survive the ravages of deadly wars and disintegration of social orders? What kinds of programmes are needed to reproduce the conditions needed for human life? 'Concrete analysis of concrete conditions' and understanding 'the how and the why of things' (Chapter 2) has always been a theoretical question as much as an empirical one.

The philosophical and theoretical developments needed for answering such types of questions go beyond European Marxism. They invite considerations of the big questions in philosophy such as ontology, epistemology, philosophical dualism and non-dualism, the philosophical and sociological foundations of modern science and technology and modern law and institutions. European Marxism does not address these questions directly, hence the fetishism of science and technology and law and institutions on the one hand and the clouding of capitalism's external relations, call it colonialism, neo-colonialism, post-colonialism, North-South or the Third World as this book has done. Underpinning all of these questions are conceptions of the relations between nature-society and human life. Liberalism's conceptions of relations between nature-society and human life have brought societies to the worst existential crisis in human history. Lenin wrote that imperialism would be the most destructive phase of capitalism, a period during which capitalism loses any progressive capacities in economy, politics, science and culture. Relationships between nature-society-people entail questions about science and technology, law and institutions, aesthetics and ethics, questions about human purpose and the place of human beings in the world.[47] Indeed 'without revolutionary theory there can be no revolutionary movement'.

Faced with extraordinary existential crisis for human life, NSMs cry out for action. 'Cut-out the theory-talk-shop, just tell us what to do', they seem to say. OSMs too cry out for 'anti-imperialist-struggles'. 'Cut out the petit bourgeois intellectualism and get on with the struggle', they seem to say. To those readers the conclusions in this book may be deeply disappointing, an anti-climax perhaps. The 'root and branch' critique of rights, liberalism, law and TMF capitalism in this book does not leave any back-alley routes to rights, liberalism, legal solutions and charters to transform TMF capitalism to a docile, humanist system. The anti-imperialist critique of rights does not provide rough and ready templates from which a manifesto for change can be drawn up. If nothing else I hope the chapters in this book will have helped at least some readers to be more self-conscious about liberal modes of thought and approach contemporary questions in different ways than they are used to.

Albert Einstein, at the beginning of the twentieth century, famously said no problem can be solved from the same level of consciousness that created it. In the epoch of imperialism European Enlightenment knowledge and the consciousness that it produced has exhausted itself even as historical capitalism heads once again to another cataclysmic collapse. The epoch of imperialism brings theory back to the very questions that the European Enlightenment project addressed: the relationships between nature, society and human life. The extraordinary destructive capacities of war technologies, mass impoverishment of entire continents, disruptions of ways of life, wanton destruction of nature, disintegration of social cohesion and collective life, the corruption of intellectual life, all point to loss of capacities to reproduce the conditions necessary for human life and result in what Zygmunt Bauman calls 'the production of wasted humans'.[48] 'Wasted humans' invite us to return to the basic questions that thinkers have grappled with since times immemorial: What is human purpose? What is human destiny? Liberalism dismisses, precisely, such ontological questions as 'useless'. If classical liberalism developed in opposition to theology, the ideology of feudalism and the institution of the Church, does it not follow that the challenge to capitalism in the epoch of imperialism can only develop in opposition to theology's successor, liberalism?

Postscript

Lawyers frequently ask me if my views on rights are not inconsistent with my professional life as a lawyer defending rights of people. They wonder about my continued engagement with civil liberties and democratic rights issues. Activists ask if they should stop taking cases to court. My usual response is something along these lines.

I inherited the Indian constitution and the UN Charter. They were written before I was born. We have no choice except to live under the institutional conditions we inherit at birth. Because we are forced to live under the institutions we inherit does not mean we must claim them or defend them. Quite the opposite. Because there is widespread racism in the academia, I do not stop working for a university. I cannot, if I wish to survive. No one sees any inconsistency in my employment in a university where there is racism and my claim that non-discrimination laws cannot address the problems of institutional racism. I am born into a patriarchal society and must necessarily live with family, friends and neighbours. I do not therefore defend patriarchy nor do I advocate aborting male children because they might turn into future patriarchs; or claim that patriarchy is a thing of the past because my own father raised his daughters to be independent women in thoughts, actions and spirit. The conflation of individual life with social institutions is a hallmark of liberal thinking. We have inherited rights-based institutions. Do we need to, for that reason, demand rights, struggle for them and place our futures in its power of promise, knowing the promises are empty for most people most of the time? What did the socialists and the freedom fighters in anti-colonial movements do? They demanded the real thing – food not right to food – national independence not right to independence, peace not right to peace, debt-repudiation not forgiveness.

Our social worlds are necessarily full of constraints. This is so because social institutions are a necessary condition of human life. Yet institutions limit human freedoms. These ideas are expressed succinctly in Buddhist and Indian philosophy in the proposition 'sarvam dukkahm'.[1] Marx wrote, '[M]en make their own history' but they make it under 'circumstances existing already, given and transmitted from the past'.[2] Freedom is always freedom from the constraints we have inherited from the *past*. The absolute freedom from all constraints in the *future* that liberalism promises is ontologically impossible. None of us can escape our place within institutions if we live in a society, but we can free ourselves from constraints that disrupt or destabilise the conditions necessary for human life.

Unease about the return of liberal imaginaries to social movements has prompted many critical and engaged activists and scholars to visualise an alternate world in negatives, by arguing what another world should *not* look like. The revolution will not be funded say women of colour in their book with the same title;[3] the revolution will not be downloaded say voices against digitised social mobilisations;[4] the revolution will not be microwaved say voices in the US organising against food standards;[5] the revolution will not be accessorised say cultural critics, and the titles of their books draw inspiration from Gil Scott-Heron's famous song,

> The revolution will not be televised, will not be televised
> Will not be televised, will not be televised
> The revolution will be no re-run brothers
> The revolution will be live

To all of the above we may add, the revolution will not ride the crest of rights, it will not be a re-run of past revolutions, it will be live.

Kumarila Bhatta (CE 660), a medieval Indian philosopher and logician and founder of the Pūrva Mīmāṃsā school of Indian philosophy, stated 'not this, not this, also is', meaning negation of something is also a positive assertion about it. Perhaps at this historical moment, when capitalism in the 'epoch of imperialism' challenges us to question the very basis of European Enlightenment modernity, even saying the revolution will not be this, will not be that, stops us from lapsing into liberalism from sheer habit, and keeps us on track in our search for answers to the questions of our times.

Notes

CHAPTER 1

1. C. Wright Mills, *The Power Elite*, pp. 20–1 (Oxford University Press. 1956 [1959]).
2. Joseph Brean, The Dark Side of 'Rights Inflation': Why Activists Should 'Reject Impulse to Frame All Grievances as Human Rights', *National Post*, 1 June 2015.
3. For a history of the organisation see International Land Coalition website at http://newsite.landcoalition.org/en/who-we-are/history (accessed 12 August 2012).
4. Ward Anseeuw, Liz Alden Wily, Lorenzo Cotula & Michael Taylor, *Land Rights and the Rush for Land: Findings of the Global Commercial Pressures on Land Research Project* (International Land Coalition. 2012).
5. Radha D'Souza, The Rights Conundrum: Poverty of Philosophy Amidst Poverty, in *Rights in Context: Law and Justice in Late Modern Society*, pp. 55–69 (Reza Banakar ed. Ashgate. 2010).
6. Karl Polanyi describes these processes in England in *The Great Transformation* (Boston Beacon Press. 1957). Marx provides analysis of these processes in *Capital*, Vols 1 and 3.
7. See Radha D'Souza, Coming Full Circle? The Return of the 'Land Question', in *Times of Crisis Inditerra: Revue Internationale sur l'Autochtonie*, available at www.reseaudialog.ca (accessed 19 November 2014).
8. Roque Planas, Chile's Mapuches Call for Regional Autonomy, NCLA (North American Congress on Latin America), 9 October 2009.
9. Keepers of the Water, Keepers of the Water Declaration, 7 September 2006, available at www.keepersofthewater.ca/keepersdeclaration2006.pdf (accessed 7 September 2016).
10. Brewster Kneen, *The Tyranny of Rights*, pp. 1–2 (The Ram's Horn. 2009).
11. For critical perspectives on human rights from a range of theoretical orientations see Jose-Manuel Barreto, *Human Rights from a Third World Perspective: Critique, History and International Law* (Cambridge Scholars Publishing. 2013); Upendra Baxi, *Human Rights in a Posthuman World: Critical Essays* (Oxford University Press. 2007); Jiwei Ci, Taking the Reasons for Human Rights Seriously, 33/2 *Political Theory*, 243–65 (2005); Costas Douzinas, *The End of Human Rights* (Hart Publishing. 2000); Tony Evans, *The Politics of Human Rights: A Global Perspective* (Pluto Press. 2001); Stefan-Lugwig Hoffman, *Human Rights in the Twentieth Century* (Cambridge University Press. 2011); Kneen, *Tyranny of Rights*; Mahmood Mamdani (ed.), *Beyond Rights Talk and Culture Talk: Comparative Essays on the Politics of Rights and Culture* (St Martin's Press. 2000); Lisa Schwartzman, Liberal Rights Theory and Social Inequality: A Feminist Critique, 14/2 *Hypatia*, 26–47 (1999); Issa Shivji, Constructing a New Rights Regime: Promises, Problems and Prospects, 8/2 *Social & Legal Studies*, 253–76 (1999); David N. Stamos, *The Myth of Universal Human Rights: Its Origins, History, and Explanation, Along with a More Humane Way* (Routledge. 2016 [2013]).
12. See Eric Hobsbawm, *The Age of Revolution: 1789–1848* (Abacus. 2010 [1962]).
13. For an extensive discussion on the contributions of liberal thinkers on slavery and indigenous rights see Domencio Losurdo, *Liberalism: A Counter History* (Gregory Elliott trans. Verso. 2014 [2006]).

14. Karl Marx, On the Jewish Question, in David McLellan, *Karl Marx Selected Writings*, p. 48 (1987 [1843]).

15. The Declaration of Independence: A Transcription, 1776 (The US National Archives & Records Administration Date, 1776).

16. Joseph R. Grodin, Rediscovering the State Constitutional Right to Happiness and Safety, 25/1 *Hastings Constitutional Law Quarterly*, 1–34 (1997–98) at 1.

17. Id.

18. UNGA A/RES/65/309 dated 19 July 2011.

19. Ibid.

20. UNGA A /RES/70/1 on 'Transforming our World: The 2030 Agenda for Sustainable Development' dated 21 October 2015.

21. UNGA Resolution A/RES/66/281 dated 28 June 2012.

22. For methodological aspects of happiness indexes see John Helliwell et al., *World Happiness Report 2015*, http://worldhappiness.report/wp-content/uploads/sites/2/2015/04/WHR15-Apr29-update.pdf; John F. Helliwell et al., *World Happiness Report 2012*, http://worldhappiness.report/ed/2012/; John F. Helliwell et al., *World Happiness Report 2013*, http://worldhappiness.report/ed/2013/ (accessed 7 April 2017).

23. See the biography for Jeffery Sachs on his personal website at http://jeffsachs.org/about/ (accessed 7 April 2017). Also ibid.

24. Helliwell et al., *World Happiness Report 2015*; Helliwell et al., *World Happiness Report 2012*; Helliwell et al., *World Happiness Report 2013*.

25. OECD, *Guidelines on Measuring Subjective Well-being* (2013), available at www.oecd.org/statistics/oecd-guidelines-on-measuring-subjective-well-being-9789264191655-en.htm (accessed October 2017).

26. Antonio Tajani, Opening Address at the European Tourism Stakeholders' Conference, Speech/10/157, European Commission Press Release Database.

27. Id.

28. For growing wealth gaps in the world generally see Zanny Minton Beddoes, For Richer, For Poorer, *The Economist*, 13 October 2012. For growing income gaps in the US see Nicholas Fitz, Economic Inequality: It's Far Worse Than You Think, *Scientific American*, 31 March 2015. For trends in income inequalities in the UK see The Poverty Site, Income Inequalities, available at www.scientificamerican.com/article/economic-inequality-it-s-far-worse-than-you-think/ (accessed 7 April 2017).

29. 2012 ICF Global Coaching Study (2012), available at www.coachfederation.org/about/landing.cfm?ItemNumber=828 (accessed October 2017).

30. The Business Leaders Initiative on Human Rights (BLIHR), The European Parliament documents 2004–09, available at www.europarl.europa.eu/meetdocs/2004_2009/documents/dv/blihr_/blihr_en.pdf. Also ABB media release dated 9 December 2003 from ABB website at www.abb.com/cawp/seitp202/bb8b64a6172963b4c1256df6003ba9ca.aspx ((websites accessed 7 April 2017). For an evaluation of the BLIHR initiative see Alvaro J. de Regil, *Business and Human Rights: Towards a New Paradigm of True Democracy and Sustainability of People and Planet or Rhetoric Rights in a Sea of Deception and Posturing* (The Jus Semper Global Alliance. January 2008).

31. The Business Leaders Initiative on Human Rights (BLIHR).

32. *Salaam Bombay* (Greetings Bombay) made in 1988 and directed by Mira Nair. The internationally acclaimed film chronicles the everyday lives of street children in Mumbai and won several awards.

33. William Blackstone, *Commentaries on the Laws of England: Book the Third With Introduction by John H. Langbein*, 109 (University of Chicago Press. 1979 [1768]).

34. *Marbury v. Madison*, 5 U.S. 137, available at www.law.cornell.edu/supremecourt/text/5/137 (US Supreme Court) (accessed 7 April 2017).

35. Milton Friedman, *Capitalism and Freedom*, pp. 10–11 (University of Chicago Press. 2002 [1962]).
36. Philip Mirowski, Postface: Defining Neoliberalism, in *The Road from Mont Pelerin: The Making of the Neoliberal Thought Collective*, pp. 417–56 (Philip Mirowski & Dieter Plehwe eds. Harvard University Press. 2009) at 436.
37. Jose E. Alvarez, International Organizations Then and Now, 100 *American Journal of International Law*, 324–47 (2006) at 325.
38. Id. at fn 6.
39. Samuel Moyn, *The Last Utopia: Human Rights in History* 1 (Harvard University Press. 2010).
40. D'Souza, The Rights Conundrum, p. 60.
41. Bailey Saunders, *The Maxims and Reflections of Goethe* 96 (The Macmillan Company. 1906).
42. Douzinas, *The End of Human Rights*, part 1.
43. Jiwei Ci, Justice, Freedom, and the Moral Bounds of Capitalism, 25/3 *Social Theory and Practice*, 409–38 (1999) at 432–3.
44. Oche Onazi, Towards a Subaltern Theory of Human Rights, 9/2 *Global Jurist Advances* (2009), Article 8.
45. Id. at 3.
46. Radha D'Souza, Rights, Action, Change: Organize for What?, in *Organize! Building from the Local for Global Justice*, pp. 71–81 (Aziz Choudry, Jill Hanley & Eric Shragge eds. PM Press. 2012) at 74.

CHAPTER 2

1. C. Wright Mills, *The Sociological Imagination*, p. 181 (Oxford University Press. 1973 [1959]).
2. Francis Fukuyama, The End of History?, *National Interest* (1989), available at www.wesjones.com/eoh.htm (accessed 2 October 2014).
3. Alex Abella, *Soldiers of Reason: The RAND Corporation and the Rise of the American Empire* (Harcourt Books. 2008). *National Interest*, a US magazine set up in 1985 to promote a return to American realism in international relations, published Fukuyama's lecture in its summer 1989 issue. The lecture became the basis for the influential book *The End of History* and the *Last Man* published with financial support from the Rand Corporation in 1992. Fukuyama's book put the resurgence of rights and democracy firmly on the agenda of states and policy makers and on the consciousness of scholars and activists.
4. For example, see R.B. Barber, *Jihad vs. McWorld* (Ballentine. 1995); H. Chavez, Address to the UN (20 September 2006); J. Derrida, *Specters of Marx: The State of the Debt, the Work of Mourning, and the New International* (Peggy Kamuf trans. Routledge. 1994); Fred Halliday, An Encounter with Fukuyama, I/193 *New Left Review* (1992); Joseph McCarney, Shaping Ends: Reflections on Fukuyama, 1/202 *New Left Review* (1993); Ralph Miliband, Fukuyama and the Socialist Alternative, I/193 *New Left Review* (1992).
5. Michael Holquist (ed.), *Dialogic Imagination Four Essays by M.M. Bakhtin* (Caryl Emerson & Michael Holquist trans. University of Texas Press. 1981).
6. Id. at 13–17.
7. Margarita Lopez Maya & Luis E. Lander, The Struggle for Hegemony in Venezuela, in *Politics in the Andes: Identity, Conflict, Reform* (Jo-Marie M. Burt & Philip Mauceri eds. University of Pittsburgh Press. 2004).
8. Margarita Lopez Maya, Venezuela After the Caracazo: Forms of Protest in a Deinstitutionalized Context, 21/2 *Bulletin of Latin American Research*, 199–218 (2002).

9. Kenneth B. Noble, Economic Riots are Spreading in Nigeria, *New York Times*, 4 June 1989.
10. Tangie Nsoh Fonchingong, Multipartyism and Democratization in Cameroon, 15/2 *Journal of Third World Studies*, 119–36 (1998).
11. Piet Koning, Privatisation and Ethno-regional Protest in Cameroon, 38/1 *Afrika Spectrum*, 5–36 (2003) at 5–6.
12. Myriam Gervais, Structural Adjustment in Niger: Implementations, Effects & Determining Political Factors, 22/63 *Review of African Political Economy*, 27–42 (1995).
13. Osaretin Idahosa, Boko Haram and the Nigerian State: A Different Perspective, 3 *Glocalism: Journal of Culture, Politics and Innovation* (2015), available at www.glocalismjournal.net/Issues/ON-GLOBAL-RISKS/Articles/Boko-Haram-And-The-Nigerian-State-A-Different-Perspective.kl (accessed 2 October 2014).
14. David B. Moore, Development Discourse as Hegemony: Towards an Ideological History – 1945–1995, in *Debating Development Discourse: Institutional and Popular Perspectives* (David B. Moore & Gerald J. Schmitz eds. St Martin's Press. 1995).
15. Michael McClintock, *Instruments of Statecraft: U.S. Guerilla Warfare, Counterinsurgency, and Counterterrorism, 1940–1990* 35 (Pantheon Books. 1992).
16. Jimmy Carter, 'Crisis of Confidence Speech' (Miller Center of Public Affairs, University of Virginia. 15 July 1979).
17. Milton Friedman, a leading neoliberal thinker, argues against delinking economics and politics, except for him the politics must always facilitate economic freedoms and free markets. See Milton Friedman, *Capitalism and Freedom* (University of Chicago Press. 2002 [1962]).
18. See F.A. Hayek, *The Road to Serfdom*, Ch. 15 (Routledge Classics. 2006 [1944]).
19. Ronald Reagan, Address to Members of the British Parliament, Ronald Reagan Presidential Library and Museum (8 June 1982), available at www.reagan.utexas.edu/archives/speeches/1982/60882a.htm (accessed 2 October 2014).
20. David Lowe, Idea to Reality: NED at 30, National Endowment for Democracy (2013), available at www.ned.org/about/history#1(accessed 2 October 2014).
21. Reagan, Address to Members of the British Parliament.
22. Ibid.
23. Lowe, Idea to Reality.
24. See Center for International Private Enterprise website at www.cipe.org/ (accessed 2 October 2014).
25. Beth Sims, *Workers of the World Undermined: American Labor's Role in US Foreign Policy* 52 (South End Press. 1992).
26. See id. at Ch. 1.
27. National Democratic Institute (NDI), Working for Democracy and Making Democracy Work (2012), available at www.ndi.org/files/NDI-Brochure-2012.pdf (accessed 2 October 2014).
28. The International Republican Institute (IRI), Building Partnerships (2012), available at www.iri.org/learn-more-about-iri/building-partnerships (accessed 2 October 2014).
29. Lowe, Idea to Reality.
30. Ibid.
31. See William Blum, *Rogue State: A Guide to the World's Only Superpower*, Ch. 13 (Zed Books and David Philip. 2006).
32. Tony Evans, *US Hegemony and the Project of Universal Human Rights*, p. 55 (Macmillan Press. 1996).
33. Id. at 56.
34. Id. at 64–5.
35. Ibid.

36. United Nations, Address Before the General Assembly (17 March 1977), available at www.presidency.ucsb.edu/ws/?pid=7183 (accessed 2 October 2014).

37. Id.

38. For an account of the role of NGOs like Amnesty International in establishing the Office of the High Commissioner for Human Rights see Andrew Clapham, Creating the High Commissioner for Human Rights: The Outside Story, 5 *European Journal of International Law* (1994).

39. Al Gore, Remarks of Vice President Al Gore at the UN World Summit for Social Development (US Department of State (12 March 1995), available at http://dosfan.lib.uic.edu/ERC/intlorg/WS_Social_Dev/950312.html (accessed 2 October 2014).

40. Hillary Clinton, Remarks of the First Lady Hillary Rodham Clinton at a Special Event at the UN Social Summit (UN Department of Economic and Social Affairs, Copenhagen) (7 March 1995).

41. Multi-donor trust-funds (MDTFs) are set up by the UN for different purposes by inviting states and private donors to contribute to UN projects and missions. States and private actors contribute to projects that they have an interest in supporting. The model marks a shift from earlier methods of funding UN projects where states were the main contributors to UN funds for different programmes and missions. For an overview of the MDTFs see http://mptf.undp.org/overview/funds (accessed 2 October 2014). For early uses of MDTFs see Sultan Barakat, The Failed Promise of Multi-donor Trust Funds: Aid Financing as an Impediment to Effective State-building in Post-conflict Contexts, 30 *Policy Studies* (2009).

42. George W. Bush, Bush's Address to the UN General Assembly: Transcript, *New York Times*, 21 September 2004.

43. UN General Assembly Resolution on 'World Summit Outcome', A/RES/60/1 adopted at the 66th session on 24 October 2005.

44. See South Asia Solidarity Group, Strange Bedfellows for Action Aid, available at www.southasiasolidarity.org/2011/08/13/strange-bedfellows-for-action-aid/ (accessed 2 October 2014).

45. For the composition for the advisory group and management of UNDEF see UNDEF website at www.un.org/democracyfund/advisory-board-0 (accessed 2 October 2014).

46. *The Economist*, Electronic Protest: Wakey-wakey, 15 February 2007.

47. James Ball, Avaaz: Can Online Campaigning Reinvent Politics?, *Guardian*, 15 January 2013; Carole Cadwalladr, Inside Avaaz – Can Online Activism Really Change the World?, *Observer*, 17 November 2013; Patrick Kingsley, Avaaz: Activism or 'Slacktivism'?, 20 July 2011.

48. Ed Pilkington, Avaaz – the Online Activist Network that is Targeting Rupert Murdoch's Bid, *Guardian*, 24 April 2011.

49. Avaaz website at www.avaaz.org/en/about.php (accessed 2 October 2014).

50. Sussane Posel, Avaaz: The Lobbyist that Masquerades as Online Activism, *Global Research* (10 December 2012).

51. For administrative reforms in India during the colonial era see Radha D'Souza, The 'Third World' and Socio-legal Studies: Neo-liberalism and Lessons from India's Legal Innovations, 14/4 *Social & Legal Studies*, 487–513 (2005); Radha D'Souza, *Interstate Conflicts Over Krishna Waters: Law, Science and Imperialism* (Orient Longmans. 2006). For administrative reforms during the colonial era in Africa see Mahmood Mamdani, *Citizen and Subject: Contemporary Africa and the Legacy of Late Colonialism* (Fountain, D. Philip and J. Currey. 1996). For the use of principles of colonial governance in international law more generally see Jedediah Purdy & Kimberly Fielding, Sovereigns, Trustees, Guardians: Private-law Concepts and the Limits of Legitimate State Power, 70 *Law & Contemporary Problems*, 165–211 (2007).

52. '... the most essential thing in Marxism, the living soul of Marxism, is the concrete analysis of concrete conditions'. Mao Tse-Tung, *On Contradictions* (Foreign Languages Press. 1937).

53. V.I. Lenin, The Right of Nations to Self-Determination, in *V.I. Lenin Selected Works in Three Volumes*, Vol. 1, pp. 597–647 (Progress Publishers. 1970 [1914]) at 600.

CHAPTER 3

1. Karl Marx & Fredrick Engels, *The German Ideology*, p. 106 (C.J. Arthur ed. International Publishers. 1981 [1846]).

2. V.I. Lenin, Imperialism the Highest Stage of Capitalism, in *V.I. Lenin Selected Works in Three Volumes*, Vol. 1, pp. 667–78 (Progress Publishers. 1970 [1917]). For an expanded discussion on Lenin's thesis on imperialism see Radha D'Souza, Imperialism and Self-determination: Revisiting the Nexus in Lenin, XLVIII/15 *Economic & Political Weekly* (Special Articles), 60–9 (2013).

3. For an expanded discussion on the distinction between colonial and capitalist societies see Radha D'Souza, Imperial Agendas, Global Solidarities and Socio-legal Scholarship on the Third World: Methodological Reflections, 49/3 *Osgoode Hall Law Journal*, 6–43 (2012). For a specific case study of the constitutional basis for (neo) colonial statehood in India see Radha D'Souza, The 'Third World' and Socio-legal Studies: Neo-liberalism and Lessons from India's Legal Innovations, 14/4 *Social & Legal Studies*, 487–513 (2005).

4. For an extensive discussion of Dutch leadership during the mercantile phase of capitalism see Jan de Vries & Ad van der Woude, *The First Modern Economy: Success, Failure, and Preservation of the Dutch Economy, 1500–1815* (Cambridge University Press. 1997).

5. See Radha D'Souza, Rights, Action, Change: Organize for What?, in *Organize! Building from the Local for Global Justice*, pp. 71–81 (Aziz Choudry, Jill Hanley & Eric Shragge eds. PM Press. 2012).

6. Radha D'Souza, The Rights Conundrum: Poverty of Philosophy Amidst Poverty, in *Rights in Context: Law and Justice in Late Modern Society*, pp. 55–69 (Reza Banakar ed. Ashgate. 2010); Radha D'Souza, Justice and Governance in Dystopia: Review Essay, 12/4 *Journal of Critical Realism*, 518–537 (2013).

7. 'Another World is Possible' is the slogan of the World Social Forum, a global social movement. See Chapter 8.

8. A historical account of the contrast between universalist claims of liberals and their political and social stances can be found in Domencio Losurdo, *Liberalism: A Counter History* (Gregory Elliott trans. Verso. 2014 [2006]).

9. Hannah Arendt, *On Revolution*, pp. 55, 71 (Penguin Books. 1990 [1963]).

10. See Jiwei Ci, Justice, Freedom, and the Moral Bounds of Capitalism, 25/3 *Social Theory and Practice*, 409–38 (1999).

11. Marx & Engels, *The German Ideology*.

12. Id. at 51.

13. Id. at 118.

14. Ibid.

15. Id. at 53.

16. Id. at 60.

17. D'Souza, The Rights Conundrum.

18. I was involved in some of these debates and arguments which were often intense, emotive and divisive.

19. For expanded discussion see D'Souza, The Rights Conundrum.

20. Ian Shapiro, *The Evolution of Rights in Liberal Theory* (Cambridge University Press. 1988 [1986]).

21. Id. at 14.

22. Id. at 273–4.

23. There is a growing body of academic literature in the fields of Law on the protection of rights of surrogate mothers, sperm and organ donors as well as in Ethics on the moral aspects of trade in these new 'items'. For reports on trade in these 'items' see Denis Campbell & Nicola Davison, Illegal Kidney Trade Booms as New Organ is 'Sold Every Hour', *Guardian*, 27 May 2012; James Melik, Fertility Trade: Eggs, Sperm and Rented Wombs, BBC News, 20 September 2012.

24. Evgeny B. Pashukanis, *Law & Marxism: A General Theory*, Ch. 3 (Barbara Einhorn trans. Pluto Press. 1989 [1929]).

25. In the words of Marx, '... the land of its excess mouths, tears the children of the earth from the breast on which they were raised, and thus transforms labour on the soil itself, which appears by its very nature as a direct wellspring of subsistence, into a mediated source of subsistence, a source purely dependent on social relations ... [as] relations posited by society, not as determined by nature'. Karl Marx, *Grundrisse: Foundations of the Critique of Political Economy (Rough Draft)*, p. 276 (Penguin Books. 1993 [1973]).

26. D'Souza, The Rights Conundrum.

27. Brewster Kneen, *The Tyranny of Rights* (The Ram's Horn. 2009).

28. See Gerry Simpson, *Great Powers and Outlaw States: Unequal Sovereigns in the International Legal Order* (Cambridge University Press. 2004).

29. For an extended discussion on competing conceptions of self-determination in the US under Woodrow Wilson and Russia under V.I. Lenin see D'Souza, Imperialism and Self-determination.

30. For a more in-depth discussion of these aspects see ibid.

31. For Samuel Moyn human rights as a programme for social movements took off in the 1970s. See *The Last Utopia: Human Rights in History*, p. 1 (Harvard University Press. 2010). Niel Stammers dates the rise of human rights to the moment when it was incorporated in the UN Charter. See *Human Rights and Social Movements* (Pluto Press. 2009). Contributors to the edited volume by Boaventura de Sousa Santos see the end of the Cold War as the moment when democratisation processes and human rights spread across the Third World. See *Democratizing Democracy: Beyond the Liberal Canon: Reinventing Social Emancipation*, Vol. 1 (Boaventura de Sousa Santos ed. Verso. 2005).

32. Radha D'Souza, Listening to the Elders as Keepers of the Water, in *Asking, We Walk: South as New Political Imaginary*, pp. 138–47 (Corrine Kumar ed. Streelekha Publications. 2013).

33. F.A. Hayek, considered one of the early founders of neoliberalism, agreed that the era of classical liberalism had ended. See F.A. Hayek, *The Road to Serfdom* (Routledge Classics. 2006 [1944]).

34. Angus Burgin, *The Great Persuasion: Reinventing Free Markets since the Depression* 1 (Harvard University Press. 2012). For Keynes' own essay on the end of laissez-faire see John Maynard Keynes, The End of Laissez-Faire (1926), in *Essays in Persuasion*, pp. 323–38 (John Maynard Keynes ed. W.W. Norton & Company. 1963).

35. Keynes argued for a 'New Liberalism'. See John Maynard Keynes, Am I a Liberal? (1925), in *Essays in Persuasion*, pp. 323–38 (John Maynard Keynes ed. W.W. Norton & Company. 1963). His vision of liberalism, which was radically different from liberalism until the end of the nineteenth century, prevailed until the revival of capitalism from the ashes of the world wars and lasted until the early 1960s. During this time, Keynesian ideas of liberalism were challenged by other liberal revisionists whose ideas found purchase during the economic crises since the middle of the 1960s and have become the dominant ideology as neoliberalism. For early neoliberal challenges to Keynesian New Liberalism see Hayek, *The Road to Serfdom*.

36. For a historical account of neoliberalism see the collection of articles in Philip Mirowski & Dieter Plehwe, *The Road from Mont Pelerin: The Making of the Neoliberal Thought Collective* (Harvard University Press. 2009).

37. In 1819 in the case of *Dartmouth Coll. v. Woodward* [(17 U.S (4 Wheat.) 518, 1819], the contractual rights of corporations under the constitutions were upheld. In 1886 in the case of *Santa Clara Cnty. v. S. Pac. R.R. Co.* [118 U.S. 394 (1886)] it was held that equal protection clauses applied equally to corporations. In 1889 in the case of *Minneapolis & St. Louis Ry. Co. v. Beckwith* [129 U.S. 26, 1889), constitutional rights to private property of corporations were affirmed. In 1931 in the case of *Russian Volunteer Fleet v. United States* [282 U.S. 481 (1931)] the rights of foreign corporations against illegal takings under the US constitution were upheld. In 1979 in the case of *Ross v. Bernhard* [396 U.S. 531 (1970)] it was held that the shareholders possess the same rights to jury trials as corporations. In 1977 in the case of *United States v. Martin Linen Supply Co.* [430 U.S. 564 (1977)] the courts assumed corporations, like natural persons, are protected by Double Jeopardy Clause rights; in 1978 in the case of *Marshall v. Barlow's, Inc.* [436 U.S. 307 (1978)] constitutional rights of corporations against warrantless search under the Fourth Amendment to the US constitution were affirmed. In 2010 in the case of *Citizens United v. Fed. Election Comm'n* [130 S. Ct. 876 (2010)] constitutional rights of corporations to free speech were upheld. As the legal history investing corporate persons (legal persons) with the same constitutional rights as natural persons (human person) shows, the process was by no means uncontested.

38. See Radha D'Souza, When Unreason Masquerades as Reason: Can Law Regulate Trade and Networked Communication Ethically?, in *Handbook of Communication Ethics*, pp. 475–93 (George Cheny, Steve May & Debabish Munshi eds. International Communication Association Routledge/Lawrence Erlbaum. 2010).

39. For more on these aspects see D'Souza, Listening to the Elders as Keepers of the Water.

40. See David A. Snow, Sarah A. Soule & Hanspeter Kriesi, Mapping the Terrain, in *The Blackwell Companion to Social Movements*, pp. 3–16 (David A. Snow, Sarah A. Soule & Hanspeter Kriesi eds. Wiley-Blackwell. 2004).

41. See Charles Tilly & Lesley J. Wood, *Social Movements 1768–2012* (Paradigm Publishers. 2013 [2004]).

42. See David A. Snow et al., *The Blackwell Companion to Social Movements*; ibid.

CHAPTER 4

1. Niccolò Machiavelli 1469–1527, *The Prince*, p. 11 (George Anthony Bull trans. Penguin. 1999).

2. Thomas M. Franck, The Emerging Right to Democratic Governance, 86/1 *American Journal of International Law*, 46–91 (1992).

3. Quoted in Arturo Santa-Cruz, *International Election Monitoring, Sovereignty and the Western Hemisphere*, p. 1 (Routledge. 2005).

4. Quoted in Arturo Santa-Cruz, The Emergence of a Transnational Advocacy Network: International Election Monitoring in the Philippines, Chile, Nicaragua, and Mexico, 2/1 *Journal of Multidisciplinary International Studies*, 1–31 (2004) at 27.

5. Radha D'Souza, Imperialism and Self Determination: Revisiting the Nexus in Lenin, XLVIII/15 *Economic & Political Weekly* (Special Articles), 60–9 (2013).

6. Ibid.

7. Radha. D'Souza, Imperial Agendas, Global Solidarities and Socio-legal Scholarship on the Third World: Methodological Reflections, 49/3 *Osgoode Hall Law Journal*, 6–43 (2012).

8. Ibid.

9. For expanded arguments see ibid. For an analysis of the specific case of India see Radha D'Souza, The 'Third World' and Socio-legal Studies: Neo-liberalism and Lessons from India's Legal Innovations, 14/4 *Social & Legal Studies*, 487–513 (2005); Radha D'Souza, Revolt and Reform in South Asia: Ghadar Movement to 9/11 and After, XLIX/8 *Economic & Political Weekly* (Special Articles), 59–73 (2014).

10. See for e.g. Tony Evans, *The Politics of Human Rights: A Global Perspective* (Pluto Press. 2001).

11. See for e.g. B.S. Chimni, *International Law and World Order: A Critique of Contemporary Approaches* (Sage. 1993).

12. On indirect rule see Radha D'Souza, *Interstate Conflicts Over Krishna Waters: Law, Science and Imperialism* (Orient Longmans. 2006); Mahmood Mamdani, *Citizen and Subject: Contemporary Africa and the Legacy of Late Colonialism* (Fountain, D. Philip & J. Currey. 1996). On the uses of the Trusteeship doctrine in the League and British imperial interests see Kevin Grant & Lisa Trivedi, A Question of Trust: The Government of India, the League of Nations, and Mohandas Gandhi, in *Imperialism on Trial: International Oversight of Colonial Rule in Historical Perspective*, pp. 21–44 (R.M. Douglas, Michael Dennis Callahan & Elizabeth Bishop eds. 2006. Lexington Books) at 24.

13. Quoted in Grant & Trivedi, A Question of Trust, p. 24, fn 11.

14. J.C. Smuts, Native Policy in Africa, 29/115 *Journal of the Royal African Society*, 248–68 (1930).

15. For a history of election monitoring see Yves Beigbeder, *International Monitoring of Plebiscites, Referenda and National Elections: Self-determination and Transition to Democracy* (Martinus Nijhoff. 1994).

16. In exceptional circumstances, as in Namibia, UN peacekeeping forces conducted elections.

17. Fareed Zakaria describes illiberal democracy as democracy (free and fair elections) without liberalism (individual liberties and rule of law). Fareed Zakaria, *The Future of Freedom: Illiberal Democracy at Home and Abroad*, p. 17 (W.W. Norton. 2004).

18. See Santa-Cruz, *International Election Monitoring*.

19. Thomas Carothers, *Critical Mission: Essays on Democracy Promotion* 10 (Carnegie Endowment for International Peace. 2004).

20. According to Carothers democracy promotion created a tension between the democracy and human rights communities. Id. at 11.

21. Madeleine Albright, US Secretary of State under the Clinton administration, is the current chairperson of the NDI. See National Democratic Institute website at www. ndi.org/supporters (accessed 10 October 2015).

22. Besides the NED, NDI donors include various US government departments, foreign governments, multilateral institutions, UN organisations and private donors including American Federation of Teachers, Chevron, Facebook, Paladin Capital Management, the Coca-Cola Company, Visa Inc. amongst many others. For the complete list of donors see National Democratic Institute website at www.ndi.org/ supporters (accessed 10 October 2015).

23. Larry Garber, *Guidelines for International Election Observing* (International Human Rights Law Group. 1984).

24. In countries like the Philippines, India, Nepal, Mexico, Columbia, China, Peru, Left movements continue to challenge what is popularly understood as the 'parliamentary path' to democracy. Indigenous peoples' movements around the world challenge liberal democracy. Social movements in the Third World generally have less faith in Western conceptions of democracy not least because of their historical experiences of liberalism under colonial rule.

25. Santa-Cruz, *International Election Monitoring*.

26. Ibid.

27. Ibid.
28. I am indebted to Nicola Perugini for drawing my attention to the paradox of IEM in Palestinian elections.
29. Eva-Lotta E. Hedman, Contesting State and Civil Society: Southeast Asian Trajectories, 35/4 *Modern Asian Studies*, 921–51 (2001) at 922.
30. Ibid.
31. Eva-Lotta E. Hedman, *In the Name of Civil Society: From Free Election Movements to People's Power in the Philippines* Ch. 5 (University of Hawai'i Press. 2006).
32. Id. at Ch. 3.
33. Id. at 49.
34. Eva-Lotta E. Hedman & John T. Sidel, *Philippines Politics and Society in the Twentieth Century: Colonial Legacies, Post-colonial Trajectories*, pp. 1–2 (Routledge. 2000).
35. National Democratic Institute for International Affairs, Reforming the Philippine Electoral Process: Developments 1986–88, p. 8.
36. Id. at 8–9.
37. Id. at Ch. 2.
38. Id. at 11.
39. Id. at 69–70; John Burgess, Philippine Election Watchers Head for Posts, *Washington Post*, 7 February 1986.
40. Burgess, *Washington Post*, Philippine Election Watchers Head for Posts.
41. National Democratic Institute for International Affairs, Reforming the Philippine Electoral Process, p. 8.
42. Hedman, *In the Name of Civil Society*, Ch. 5.
43. Id. at 94.
44. NDI, 'Citizen Participation' programmes include technical assistance to organise civil and voter education, budget oversight and other skills 'to make governments accountable'. See www.ndi.org/citizen-participation (accessed 14 October 2015).
45. The 'Debates' programmes include projects to export the American presidential debate model around the world. See www.ndi.org/debates (accessed 14 October 2015).
46. 'Democracy and Technology' programmes support and train activists to use new technologies to 'access information across borders and issues areas'. See www.ndi.org/democracy-and-technology (accessed 14 October 2015).
47. See NDI 'Democratic Governance' programmes at www.ndi.org/governance (accessed 14 October 2015).
48. See NDI, Gender, Women and Democracy, available at www.ndi.org/gender-women-democracy (accessed 14 October 2015).
49. See NDI, Political Inclusion of Marginalised Groups, available at www.ndi.org/political-inclusion-of-marginalized-groups (accessed 14 October 2015).
50. See NDI, 'Political Parties' programme at www.ndi.org/political-parties (accessed 14 October 2015).
51. See International Republican Institute website at International Republican Institute, What We Do, available at www.iri.org/what-we-do (accessed 14 October 2015).
52. For a list of organisations accredited by the Republic of Philippines Commission on Elections see www.comelec.gov.ph/?r=References/Links/linksnongoveph (accessed 14 October 2015).
53. IDEA is an international NGO founded by states. It is not a UN organisation but has observer status. IDEA is funded by contributions from member states and other multilateral organisations. See International IDEA website at www.idea.int/about/faq/ (accessed 14 October 2015).
54. EISA is an NGO funded by Canadian International Development Agency (CIDA); Danida; Department for International Development (DIFD) (UK); Embassy of Finland Pretoria; Foreign & Commonwealth Office (FCO) (UK); National

Democratic Institute; Norwegian Foreign Affairs Ministry; Swedish International Development Agency (Sida); Swiss Agency for Development and Cooperation (SDC); United Nations Democracy Fund (UNDEF). EISA's Board of Directors are intellectuals: academics and media persons from the region. See EISA 'Donors' and 'Partnerships' and 'Board of Directors', Electoral Institute for Sustainable Elections in Africa, available at https://eisa.org.za/ (accessed 14 October 2015).

55. Elections Canada is a statutory agency set up to conduct elections in Canada. It engages in international activities including participating in IEM teams and knowledge exchanges. See Elections Canada, available at www.elections.ca/content. aspx?section=abo&document=index&lang=e (accessed 14 October 2015).

56. The National Electoral Institute of Mexico (INE) is a statutory authority set up pursuant to electoral reforms to conduct elections to all public offices. The INE is part of an international network of electoral authorities and participates in IEMs. See www2.ine.mx/archivos3/portal/historico/contenido/International_Activity_2008_2009/#1 (accessed 14 October 2015).

57. The IFES is a US-based private international NGO that provides electoral services to election officials, social groups and research organisations in one hundred and forty-five countries. It was set up in 1987 after President Reagan's Westminster speech (see Chapter 2) as a NED-funded bipartisan organisation to 'support credible elections', and work with 'election management bodies around the world on all aspects of election administration and across all phases of the electoral cycle, including long-term institutional capacity building'. In addition, IFES has developed an electoral integrity portfolio focused on three principle areas – election dispute resolution, fraud and malpractice mitigation, and political finance regulation. The board of directors comprise corporate CEOs, US businessmen, political consultants (including lobbying and public relation firms) and academics. See under 'Board' at the International Foundation for Electoral Systems website at www.ifes.org/about/board (accessed 14 October 2015).

58. The Carter Center is a private US charitable foundation set up by former President Jimmy Carter under whose presidency 'democracy promotion' became a foreign policy instrument of the US. The Center has been at the forefront of election observations in landmark elections in Nicaragua, Panama and other milestone elections that established IEMs as an international norm and practice. Although best known for its leading role in promoting IEMs internationally the Center also undertakes other philanthropic activities. See the Carter Center at www.cartercenter.org/about/faqs/index.html (accessed 14 October 2015).

59. The UNDESA is part of the UN Secretariat, the administrative organ of the UN. It was restructured in 1997 following UN reforms after the Cold War ended. UNDESA's responsibilities include norm-setting. UNDESA has been a key site within the UN for the development of IEMs as an international norm. See United Nations Department of Economic and Social Affairs website at www.un.org/development/desa/en/what-we-do.html

60. UNDP is a nodal agency for economic development programmes in the Third World. See United Nations Development Programme, available at www.undp.org/content/undp/en/home/operations/about_us.html (accessed 14 October 2015).

61. UNEAD was set up as a division within the UN Peacekeeping mission and located in the Department of Political Affairs in the UN Secretariat. See United Nations Department of Political Affairs website at www.un.org/undpa/overview (accessed 14 October 2015).

62. For example, William Sweeney, a communication consultant is the president and CEO of the IFES. See IFES website at www.ifes.org/ (accessed 10 October 2015).

63. Arturo Santa-Cruz, Redefining Sovereignty, Consolidating a Network: Monitoring the 1990 Nicaraguan Elections, XXIV/1 *Revista De Cencia Politica*, 189–208 (2004) at 201.

64. David Stoelting, The Challenge of UN-monitored Elections in Independent Nations, 28 *Stanford Journal of International Law*, 371–424 (1991–92) at 372; Beigbeder, *International Monitoring of Plebiscites*.

65. Article 2(7) of the UN Charter states: 'Nothing contained in the present Charter shall authorize the United Nations to intervene in matters which are essentially within the domestic jurisdiction of any state or shall require the Members to submit such matters to settlement under the present Charter; but this principle shall not prejudice the application of enforcement measures under Chapter VII.' Chapter VII provides for UN interventions for peacekeeping and external aggression.

66. Quoted in Stoelting, The Challenge of UN-monitored Elections, p. 372.

67. For the undeclared war on Nicaragua see articles in Thomas W. Walker, *Reagan versus the Sandinistas: The Undeclared War on Nicaragua* (Westview Press. 1987). For a detailed analysis of US intervention in the electoral process see William I. Robinson, *A Faustian Bargain: US Intervention in the Nicaraguan Elections and American Foreign Policy in the Post-Cold War Era* (Westview Press. 1992).

68. William I. Robinson, A Case Study of Globalisation Processes in the Third World: A Transnational Agenda in Nicaragua, 11/1 *Global Society*, 61–91 (1997) at 65.

69. For a discussion on the class and social composition of the Sandinistas see Elizabeth Dore & John Weeks, *The Red and the Black: The Sandinistas and the Nicaraguan Revolution*, Research Papers (Institute of Latin American Studies, University of London. 1992); for post-election reforms of state and society see ibid.; for the counterinsurgency see various articles in Walker, *Reagan versus the Sandinistas*.

70. Peter Kornbluh, The Covert War, in *Reagan versus the Sandinistas: The Undeclared War on Nicaragua*, p. 29 (Thomas W. Walker ed. Westview Press. 1987).

71. Dore & Weeks, *The Red and the Black*, p. 30.

72. Robinson, *A Faustian Bargain*, p. 3.

73. UN Resolution 2625 states: 'No State may use or encourage the use of economic political or any other type of measures to coerce another State in order to obtain from it the subordination of the exercise of its sovereign rights and to secure from it advantages of any kind, ...'. UNGA Resolution A/RES/25/2625 adopted at the 25th session, available at www.un-documents.net/a25r2625.htm (accessed 14 October 2015).

74. ICJ Communique No. 84/10 dated 9 April 1984, available at www.icj-cij.org/docket/files/70/9855.pdf at 1 (accessed 14 October 2015).

75. Id. at 2.

76. ICJ Communique No. 84/18 dated 10 May 1984, available at www.icj-cij.org/docket/files/70/9871.pdf at 1 (accessed 14 October 2015).

77. Robinson, *A Faustian Bargain*; Santa-Cruz, Redefining Sovereignty.

78. Robinson, *A Faustian Bargain*, Ch. 5.

79. The Center for Democratic Consultation was set up with NED funds in Costa Rica to promote an alliance of social movements in Nicaragua opposed to the Sandinistas. See id. at 93–6.

80. Id. at 98–9.

81. Id. at 101–5.

82. Id. at 99–101.

83. For more on the context for US intervention see Thomas Carothers, *In the Name of Democracy: U.S. Policy Toward Latin America in the Reagan Years*, Ch. 3 (University of California Press. 1991) at 77–116; Roy Gutman, *Banana Diplomacy: The Making of American Policy in Nicaragua, 1981–1987* (Simon and Schuster. 1988); Santa-Cruz, Redefining Sovereignty; Robinson, *A Faustian Bargain*.

84. ICJ Communique No. 91/28 dated 27 September 1991.
85. 'Enhancing the Effectiveness of the Principle of Periodic and Genuine Elections', UNGA Resolution A/Res/43/157 at the 75th plenary meeting on 8 December 1988.
86. Garber, *Guidelines for International Election Observing*.
87. Id. at 1–10.
88. Article 1 states: 'All peoples have the right of self-determination. By virtue of that right they freely determine their political status and freely pursue their economic, social and cultural development.' Article 2 affirms sovereignty over natural resources and Article 3 extends the principle of self-determination to non self-governing territories. Article 55 affirms respect for self-determination in interstate relations.
89. UNGA Resolution 2625 clarifies the UN's understanding of self-determination and for the purposes of IEM states explicitly that: 'Every State has an inalienable right to choose its political, economic, social and cultural systems, without interference in any form by another State.'
90. The ICJ Advisory Opinion in the Western Sahara case states that the exercise of self-determination of people must be free from outside influence and a genuine expression of the people's will. International Court of Justice, Western Sahara, Advisory Opinion of 16 October 1975, ICJ Reports, para. 55 at 34 (1975).
91. UNGA Resolution A/Res/44/146 at the 82nd plenary meeting on 15 December 1989.
92. UNGA Resolution A/Res/44/147 adopted on 15 December 1989 at the 82nd plenary meeting.
93. The resolutions can be accessed from the UN Department of Political Affairs website at www.un.org/wcm/content/site/undpa/main/issues/elections/resolutions (accessed 14 October 2015).
94. UNGA Resolution A/Res/46/137 dated 9 March 1992.
95. UNGA Resolution A/Res/47/138 dated 1 March 1993.
96. UNGA Resolution on the report of the Third Committee [(A/49/610/Add.2)] A/Res/49/190 dated 9 March 1995.
97. UNGA Resolution A/Res/52/129 dated 26 February 1998.
98. See Raul Cordenillo & Andrew Ellis, *The Integrity of Elections: The Role of Regional Organisations* (International Institute for Democracy and Electoral Assistance (IDEA). 2012).
99. See the Pacific Islands, Australia and New Zealand Electoral Administrators (PIANZEA) Network, available at www.pianzea.org/about.html (accessed 14 October 2015).
100. See Association of Asian Election Authorities (AAEA) website at http://eci.nic.in/eci_main1/inter_corp_pdf/AAEA.pdf (accessed 14 October 2015).
101. UNGA Resolution A/Res/52/129 dated 26 February 1998.
102. The Declaration of Principles for Election Observation and Code of Conduct for International Election Observers Electoral Assistance, Department of Political Affairs, United Nations, available at www.un.org/wcm/content/site/undpa/main/issues/elections (accessed 14 October 2015).
103. UNGA Resolution A/Res/47/130 dated 22 February 1993.
104. Report of the Secretary-General, UN Doc. A/59/2005 & annex (2005).
105. For a summary and comment on the UN report see Anne-Marie Slaughter, Notes and Comments: Security, Solidarity, and Sovereignty: The Grand Themes of UN Reform, 99 *American Journal of International Law* (2005).
106. Electoral Assistance, Department of Political Affairs, United Nations, available at www.un.org/wcm/content/site/undpa/main/issues/elections (accessed 14 October 2015).
107. Judith Kelley, Assessing the Complex Evolution of Norms: The Rise of International Election Monitoring, 62/2 *International Organization*, 221–56 (2008) at 229.

108. See David A. Armstrong, Stability and Change in the Freedom House Political Rights and Civil Liberties Measures, 48/5 *Journal of Peace Research*, 653–62 (2011); Christopher G. Bradley, International Organizations and the Production of Indicators: The Case of Freedom House, in *The Quiet Power of Indicators: Measuring Governance, Corruption, and Rule of Law*, pp. 27–74 (Sally Engle Merry, Kevin E. Davis & Benedict Kingsbury eds. Cambridge University Press. 2015).

109. John Bolton, Panel on 'The 1992 Presidential Campaign and International Law and Institutions', American Society of International Law, 86 *Proceedings of the American Society of International Law*, 88–96 (1992) at 88.

110. Scholarly analyses of IEMs generally describe them as *sui generis* developments that actors accept because of their circumstances. Their analyses do not consider causal factors or the issues at stake for key contestants in the process. For example see Beigbeder, *International Monitoring of Plebiscites*; Judith G. Kelley, *Monitoring Democracy: When International Election Observation Works, and Why It Often Fails* (Princeton University Press. 2012). In contrast, Arturo Santa-Cruz considers IEMs in national, international and historical context but limits the consideration to normative developments that became acceptable to diverse actors because US and Western norms have diffused sufficiently to become universal norms. See Santa-Cruz, *International Election Monitoring*.

111. Namibia was under the UN Trusteeship Council as a former League of Nations Mandate. The independence of Namibia remained a contentious issue for seven decades in the UNGA because of opposition from South Africa. South Africa eventually consented to elections in 1980 and the UN organised its first international election. See United Nations Peacekeeping, Past Operations: United Nations Transition Assistance (UNTAG) (Background), available at www.un.org/en/peacekeeping/missions/past/untagFT.htm#Background (accessed 14 October 2015).

112. Bolton, Panel on 'The 1992 Presidential Campaign', pp. 88–9.

113. Id. at 90.

114. Ibid.

115. Santa-Cruz, *International Election Monitoring*.

116. University of Pittsburgh, The Dick Thornburg Papers (Biography), available at www.library.pitt.edu/thornburgh/biography.html (accessed 14 October 2015); also see Dick Thornburgh, Today's United Nations in a Changing World, 9 *American University Journal of International Law & Policy*, 215–23 (1993–94).

117. For Boutros-Ghali's account of why the US opposed his reappointment see Boutros Boutros-Ghali, *Unvanquished, a United Nations-United States Saga* (I.B Tauris & Co. Ltd. 1999).

118. Id. at 23.

119. That regime change in Iraq and Libya was raised in the UNSC as far back as 1992, and the predetermined nature of war in the two countries over a decade later appears not to have received the importance it deserves.

120. Boutros-Ghali, *Unvanquished*, p. 25.

121. Ibid.

122. Maurice Bertrand, *The United Nations: Past, Present and Future*, pp. 123–5 (Kluwer Law International. 1997).

123. For example, see the themes addressed at the *Proceedings of the American Society of International Law* and the high profiles of political representatives, policy makers, think tank institutions and academic contributors to the proceedings.

124. See Franck, The Emerging Right to Democratic Governance.

125. See presentations and discussions at the annual conference of the American Society of International Law in 1992. American Society of International Law, National Sovereignty Revisited: Perspectives on the Emerging Norm of Democracy in

International Law, 86 *Proceedings of the American Society of International Law,* 249–71 (1992).

126. Kelley, Assessing the Complex Evolution of Norms (2008).

CHAPTER 5

1. W.S. Holdsworth, The Indian States and India, 46 *Law Quarterly Review*, 411, 413 (1930).

2. Richard Mulgan, *Holding Power to Account*, p. 15 (Palgrave Macmillan. 2003).

3. Amanda Sinclair, The Chameleon of Accountability: Forms and Discourses, 20 *Accounting, Organizations and Society*, 555 (1995).

4. Melvin J. Dubnick, Accountability as a Cultural Keyword, in *The Oxford Handbook of Public Accountability*, pp. 23–38 (Mark Bovens, Robert E. Goodin & Thomas Schillemans eds. Oxford University Press. 2014) at 28.

5. The International Forum for Democratic Studies at the National Endowment for Democracy publishes the influential *Journal of Democracy*. It counts Francis Fukuyama, Condoleezza Rice, the former Secretary of State, and Zbigniew Brzezinski, former National Security Advisor amongst its editors and advisors on democratisation. See National Endowment for Democracy website at www.ned.org/ideas/research-council/ (accessed 9 February 2016).

6. Andreas Schedler, *The Politics of Uncertainty: Sustaining and Subverting Electoral Authoritarianism* 2 (Oxford University Press. 2013).

7. Id. at 383.

8. Ibid.

9. Id. at 384.

10. Harry D. Gould, *The Legacy of Punishment in International Law*, pp. 3, 16 (Palgrave Macmillan. 2010).

11. Id. at 119. For an extensive and useful discussion on the history of the right to punish in international law see id. at Ch. 2.

12. Mark Bovens, The Concept of Public Accountability, in *The Oxford Handbook of Public Management*, pp. 182–208 (Ewan Ferlie, Laurence E. Lynn Jr & Christopher Pollitt eds. 2007. Oxford University Press) at 182–3.

13. Id. at 184–6.

14. Anne-Marie Slaughter is the CEO and President of the policy think tank New America Foundation. See Munk Debates, available at www.munkdebates.com/debates/obamas-foreign-policy/speakers-con/anne-marie-slaughter (accessed 9 February 2016).

15. Anne-Marie Slaughter, Disaggregated Sovereignty: Towards the Public Accountability of Global Government Networks, in *Global Governance and Public Accountability*, pp. 35–66 (David Held & Mathais Koenig-Archibugi eds. Blackwell. 2005) at 35; also see Anne-Marie Slaughter, *A New World Order* (Princeton University Press. 2005).

16. Slaughter, Disaggregated Sovereignty, pp. 35, 38.

17. Anne-Marie Slaughter, Sovereignty and Power in a Networked World Order, 40 *Stanford Journal of International Law*, 283–327 (2004).

18. Id. at 62.

19. For expanded discussion of Slaughter's arguments see Slaughter, Disaggregated Sovereignty.

20. Id. at 61.

21. Id. at 61–2.

22. Id. at 39.

23. Ibid.

24. Id. at 48.

25. Ibid.

26. Id. at 49.

27. Id. at 48–9.

28. See Karuna Mantena, *Alibis of Empire: Henry Maine and the Ends of Liberal Imperialism* (Princeton University Press. 2010).

29. For a summary of the issues in the trial see Susan B.V. Ellington, United States v. Noriega as a Reason for an International Criminal Court, 11/2 *Dickinson Journal of International Law*, 451–75 (1992–93); on extraterritorial jurisdiction and immunity for heads of state see Adam Isaac Hasson, Extraterritorial Jurisdiction and Sovereign Immunity on Trial: Noriega, Pinochet, and Milosevic – Trends in Political Accountability and Transnational Criminal Law, 25/11 *Boston College International and Comparative Law Review*, 125–58 (2002); for lessons from the Noriega trial see id. at 156–8. For the legality of Operation Just Cause and Noriega's arrest see discussion at the American Society of International Law (ASIL): American Society of International Law, Panel Discussion: 'The Panamanian Revolution: Diplomacy, War and Self-determination in Panama (I & II) Self Determination And Intervention in Panama (ii)', 84 *Proceedings of the American Society of International Law*, 182–203 (1990); American Society of International Law, Panel Discussion: 'The Panamanian Revolution: Diplomacy, War and Self-determination in Panama (I & II) Self Determination And Intervention in Panama (i)', 84 *Proceedings of the American Society of International Law* (1990); American Society of International Law, *Proceedings of the American Society of International Law*, 236–56 (1990).

30. The International Criminal Tribunal for the former Yugoslavia or ICTY is the common name for the International Tribunal for the Prosecution of Persons Responsible for Serious Violations of International Humanitarian Law Committed in the Territory of the Former Yugoslavia since 1991.

31. See collection of essays in Ellen L. Lutz & Caitlin Reiger, *Prosecuting Heads of State* (Cambridge University Press. 2009). Lutz et al. provide quantitative analysis of prosecutions of heads of states. They aggregate the data for international and national prosecution of heads of states. The moral stance of outrage against heinous crimes by political leaders may be common to both types of trials. However, the philosophical and jurisprudential premises for national and international trials of political leaders follow very different reasoning that are not easily reconcilable.

32. See John Quigley, The Legality of the United States Invasion of Panama, 15 *Yale Journal of International Law*, 276–315 (1990).

33. Panama Suspends U.S. Tie and Charges Aggression After Riot in Canal Zone, *New York Times*, 10 January 1964.

34. Quigley, The Legality of the United States Invasion of Panama.

35. Thomas Carothers, *In the Name of Democracy: U.S. Policy Toward Latin America in the Reagan Years*, Ch. 5 (University of California Press. 1991).

36. Id. at Ch. 5; Quigley, The Legality of the United States Invasion of Panama.

37. Carothers, *In the Name of Democracy*, Ch. 5.

38. Ibid.

39. See ibid.; Quigley, The Legality of the United States Invasion of Panama.

40. Carothers, *In the Name of Democracy*, Ch. 5.

41. Doyle McManus, Bush Orders Aid for Foes of Noriega: CIA Funds Election Efforts in Bid to Oust Panama Chief, *Los Angeles Times*, 23 April 1989.

42. Carothers, *In the Name of Democracy*, Ch. 5; also Philip Agee, 1984–1989, Panama: If NED Fails, Send in the Marines, *Covert Action Information Bulletin* (Fall, 1992), available at http://coat.ncf.ca/our_magazine/links/issue43/articles/1984_1989_panama.htm (accessed 9 February 2016).

43. National Republican Institute for International Affairs and National Democratic Institute for International Affairs, The May 7, 1989 Panamanian Elections:

International Delegation Report, (Atlanta, GA, 1989), available at www.ndi.org/sites/default/files/289_pa_89elections.pdf (accessed 23 July 2014).
44. Ellington, United States v. Noriega.
45. Carothers, *In the Name of Democracy*, Ch. 5.
46. See William L. Furlong, Panama: The Difficult Transition Towards Democracy, 35 *Journal of Interamerican Studies and World Affairs* (1993); Margaret E. Scranton, Consolidation After Imposition: Panama's 1992 Referendum, 35/3, *Journal of Interamerican Studies and World Affairs*, 65–102.
47. Carothers, *In the Name of Democracy*, Ch. 5.
48. American Society of International Law, Panel Discussion: 'The Panamanian Revolution: Diplomacy, War and Self-determination in Panama (I & II) Self Determination And Intervention in Panama (ii)', p. 196.
49. BBC Archives, US Forces Oust General Noriega, 20 December 1989.
50. Ellington, United States v. Noriega.
51. BBC Archives, US Forces Oust General Noriega.
52. Don Shannon, U.N. Assembly Condemns U.S. Invasion, *Los Angeles Times*, 30 December 1989.
53. Quigley, The Legality of the United States Invasion of Panama.
54. Kenneth Freed, Update: Invasion Ghosts: Panama Tries to Bury Rumors of Mass Graves: Allegations Persist that up to 4000 Civilians were Killed in the US Invasion, *Los Angeles Times*, 27 October 1990; Larry Rohter, Panama and U.S. Strive to Settle on Death Toll, *New York Times*, 1 April 1990.
55. Geoffrey S. Corn & Sharon G. Finegan, America's Longest Held Prisoner of War: Lessons Learned from the Capture, Prosecution, and Extradition of General Manuel Noriega, 71 *Louisiana Law Review* (2010–11).
56. Ellington, United States v. Noriega, 474; Larry Rohter, The Noriega Verdict; U.S. Jury Convicts Noriega of Drug-trafficking Role as the Leader of Panama, *New York Times*, 10 April 1992.
57. Rohter, The Noriega Verdict.
58. Quoted in Hasson, Extraterritorial Jurisdiction and Sovereign Immunity on Trial, p. 130.
59. Ellington, United States v. Noriega; Quigley, The Legality of the United States Invasion of Panama.
60. Peter Zirnite, *Reluctant Recruits: The US Military and the War on Drugs* (Washington Office on Latin America. 1997), available at www.tni.org/files/download/Reluctant%20recruits%20report_0.pdf (accessed 21 December 2015).
61. Ibid.
62. Ibid.
63. Martin Jelsma, The Development of International Drug Control: Lessons Learned and Strategic Challenges for the Future, Working Paper, Global Commission on Drug Policies, Geneva (2011), p. 7.
64. Bruce Michael Bagley, US Foreign Policy and the War on Drugs: Analysis of a Policy Failure, 30(2/3) *Journal of Interamerican Studies and World Affairs*, 189–212 (1988); Donald Mabry, The US Military and the War on Drugs in Latin America, 30(2/3) *Journal of Interamerican Studies and World Affairs*, 53–76; Raphael Francis Perl, Congress, International Narcotics Policy, and the Anti-Drug Abuse Act of 1988, 30(2/3) *Journal of Interamerican Studies and World Affairs*, 19–51; Zirnite, *Reluctant Recruits*.
65. Zirnite, *Reluctant Recruits*, p. 3.
66. Ibid.
67. Jelsma, The Development of International Drug Control, p. 8.
68. Id. at 7.
69. Id. at 6.

70. The U.N. Draft Convention against Illicit Traffic in Narcotic Drugs and Psychotropic Substances: A Report on the Status of the Draft Convention, the U.S. Negotiating Position, and Issues for the Senate: Prepared for the Use of the Senate Caucus on International Narcotics Control (Washington, DC: US Government Printing Office. 1987).

71. Jelsma, The Development of International Drug Control, p. 2.

72. U.N. Draft Convention against Illicit Traffic in Narcotic Drugs and Psychotropic Substances, p. 9.

73. Id. at 2.

74. Id. at 6.

75. Id. at 9.

76. Id. at 1.

77. Id. at 10.

78. Ellen Warlow, Remarks: Panel on Transnational Crime, 90 *American Society of International Law Proceedings* (1996).

79. Roger S. Clark, *The United Nations Crime Prevention and Criminal Justice Program: Formulation of Standards and Efforts at their Implementation*, p. 15 (University of Pennsylvania Press. 1994).

80. In 1990 the Council of Europe adopted the Convention on Laundering, Search, Seizure and Confiscation of the Proceeds from Crime. In November 1994 the UN World Ministerial Conference on Organized Transnational Crime adopted the Naples Political Declaration and Global Action Plan against Organized Transnational Crime. The Naples Declaration led to the adoption of the United Nations Convention against Transnational Organized Crime of 2000.

81. UN General Assembly Resolution 55/25 adopted on 15 November 2000.

82. United Nations Convention against Transnational Organized Crime and the Protocols Thereto (2004).

83. Id. at Articles 6, 7.

84. Id. at Articles 8, 9.

85. Id. at Articles 11, 12, 13, 14.

86. Id. at Article 16.

87. Id. at Article 18.

88. Id. at Article 15.

89. David Edgerton, *Warfare State: Britain, 1920–1970* (Cambridge University Press. 2005). Also see C. Wright Mills, The Structure of Power in American Society, in *Politics and People: The Collected Essays of C. Wright Mills*, pp. 23–38 (Irving Louis Horowitz ed. Oxford University Press. 1963); C. Wright Mills, *The Power Elite* (Oxford University Press. 1959 [1956]).

90. Mike Maguire, The Needs and Rights of Victims of Crime, 14 *Crime & Justice* (1991).

91. Ibid.

92. Robert Elias, Has Victimology Outlived its Usefulness?, 6/1 *Journal of Human Justice*, 4–25 (1994).

93. James M. Dolliver, Victims' Rights Constitutional Amendment: A Bad Idea Whose Time Should Not Come, 34 *Wayne Law Review*, 87–93 (1987–88); Elias, Has Victimology Outlived its Usefulness?

94. See David Miers, Positivist Victimology: A Critique, 1 *International Review of Victimology*, 3–22 (1989); David Miers, Positivist Victimology: A Critique Part 2: Critical Victimology, 1 *International Review of Victimology*, 219–30 (1990); R.I. Mawby & S. Walklate, Perspectives on Victimology, in *Critical Victimology: International Perspectives*, pp. 7–23 (R.I. Mawby & S. Walklate eds. Sage. 1994). For a critique see Elias, Has Victimology Outlived its Usefulness?

95. LeRoy L. Lamborn, The United Nations Declaration on Victims: Incorporating 'Abuse of Power', 19 *Rutgers Law Journal*, 59–95 (1987–88); Maguire, The Needs and Rights of Victims of Crime.

96. International Penal and Penitentiary Commission, International Penal and Penitentiary Commission, 4 *International Organization*, 543–44 (1950).

97. Clark, *The United Nations Crime Prevention and Criminal Justice Program*, pp. 11–12.

98. Quoting John Gallagher, in Anil Seal in Daniel Gorman, Empire, Internationalism, and the Campaign against the Traffic in Women and Children in the 1920s, 19/2 *Twentieth Century British History*, 186–216 (2008) at 189.

99. Ibid.

100. Ibid.

101. Id. at 193.

102. Roger S. Clark, Human Rights and the U.N. Committee on Crime Prevention and Control, 506 *Annals, AAPSS* (1989).

103. Clark, *The United Nations Crime Prevention and Criminal Justice Program* 24; ibid.

104. See Lamborn, The United Nations Declaration on Victims.

105. United Nations Audiovisual Library of International Law, Procedural History: Declaration of Basic Principles of Justice for Victims of Crime and Abuse of Power, available at http://legal.un.org/avl/ha/dbpjvcap/dbpjvcap.html (accessed 9 February 2016).

106. Agenda item 'Crime and the Abuse of Power: Offences and Offenders Beyond the Reach of the Law?', ibid.

107. Ibid.

108. See Lamborn, The United Nations Declaration on Victims.

109. Sixth United Nations Congress on the Prevention of Crime and the Treatment of Offenders (1981).

110. World Society of Victimology, available at www.worldsocietyofvictimology.org/about-us/history-and-overvie (accessed 9 February 2016).

111. Lamborn, The United Nations Declaration on Victims, p. 63.

112. UNGA Resolution A/RES/40/34, adopted on 29 November 1985 at the 96th plenary meeting. Declaration of Basic Principles of Justice for Victims of Crime and Abuse of Power, Art. 20.

113. General Assembly Resolution 95 (I) of 11 December 1946 (Affirmation of the Principles of International Law recognized by the Charter of the Nürnberg Tribunal) and Introductory note by Antonio Cassese, United Nations Audiovisual Library of International Law, available at http://legal.un.org/avl/ha/criminallaw.html (accessed 9 February 2016).

114. William Schabas, *Unimaginable Atrocities: Justice, Politics, and Rights at the War Crimes Tribunals*. Ch. 3 (Oxford University Press. 2012).

115. Gould, *The Legacy of Punishment*.

116. See Conan Fischer, *The Ruhr Crisis 1923–1924* (Oxford University Press. 2003); Bruce Kent, *The Spoils of War: The Politics, Economics, and Diplomacy of Reparations 1918–1931* (Clarendon Press, Oxford University Press. 1989).

117. See Ian Clark, *The Post-Cold War Order: The Spoils of Peace* (Oxford University Press. 2001).

118. William A. Schabas, *An Introduction to the International Criminal Court*, pp. 8–11 (Cambridge University Press, 4th edn. 2011).

119. Samantha Power, *'A Problem from Hell': America and the Age of Genocide* (Basic Books. 2002).

120. Id. at 268. For a profile of Power published in the *New Yorker* see Evan Osnos, Profiles: In the Land of the Possible: Samantha Power has the President's Ear. To What End?, *New Yorker*, 22 & 29 December 2014.

121. Power, 'A Problem from Hell', pp. 268–9.
122. Ellen L. Lutz & Caitlin Reiger, Introduction, in *Prosecuting Heads of State*, p. 7 (Ellen L. Lutz & Caitlin Reiger eds. Cambridge University Press. 2009).
123. Ibid.
124. Schabas, Unimaginable Atrocities, p. 78.
125. Schabas, *An Introduction to the International Criminal Court*, pp. 11–16; Schabas, Unimaginable Atrocities, pp. 14–16.
126. Schabas, *An Introduction to the International Criminal Court*, pp. 69, 84–5, 88–9.
127. Ibid.
128. For the role of the US in the founding of the ICC see id. at 25–34.
129. See Rome Statute of the International Criminal Court (1998).
130. Id. at Preamble.
131. Schabas, *An Introduction to the International Criminal Court*, pp. 34–5.
132. Id. at 34–9. Also see Schabas, Unimaginable Atrocities, p. 86.
133. In May 2014, the ICC agreed to investigate allegations of war crimes in Iraq by the UK. Earlier, in 2006 the ICC had declined to investigate similar allegations, Ian Cobain, ICC to Examine Claims that British Troops Carried Out War Crimes in Iraq, *Guardian*, 13 May 2014. The ICC is currently investigating crimes in Afghanistan, Colombia, Guinea, Iraq, Nigeria, Palestine and Ukraine. See ICC Situations and Cases at www.icc-cpi.int/ (accessed 9 February 2016). For articles and analysis on ICC's trial of African leaders see Mahmood Mamdani, Darfur, the ICC and the New Humanitarian Order: How the ICC's 'Responsibility to Protect' is Being Turned into an Assertion of Neocolonial Domination, *Pambazuka News*, 17 September 2008. Also see ICC, A Tool to Recolonise Africa, *African Business Magazine*, 1 September 2011; Solomon Dersso, The International Criminal Court's Africa Problem, *Al Jazeera*, 11 June 2013; Policy Brief No. 8: The African Union and the International Criminal Court: An Embattled Relationship?, March 2013; Alana Tiemessen, The International Criminal Court and the Politics of Prosecutions, 18/4–5 *International Journal of Human Rights*, 444–61 (2014).
134. Mahmood Mamdani, *Saviors and Survivors: Darfur, Politics and the War on Terror* (Doubleday. 2010).
135. Schabas, Unimaginable Atrocities, pp. 53–4.
136. Somini Sengupta, Omar al-Bashir Case Shows International Criminal Court's Limitations, *New York Times*, 15 June 2015; Simon Tisdall, Omar al-Bashir Case Suggests South African Foreign Policy is Going Rogue, *Guardian*, 15 June 2015.
137. See Dahr Jamail, Iraq: War's Legacy of Cancer, *Al Jazeera*, 15 March 2013.
138. See Human Rights Watch, Israel: White Phosphorus Use Evidence of War Crimes, 25 March 2009, available at www.hrw.org/news/2009/03/25/israel-white-phosphorus-use-evidence-war-crimes (accessed 21 December 2016).
139. See Human Rights Watch, Cluster Bombs in Afghanistan, *Human Rights News*, October 2001.
140. Maurice Bertrand, *The United Nations: Past, Present and Future*, pp. 122–5 (Kluwer Law International. 1997).
141. Id. at 124.
142. William R. Pace & Mark Thieroff, Participation of Non-governmental Organisations, in *The Making of the Rome Statute, Issues, Negotiations and Results*, pp. 391–420 (Roy S. Lee ed. Kluwer Law International. 1999).
143. For example, see Power, 'A Problem from Hell'.
144. Pace & Thieroff, Participation of Non-governmental Organisations, p. 391.
145. Amnesty international Limited, Report and Financial Statements for the Year Ended 31 December 2013, available at www.amnesty.org/en/who-we-are/accountability/financial-reports (accessed 9 February 2016).

146. For example, see Francis Boyle & Dennis Bernstein, Interview: Amnesty on Jenin, *CovertAction Quarterly*, 9–12 (2002); Daniel Kovalick, Amnesty International and the Human Rights Industry, *Counterpunch*, 8 November 2012; Ann Wright & Coleen Rowley, Amnesty's Shilling for US Wars, Consortiumnew.org, 18 June 2012.

147. See Amy Goodman, Debate: Is Human Rights Watch Too Close to the U.S. Gov't to Criticize its Foreign Policy: Reed Brody and Keane Bhatt, *Democracy Now*, 11 June 2014.

148. See Parliamentarians for Global Action website at www.pgaction.org/membership/sponsors.html (accessed 9 February 2016).

149. ICHRDD's claim to be independent and 'non-governmental' was contested by me during the anti-globalisation campaigns. See Radha D'Souza, Parallel People's APEC: Two Meetings, Two Views, *Six Nations Solidarity*, 1995, available at http://sisis.nativeweb.org/global/apecradha.html (accessed 9 February 2016). ICHRDD, later renamed Rights and Democracy, was closed down by the Ministry of Foreign Affairs on 3 April 2012.

150. No Peace Without Justice, Emma Bonino, available at www.npwj.org/content/Emma-Bonino.html (accessed 9 February 2016).

151. The American NGO Coalition for the ICC (AMICC) website describes the network as a coalition that examines the moral, ethical and religious considerations surrounding the Court. The network views crime as individual moral wrongdoing and extends principles that apply to elected representative within national jurisdictions to foreign nationals in the international forums such as the ICC. See www.amicc.org/about/faith/ (accessed 9 February 2016).

152. Pace & Thieroff, Participation of Non-governmental Organisations, p. 392.

153. For case studies on the scope and extent of extraterritorial jurisdiction see Luc Reydams, *Universal Jurisdiction: International and Municipal Legal Perspectives* (Oxford University Press. 2004).

154. Gould, *The Legacy of Punishment*, Ch. 2.

155. Lutz & Reiger, *Prosecuting Heads of State*, p. 37.

156. Craig Whitlock, Spain's Judges Cross Borders in Rights Cases, *Washington Post*, 24 May 2009.

157. Ashifa Kassam, Spain Moves to Curb Legal Convention Allowing Trial of Foreign Rights Abuses, *Guardian*, 11 February 2014; Jim Yardley, Spain Seeks to Curb Law Allowing Judges to Pursue Cases Globally, *New York Times*, 10 February 2014.

158. Reydams, *Universal Jurisdiction*, p. 222.

159. Richard Mulgan, 'Accountability': An Ever-expanding Concept?, 78 *Public Administration*, 556 (2000).

160. Dubnick, Accountability as a Cultural Keyword.

161. Id. at 31.

CHAPTER 6

1. John Maynard Keynes, Economic Possibilities for Our Grandchildren (1930), in *Essays in Persuasion*, pp. 358–73 (John Maynard Keynes ed. W.W. Norton & Company. 1963) at 372.

2. Theodore J. Lowi, Risk and Rights in the History of American Governments, 119/4 *Daedalus*, 17–40 (1990) at 21.

3. See Donald A. Mackenzie, *An Engine, Not a Camera: How Financial Models Shape the Markets* (MIT Press. 2006).

4. Davita Silfen Glasberg, *The Power of Collective Purse Strings: The Effects of Bank Hegemony on Corporations and the State*, p. 150 (University of California Press. 1989).

5. Ibid.

6. George C. Abbott, A Re-examination of the 1929 Colonial Development Act, 24/1 *Economic History Review*, 68–81 (1971).

7. Cheryl Payer, *The Debt Trap* (Monthly Review Press. 1975).

8. Sue Branford & Bernardo Kucinski, *The Debt Squads: The US, the Banks and Latin America*, pp. 35–8, 63 (Zed. 1988).

9. Id. at 68–9; Harold Karan Jacobson, *China's Participation in the IMF, the World Bank, and GATT: Toward a Global Economic Order*, pp. 29–30 (University of Michigan Press. 1990).

10. Jacobson, *China's Participation in the IMF*, p. 29.

11. Branford & Kucinski, *The Debt Squads*, pp. 43–4.

12. Id. at 42.

13. Glasberg, *The Power of Collective Purse Strings*, p. 148.

14. Ranjit Sau, *Unequal Exchange, Imperialism and Underdevelopment: An Essay on the Political Economy of World Capitalism* (Oxford University Press. 1978).

15. Glasberg, *The Power of Collective Purse Strings*, Ch. 6.

16. Id. at 145–6.

17. Branford & Kucinski, *The Debt Squads*, p. 95.

18. Id. at 105.

19. Quoted in ibid.

20. Graeme F. Rea, Restructuring Sovereign Debt – Will There be New International Law and Institutions?, 77 *Proceedings of the American Society of International Law*, 312–17 (15 April 1983) at 313.

21. Harris Black, *Allied Bank International v. Banco Credito Agricola De Cartago*: Applying the Act of State Doctrine to Actions against Foreign Debtors – Comment on the Case, 13 *Brooklyn Journal of International Law*, 183–96 (1987).

22. Ibid.

23. *A.I. Credit Corp. v. Government of Jamaica*, 666 F. Suppl. 629 (S.D.N.Y, 1987).

24. Joel P. Trachtman, Foreign Investment, Regulation and Expropriation: A Debtor's Jubilee, 89 *Proceedings of the American Society of International Law*, 103–9 (1995) at 104–5.

25. David Suratgar, Opening Remarks by the Chairman, 79 *Proceedings of the American Society of International Law*, 126–36 (1985) at 127.

26. Mr Brower, Discussion: ASIL Panel on Restructuring Sovereign Debt – Will There be New International Law and Institutions?, ed. Lisa Helling, *Proceedings of the American Society of International Law*, 312–35 (1983) at 335.

27. For in-depth analysis of debt-equity swaps in corporate rescue plans see Shubhrendu Chatterji & Paul Hedges, *Loan Workouts and Debt for Equity Swaps: A Framework for Successful Corporate Rescues* (John Wiley & Sons. 2001). For an overview of Chapter 11 of the US Bankruptcy Code on loan work-outs see Christopher R. Kaup & J. Daryl Dorsey, Chapter 11 Bankruptcy: A Primer, 28 *GPSolo*, 49–51 (2011). For an evaluation of the reorganisation process in bankruptcy proceedings under Chapter 11 of the US Bankruptcy Code see Edward I. Altman, Comment: Evaluating the Chapter 11 Bankruptcy-reorganization Process, 1/Winter *Columbia Business Law Review*, 1–25 (1993). For corporate rescue law in the UK see Vanessa Finch, Corporate Rescue: A Game of Three Halves, 32/2 *Legal Studies*, 302–24 (2012). For an analysis of US corporate rescue plans when one party is a foreign actor see Henry Dahl, USA: Bankruptcy Under Chapter 11, 5 *International Business Law Journal*, 555–66 (1992). For a comparison of corporate rescue provisions in the US and UK see Gerard McCormack, *Corporate Rescue Law – an Anglo-American Perspective* (Edward Elgar. 2008).

28. McCormack, *Corporate Rescue Law*.

29. Chatterji & Hedges, *Loan Workouts and Debt for Equity Swaps*; Finch, Corporate Rescue; McCormack, *Corporate Rescue Law*, p. 253.

30. Bevis Longstreth, 'In Search of a New Safety Net for the Financial Services Industry', Speech to the New York Regional Group of the American Society of Corporate Secretaries, New York, available at www.sec.gov/news/speech/1983/021083 longstreth.pdf (accessed 20 February 2015).

31. Nora Lustig, *Mexico: The Remaking of an Economy* (Brookings Institution Press. 1998).

32. For Mexico-US relations see Arturo Santa-Cruz, *Mexico-United States Relations: The Semantics of Sovereignty* (Routledge. 2012).

33. Raul Hinojosa-Ojeda, *North American Integration and Concepts of Human Rights: Reflections on 150 Years of Treaty Making* (1998); Robert E. Lutz, The Mexican War and the Treaty of Guadalupe Hidalgo: What's Best and Worst About Us, 5 *Southwest Journal of Law & Trade in the Americas*, 27–30 (1998). See id. at 27.

34. Glasberg, *The Power of Collective Purse Strings*, p. 150.

35. Id. at 154.

36. Id. at 150–1.

37. Id. at 154.

38. Id. at 148.

39. Id. at 164.

40. Statement by Paul A. Volcker, Chairman, Board of Governors of the Federal Reserve System before the Committee on Banking, Finance and Urban Affairs House of Representatives, 2 February 1983, available at https://fraser.stlouisfed.org/docs/ historical/volcker/Volcker_19830202.pdf (accessed 20 February 2015).

41. Glasberg, *The Power of Collective Purse Strings*, p. 169.

42. Id. at 157.

43. Russell Munk, Exchange Stabilization Fund Loans to Sovereign Borrowers: 1982–2010, 73 *Law and Contemporary Problems*, 215–40 (2010).

44. C. Randall Henning, The Exchange Stabilization Fund: Slush Money or War Chest?, Policy Analysis in International Economics No. 57, Institute for International Economics (1999).

45. Munk, Exchange Stabilization Fund Loans, p. 221.

46. Ibid.

47. Branford & Kucinski, *The Debt Squads*, p. 18; also Jacobson, *China's Participation in the IMF*, p. 30.

48. See Jacobson, *China's Participation in the IMF*, p. 31.

49. George L. Head, Underwriting – in Five Easy Lessons?, 35/2 *Journal of Risk and Insurance*, 307–10 (1968) at 308.

50. Jacobson, *China's Participation in the IMF*, p. 29.

51. Ibid.

52. Ibid.

53. The Articles of Agreement of the IMF privilege the five largest subscribers to the IMF's capital contributions. The five largest contributors appoint five permanent executive directors. There is a *de facto* understanding in place since 1944 known as the 'gentleman's agreement' under which the president of the World Bank is a US nominee and the president of the IMF is a European nominee. See Joshua E. Keating, Why is the IMF Chief Always a European?, *Financial Post*, 18 May 2011.The voting powers of contributing states are proportionate to the quotas – the contributions that states make to the IMF as a condition of their membership of the organisation. See IMF website at www.imf.org/external/np/sec/memdir/members.aspx (accessed 20 February 2015). When the IMF was set up the US quota was over 39 per cent of the total contributions at that time. The US quota has since reduced to 17.69 per cent and it controls 16.5 per cent of the votes. Japan, the second largest contributor, trails behind with 6.23 per cent of the votes (see IMF website). As the single largest

contributor to the IMF funds the US continues to have the largest voting power in the IMF in spite of the reduced contributions.

54. Glasberg, *The Power of Collective Purse Strings*, p. 171.
55. See Branford & Kucinski, *The Debt Squads*, p. 13; id. at 147; Joseph Gold, Mexico and the Development of the Practice of the International Monetary Fund, *World Development*, 1127–42 (16 October 1988) at 1130.
56. Jacobson, *China's Participation in the IMF*, pp. 31–2.
57. Gold, Mexico and the Development of the Practice of the International Monetary Fund, pp. 1130–1.
58. Glasberg, *The Power of Collective Purse Strings*, p. 165.
59. William E. Holder, Exchange Rate Policies: The Role and Influence of the International Monetary Fund, 80 *Proceedings of the American Society of International Law*, 29–35 (1986) at 30.
60. Ibid.; Gerald M. Meier, The 'Jamaica Agreement,' International Monetary Reform, and the Developing Countries, 11 *International Journal of Law & Economics*, 67–89 (1976–1977).
61. Glasberg, *The Power of Collective Purse Strings*, pp. 161–2.
62. Id. at 166.
63. Quoted in id. at 167.
64. Roger Thomas, Panel Discussion: International Debt Focus on Mexico, 82 *American Society of International Law Proceedings*, 479–82 (1988) at 481–2.
65. John W. Head, Suspension of Debtor Countries' Voting Rights in the IMF: An Assessment of the Third Amendment to the IMF Charter, 33 *Virginia Journal of International Law*, 591–646 (1992–93).
66. Daniel D. Bradlow, Rapidly Changing Functions and Slowly Evolving Structures: The Troubling Case of the IMF, 94 *American Society of International Law Proceedings*, 152–9 (2000).
67. Ibid.
68. Ibid.
69. See Board of Directors on IIE website at www.iie.com/institute/board.cfm#33 (accessed 20 February 2015).
70. John Williamson, A Short History of the Washington Consensus, 15 *Law and Business Review of the Americas*, 7–23 (2009) at 9.
71. Id. at 9–10.
72. See Chatterji & Hedges, *Loan Workouts and Debt for Equity Swaps*.
73. Lee C. Buchheit et al., Revisiting Sovereign Bankruptcy (Committee on International Economic Policy and Reform, Brookings Institution, 2013), available at www.brookings.edu/research/reports/2013/10/sovereign-debt (accessed 20 February 2015); Commonwealth Secretariat, 'Report of Experts' Group Meeting on Sovereign Debt -Restructuring (United Nations Financing for Development Office, Centre for International Governance Innovation, 18 May 2012); Kenneth Rogoff and Jeromin Zettelmeyer, Bankruptcy Procedures for Sovereigns: A History of Ideas, 1976–2001, 49/3 *IMF Staff Papers*, 470–507 (2002).
74. Anne Krueger, International Financial Architecture for 2002: A New Approach to Sovereign Debt Restructuring, Address given at the National Economists' Club Annual Members' Dinner, American Enterprise Institute, Washington, DC, 26 November 2001, available at www.imf.org/external/np/speeches/2001/112601.htm (accessed 20 February 2015). On the problems of extending bankruptcy proceedings for private debt recovery to sovereign debt recovery see Jonathan P. Thomas, Bankruptcy Proceedings for Sovereign State Insolvency and their Effect on Capital Flows, *International Review of Economics and Finance*, 341–61 (13 March 2004).
75. Quoted in Rogoff & Zettelmeyer, Bankruptcy Procedures for Sovereigns, p. 418.

76. Charles Gore, The Rise and Fall of the Washington Consensus as a Paradigm for Developing Countries, 28/5 *World Development*, 789–804 (2000).

77. Draft Resolution II of the Second Committee on 'Unilateral Economic Measures as a Means of Political and Economic Coercion against Developing Countries', Agenda Item 95 on Macroeconomic Policy Question, General Assembly 56th session, 90th plenary meeting on Friday 21 December 2001, A/56/PV.90.

78. UNGA Resolution 57/240.

79. Bhumika Muchhala, United Nations: Historic Vote on a Multilateral Sovereign Debt Mechanism, *Social Watch: Poverty Eradication and Gender Justice* (25 September 2014), available at www.socialwatch.org/node/16653 (accessed 11 February 2016); ibid.

80. Ibid.

81. 'Towards the Establishment of a Multilateral Legal Framework for Sovereign Debt Restructuring Processes', UNGA Resolution A/68/L.57/Rev2.

82. Muchhala, United Nations: Historic Vote; ibid.

83. See Antonio R. Parra, Panel: ICSID and the Rise of Bilateral Investment Treaties: Will ICSID be the Leading Arbitration Institution in the Early 21st Century?, 94 *American Society of International Law Proceedings*, 41–4 (2000).

84. James Petras and Henry Veltmeyer show how the crises of TMF capitalism invited varying responses from different types of political and social movements in Latin America. Henry Veltmeyer & James Petras, *Social Movements in Latin America: Neoliberalism and Popular Resistance* (Palgrave Macmillan. 2011).

85. For brief histories of the Jubilee 2000 see Soren Ambrose, Social Movements and the Politics of Debt Cancellation, 6/1 *Chicago Journal of International Law*, 267–85 (2005); Kristen E. Gwinn, The Debt Relief Movement, in *Encyclopedia of Activism and Social Justice*, pp. 434–5 (Gary L. Anderson & Kathryn G. Herr eds. Sage. 2007); Ann Pettifor, The Jubilee 2000 Campaign: A Brief Overview, in *Sovereign Debt at the Crossroads: Challenges and Proposals for Resolving the Third World Debt Crisis*, pp. 297–318 (Chris Jochnick & Fraser A. Preston eds. Oxford University Press. 2006).

86. Pettifor, The Jubilee 2000 Campaign, p. 299.

87. Ibid.

88. Joshua William Busby, Bono Made Jesse Helms Cry: Jubilee 2000, Debt Relief, and Moral Action in International Politics, 51/2 *International Studies Quarterly*, 247–75 (2007) at 247–8.

89. Gwinn, The Debt Relief Movement, pp. 434–5.

90. Radha D'Souza, The WSF Revisited: Back to Basics?, available at www.coloursofresistance.org/271/the-wsf-revisited-back-to-basics/ (accessed 20 February 2015).

91. See Odette Lienau, *Rethinking Sovereign Debt: Politics, Reputation, and Legitimacy in Modern Finance* (Harvard University Press. 2014).

92. See ibid.

93. Edward Cody, Castro Takes up Cause of Latin American Debtors, *Washington Post*, 3 July 1985. For a discussion on the reasons why debt cancellation is preferable to debtors' cartel from the perspectives of one international negotiator for the banking sector see Christine A. Bogdanowicz Bindert, Discussion: Panel on Restructuring Sovereign Debt, 77 *American Society of International Law Proceedings*, 326–35 (1983) at 333.

94. See Klaus Friedrich Veigel, *Dictatorship, Democracy and Globalization: Argentina and the Cost of Paralysis, 1973–2001*, p. 143 (Pennsylvania State University Press. 2009).

95. Samuel Moyn, Imperialism, Self-determination, and the Rise of Human Rights, in *The Human Rights Revolution: An International History*, pp. 159–78 (Akira Iriye et al. eds. Oxford University Press. 2012) at 172.

96. Razeen Sally, *Classical Liberalism and International Economic Order: Studies in Theory and Intellectual History* (Routledge. 1998).

97. Radha D'Souza, *Interstate Conflicts Over Krishna Waters: Law, Science and Imperialism*, p. 592 (Orient Longmans. 2006).

CHAPTER 7

1. Thomas Munro (1761–1827), Governor of Madras Presidency in India under the East India Company for over thirty years. Quoted in C. Ramachandran, *East India Company and South Indian Economy* , p. 171 (New Era Publications. 1980).

2. On NBA see William F. Fisher, *Toward Sustainable Development: Struggling Over India's Narmada River* (M.E. Sharpe. 1995). Also Sanjeev Khagram, *Dams and Development: Transnational Struggles for Water and Power* (Cornell University Press. 2004). For a critique of the movement see Radha D'Souza, Three Actors, Two Geographies, One Philosophy: The Straightjacket of Social Movements, in *Social Movements and/in the Postcolonial: Dispossession, Development and Resistance in the Global South* , pp. 227–49 (Alf Nielsen & Sarra Motta eds. Palgrave Macmillan. 2010).

3. Article IV, Section 10 of the Articles of Agreement establishing the World Bank states: 'The Bank and its officers shall not interfere in the political affairs of any member; nor shall they be influenced in their decisions by the political character of the member or members concerned. Only economic considerations shall be relevant to their decisions, and these considerations shall be weighted impartially in order to achieve the purposes stated in Article I.' Under Article III, Section 5(b) the Bank must ensure that funds loaned will be only used for the purposes for which they were loaned, '... with due attention to considerations of economy and efficiency and without regard to political or other non-economic influences or considerations'. Article V, Section 5(c) states that the President, staff and officers of the Bank owe their duty to the Bank and '... to no other authority. Each member of the Bank shall respect the international character of this duty and shall refrain from all attempts to influence any of them in the discharge of their duties.'

4. Nicholas H. Moller, The World Bank: Human Rights, Democracy and Governance, 15/1 *Netherlands Quarterly of Human Rights*, 21–45 (1997) at 23–5.

5. Ibrahim F.I. Shihata, The World Bank and Human Rights: An Analysis of the Legal Issues and the Record of Achievements, 17/1 *Denver Journal of International Law and Policy*, 39–66 (1988) at 48.

6. Ibid. See also Ibrahim F.I. Shihata, *The World Bank in a Changing World*, Vol. I (Martinus Nijhoff. 1991).

7. Shihata, The World Bank and Human Rights, p. 49.

8. Ibrahim F.I. Shihata, *The World Bank in a Changing World*, Vol. II, p. 568 (Martinus Nijhoff. 1995).

9. For purpose of the Act see The International Development and Finance Act of 1989, available at www.govtrack.us/congress/bills/101/hr2494/text (accessed 20 February 2015).

10. Under its Articles of Agreement the WB is an independent international organisation. The WB governors are not required to follow any directives issues by their home governments. The US nominates a permanent executive director and under convention the US nominee is the president of the WB. The question of whether the US can direct its nominees to vote in certain ways has always remained controversial. See Bartram S. Brown, *The United States and the Politicization of the World Bank* (Kegan Paul International. 1992). The abstention directive some believe circumvented a head-on engagement with this contentious question. See M.J. Peterson, Narmada Dams Controversy, *International Dimensions of Ethics Education*

in Science and Engineering (2010), available at http://scholarworks.umass.edu/cgi/ viewcontent.cgi?article=1015&context=edethicsinscience (accessed 20 February 2015).

11. Congressional veto over executive action was overruled by the US Supreme Court in the case of *I.N.S v. Chadha*. The Act was substantially amended after the ruling. Meyer identifies three phases in the evolution of the Foreign Assistance Act 1961. For an analysis of the evolution of the Act until 1988 see Jeffrey Meyer, Congressional Control of Foreign Assistance, 13/1 *Yale Journal of International Law*, 69–110 (1988).

12. See Brown, *The United States and the Politicization of the World Bank*.

13. See ibid.

14. Bradford Morse & Thomas Berger, *Sardar Sarovar: Report of the Independent Review*, Ottawa, Canada: The Independent Review (1992).

15. See Operational Manual on Environmental and Social Safeguard policies at http:// web.worldbank.org/ (accessed 20 February 2015).

16. See articles in Fisher, *Toward Sustainable Development*.

17. Robert Wade, Greening the Bank: The Struggle Over the Environment 1970–1995, in *The World Bank: Its First Half Century*, Vol. 2, pp. 611–734 (Devesh Kapur, John P. Lewis & Richard Webb eds. Brookings Institution Press. 1997); also Peterson, Narmada Dams Controversy.

18. Wade, Greening the Bank; also Peterson, Narmada Dams Controversy.

19. See annual reports of IRN from the International Rivers website at www. internationalrivers.org/ (accessed 20 February 2015).

20. Information on different campaigns can be found at the International Rivers website at www.internationalrivers.org/.

21. For an extended discussion see D'Souza, Three Actors.

22. For a discussion on Africa on this issue see Issa Shivji, Constructing a New Rights Regime: Promises, Problems and Prospects, 8/2 *Social & Legal Studies*, 253–76 (1999).

23. For early campaigns to link 'human' rights with aid and overseas assistance see Andre Frankovits & Eric Sidoti, *The Rights Way to Development: A Human Rights Approach to Development Assistance* (The Human Rights Council of Australia. 1995).

24. See for e.g. Charles Gore, The Rise and Fall of the Washington Consensus as a Paradigm for Developing Countries, 28/5 *World Development*, 789–804 (2000); Tony Weiss, A Precarious Balance: Neoliberalism, Crisis Management, and the Social Implosion in Jamaica, 85 *Capital & Class*, 115–47 (2005).

25. Dani Rodrik & World Bank, Goodbye Washington Consensus, Hello Washington Confusion? A Review of the World Bank's 'Economic Growth in the 1990s: Learning from a Decade of Reform', 44/4 *Journal of Economic Literature*, 978–87 (2006).

26. See Barbara Nunberg, Public Sector Management Issues in Structural Adjustment Lending, World Bank Discussion Paper No. 99 (1990).

27. For a comparative study of reforms of the bureaucracy in New Zealand and Denmark see Robert Gregory & Jorgen G. Christensen, Similar Ends, Differing Means: Contractualism and Civil Service Reform in Denmark and New Zealand, 17/1 *Governance: An International Journal of Policy, Administration and Institutions*, 59–82 (2004). For an in-depth analysis of the role of the WB in restructuring the bureaucracy in the Philippines see Robin Broad, *Unequal Alliance: The World Bank, the International Monetary Fund, and the Philippines* (University of California Press. 1988).

28. Christine A. Bogdanowicz-Bindert, The Debt Crisis: The Baker Plan Revisited, 28/3 *Journal of Interamerican Studies and World Affairs*, 33–45 (1986).

29. Jonathan P. Thomas, Bankruptcy Proceedings for Sovereign State Insolvency and their Effect on Capital Flows, 13/3 *International Review of Economics and Finance*, 341–61 (2004).

30. Thomas L. Palley, The Rise and Fall of Export-led Growth, Working Paper No. 675, Levy Economics Institute (2011).

31. Sebastian Edwards, The Mexican Peso Crisis: How Much Did We Know? When Did We Know It?, 21 *World Economy* (1998) at 3. Also Rodrik & Bank, Goodbye Washington Consensus.

32. See *The New Institutional Economics and Third Word Development* (John Harriss, Janet Hunter & Colin M. Lewis, eds. Routledge. 1995). Also Rodrik & Bank, Goodbye Washington Consensus.

33. Douglass C. North, The New Institutional Economics and Third World Development, in *The New Institutional Economics and Third Word Development*, pp. 17–26 (John Harriss, Janet Hunter & Colin M. Lewis eds. Routledge. 1995) at 23.

34. See articles in Harriss et al., *The New Institutional Economics*. Also Daniel D. Bradlow & Claudio Grossman, Limited Mandates and Intertwined Problems: A New Challenge for the World Bank and the IMF, 17/3 *Human Rights Quarterly*, 411–42 (1995).

35. See BankTrack webpage at www.banktrack.org/show/pages/history (accessed 20 February 2015). Also see discussion in Benjamin J. Richardson, *Socially Responsible Investment Law: Regulating the Unseen Polluters*, Ch. 6 (Oxford University Press. 2008) and N. O'Sullivan & B. O'Dwyer, Stakeholder Perspectives on a Financial Sector Legitimation Process: The Case of NGOs and the Equator Principles, 22/4 *Accounting Auditing & Accountability Journal*, 553–87 (2009).

36. O'Sullivan & O'Dwyer, Stakeholder Perspectives.

37. Richardson, *Socially Responsible Investment Law*, pp. 413–14.

38. Richard V. Ericson, Aaron Doyle & Dean Barry, *Insurance as Governance* , p. 4 (University of Toronto Press. 2003).

39. See id. at 72.

40. Ulrich Beck, *Risk Society: Towards a New Modernity* (Mark Ritter trans. Sage. 1992); also Anthony Giddens, The Consequences of Modernity (Polity and Blackwell. 1990); Anthony Giddens, *Modernity and Self-identity: Self and Society in the Late Modern Age* (Polity. 1991).

41. See Alvaro Santos, The World Bank's Uses of the 'Rule of Law' Promise in Economic Development, in *The New Law and Economic Development* p. 275 (David M. Trubek & Alvaro Santos eds. Cambridge University Press. 2006).

42. Ibrahim R.I. Shihata, The Multilateral Investment Guarantee Agency, 80 *American Society of International Law Proceedings*, 21–7. See also the Q&A after Shihata's speech at the ASIL conference (1986).

43. Article 11(a)(i), Convention Establishing the Multilateral Investment Guarantee Agency.

44. Article 11(a)(ii), Convention Establishing the Multilateral Investment Guarantee Agency.

45. Article 11(a)(iii), Convention Establishing the Multilateral Investment Guarantee Agency.

46. Article 11(a)(iv), Convention Establishing the Multilateral Investment Guarantee Agency. Terrorist attacks targeting a specific investor can be covered only if the investor and the host country make a joint request to the WB under Article 11(b).

47. John Coyle, The Treaty of Friendship, Commerce and Navigation in the Modern Era, 51/2 *Columbia Journal of Transnational Law*, 302–59 (2013); Kenneth J. Vandevelde, The Bilateral Investment Treaty Program of the United States, 21/2 *Cornell International Law Journal*, 201–76 (1988); Kenneth J. Vandevelde, The BIT Program: A Fifteen-year Appraisal: Panel on the Development and Expansion of Bilateral Investment Treaties, 86 *American Society of International Law Proceedings*, 532–40 (1992). Also see Wolfgang Alschner, Americanization of the BIT Universe: The

Influence of Friendship, Commerce and Navigation (FCN) Treaties on Modern Investment Treaty Law, 2 *Goettingen Journal of International Law*, 455–86 (2013).

48. Joseph M. Cardosi, Precluding the Treasure Hunt: How the World Bank Group Can Help Investors Circumnavigate Sovereign Immunity Obstacles to ICSID Award Execution, 41/1 *Pepperdine Law Review*, 117–56 (2013–14).

49. Coyle, The Treaty of Friendship; Vandevelde, The Bilateral Investment Treaty Program; Vandevelde, The BIT Program. Also see Alschner, Americanization of the BIT Universe.

50. Latin American states were the first states to become formally independent and the first to test the limits of the right of nations to self-determination. In the early 1800s Latin American states invited foreign investments to modernise and develop their economies offering them equal national treatment. By the 1830s most Latin American states defaulted on their bond obligations. US and UK investors turned to their home governments for protection of their investments. See Christopher K. Dalrymple, Politics and Foreign Direct Investment: The Multilateral Investment Guarantee Agency and the Calvo Clause, 29/1 *Cornell International Law Journal*, 161–89 (1996) at 164.

51. Id. at 164–5.

52. Ericson et al., *Insurance as Governance*, p. 71.

53. Id. at 71–2.

54. George L. Priest, The New Legal Structure of Risk Control, 119/4 *Daedalus*, 207–27 (1990) at 215.

55. Ibid.

56. See Michael Likosky, *Law, Infrastructure and Human Rights* (Cambridge University Press. 2006).

57. For case studies on infrastructure projects and human rights risks see ibid.

58. See David H. Lempert, A Dependency in Development Indicator for NGOs and International Organizations, 9/2 *Global Jurist*, Article 6 (2009).

59. *Insurance Regulation for Sustainable Development: Protecting Human Rights Against Climate Risk and Natural Hazards*, p. 1 (Cambridge Institute for Sustainability and Leadership. 2016). For human rights and insurance issues in infrastructure industries see Likosky, *Law, Infrastructure and Human Rights*.

60. See Theodore J. Lowi, Risk and Rights in the History of American Governments, 119/4 *Daedalus*, 17–40 (1990). Lowi's arguments refer to American state and society. The underlying reasoning for the arguments are relevant for other G7 states and risk regulation more generally.

61. Priest, The New Legal Structure of Risk Control.

62. George Priest, The Invention of Enterprise Liability: A Critical History of the Intellectual Foundations of Modern Tort Law, 14/3 *Journal of Legal Studies*, 461–527 (1985).

63. See Lowi, Risk and Rights in the History of American Governments, p. 38.

64. Christopher Wright & Alexis Rwabizambuga, Institutional Pressures, Corporate Reputation, and Voluntary Codes of Conduct: An Examination of the Equator Principles, 111/1 *Business and Society Review*, 89–117 (2006).

65. World Bank, *Governance and Development* (World Bank. 1992).

66. Thomas Weiss, Governance, Good Governance and Global Governance: Conceptual and Actual Challenges, 21/5 *Third World Quarterly*, 795–814 (2000) at 801. For more detailed analysis see World Bank, *Sub-Saharan Africa: From Crisis to Sustainable Growth, A Long-term Perspective Study* (1989).

67. See Weiss, Governance, Good Governance.

68. The analysis and management skills are considered necessary for management of public finances including debt management and cutbacks to public expenditure.

69. The reforms include wage increases for civil servants at top levels so as to attract skilled professionals in the labour market and reduce wage gaps between public and private sectors; also trimming staffing at lower levels and wage cuts to reduce public expenditure. Re-training is needed to re-educate public servants about their new roles as contractors of public services which is a different role from public servants as providers of public services in the past. See Nunberg, Public Sector Management Issues; World Bank, *The Reform of Public Sector Management: Lessons from Experience* (Country Economics Department, World Bank. 1991).

70. Revenue policies include low taxation levels that are attractive for investors and market-oriented social safety nets for those disadvantaged by LPG reforms. See Nunberg, Public Sector Management Issues; World Bank, *Reform of Public Sector Management.*

71. Anti-corruption policies are justified as necessary for efficient administration to avoid 'slippage' of revenues and decentralisation policies are promoted as democratic governance, where each sector can adapt itself to the overall goals of the game more effectively. See Nunberg, Public Sector Management Issues; World Bank, *Reform of Public Sector Management.*

72. Establishing independent regulatory authorities for each sector of the economy, voluntary codes of conduct and professional codes, establishing performance indicators. See Nunberg, Public Sector Management Issues; World Bank, *Reform of Public Sector Management.*

73. Public enterprise reforms include privatisation of publicly owned enterprises, market-oriented management of enterprises and public-private partnerships especially in infrastructure projects. World Bank Independent Evaluation Group (IEG), *Public Sector Reform: What Works and Why?: An IEG Evaluation of World Bank Support* (2008). Also Nunberg, Public Sector Management Issues; World Bank, *Reform of Public Sector Management.*

74. World Bank IEG, *Public Sector Reform.*

75. World Bank, *Governance and Development.* Id. at 13.

76. World Bank IEG, *Public Sector Reform*, p. xiii.

77. The WB uses management techniques to govern the Third World. See Bill Cooke, The Managing of the (Third) World, 11/5 *Organization*, 603–29 (2004). Neoliberalism introduced corporate management techniques to civil services. See Gregory & Christensen, Similar Ends, Differing Means.

78. World Bank, *Sub-Saharan Africa*, p. 6.

79. Shihata, *The World Bank in a Changing World*, Vol. I; Shihata, *The World Bank in a Changing World*, Vol. II.

80. Ibid. Also Shihata, The World Bank and Human Rights.

81. North, The New Institutional Economics, p. 25.

82. Ibid.

83. Id. at 25–6.

84. Robert Bates, Social Dilemmas and Rational Individuals, in *The New Institutional Economics and Third Word Development*, pp. 27–48 (John Harriss et al. eds. Routledge. 1995); see id. at 27–48.

85. Santos, The World Bank's Uses of the 'Rule of Law' Promise, pp. 253–4, fn 1.

86. World Bank, *Reform of Public Sector Management*, pp. 11, 30.

87. Nancy Zucker Boswell, Combating Corruption: Are International Institutions Doing their Job?, 90 *American Society of International Law Proceedings*, 98–105 (1996) at 99.

88. Ibid.

89. Id. at 106.

90. Thomas J. White, US Efforts to Combat Foreign Corrupt Practices, 92 *American Society of International Law Proceedings*, 162–5 (1998). Also Thomas J. White, U.S.

Efforts to Combat Foreign Corrupt Practices, 4/3 *Science and Engineering Ethics*, 263–8 (1998).

91. See Chapter 5 on US initiatives to internationalise corruption in the wake of the Panama invasion and the trial of President Noriega.

92. White, US Efforts to Combat Foreign Corrupt Practices.

93. Id. at 163.

94. World Bank, *Governance and Development*, p. 13.

95. Id. at 14.

96. Ibid.

97. Ibid.

98. Id. at 15.

99. See Patricia J. Arnold, The Political Economy of Financial Harmonization: The East Asian Financial Crisis and the Rise of International Accounting Standards, 37/6 *Accounting, Organizations and Society*, 361–81 (2012).

100. Professional Services: The Economist, Attack of the Bean-counters: Lawyers Beware: The Accountants are Coming After Your Business, *The Economist*, 21 March 2015.

101. World Bank, *Governance and Development*, pp. 22–3.

102. Id. at 24.

103. Ibid.

104. World Bank, *Governance and Development*.

105. Id. at 25.

106. Id. at 26.

107. See *Incite! Women of Colour Against Violence, the Revolution Will Not Be Funded: Beyond The Non-profit Industrial Complex* (South End Press. 2007).

108. On the question of higher education and activist scholarship see Radha D'Souza, The Prison Houses of Knowledge: Activist Scholarship and Revolution in the Era of 'Globalisation', 44/1 *McGill Journal of Education*, 1–20 (2009).

109. See R. Edward Freeman & David L. Reed, Stockholders and Stakeholders: A New Perspective on Corporate Governance, XXV/3 *California Management Review*, 88–106 (1983).

110. North, The New Institutional Economics, p. 18.

111. Id. at 22.

112. Robert Bates, Social Dilemmas and Rational Individuals; see id. at 32.

113. Ibid., drawing on J.E. Stiglitz, The New Development Economics, 14/2 *World Development*, 257–65 (1986) and Y. Barze, *Economic Analysis of Property Rights* (Cambridge University Press. 1989).

114. Id. at 33–4.

115. John Toye, The New Institutional Economics and its Implications for Development Theory, in *The New Institutional Economics and Third World Development*, pp. 49–68 (John Harriss et al. eds. Routledge. 1995) at 55.

116. Id. at 60.

117. Id. at 61.

118. Id. at 59.

119. For a history of futures studies see Hyeonju Son, The History of Western futures Studies: An Exploration of the Intellectual Traditions and Three-phase Periodization, 66 *Futures*, 120–37 (2015). Also see Hazel Henderson, Viewing 'The New Economy' from Diverse Forecasting Perspectives, 30/4 *Futures*, 267–75 (1998).

120. Toye, The New Institutional Economics, p. 63.

121. For HMRC reports see Rowena Mason, HMRC to Sell Taxpayers' Financial Data, *Guardian*, 18 April 2014; Keith Perry, HMRC Plans to Sell Taxpayers' Data to Private Firms, *Telegraph*, 18 April 2014. For sale of NHS databases see Laura Donnelly, Hospital Records of All NHS Patients Sold to Insurers, *Independent*, 23 February

2014; Randeep Ramesh, NHS Patient Data to be Made Available for Sale to Drug and Insurance Firms, *Guardian*, 19 January 2014.

122. Ishaan Tharoor, Anna Hazare's Hunger Fasts Rock India, *Time Magazine*, 7 December 2011.

123. Amita Baviskar, Winning the Right to Information in India: Is Knowledge Power?, in *Citizen Action and National Policy Reform: Making Change Happen*, pp. 130–52 (J. Gaventa & R. McGee eds. Zed Books. 2010).

124. See id.

125. The Lokpal and Lokayuktas Act, 2013 1 of 2014 (2013).

126. Samantha Subramanian, The Agitator: India's Anti-corruption Crusader Enters Politics, *New Yorker*, 2 September 2013.

127. See Ramon Magsaysay Award at www.rmaf.org.ph/newrmaf/main/the_foundation/about (accessed 10 February 2017).

128. Subramanian, The Agitator.

129. See Bhanwar Megwanshi, India: The Communal Character of Anna Hazare's Movement (5 September 2011), available at www.sacw.net/article2266.html (accessed 20 February 2015).

130. See Art of Living Foundation at www.artofliving.org/art-living-overview (accessed 20 February 2015).

131. Simon Denyer, India's Anti-corruption Movement Aims to Galvanize Democracy, *Washington Post*, 12 August 2011.

132. Subramanian, The Agitator.

133. 1 of 2014 (2013).

134. Mukul Sinha, India: Was Anna's Movement Really Against Corruption or a RSS Sponsored Ploy? Kiran Bedi Spills the Beans, South Asia Citizens Web (13 January 2014), available at www.sacw.net/article7255.html (accessed 20 February 2015).

135. Barack Obama, India's Reformer-in Chief, *Time Magazine*, 16 April 2015.

136. See for e.g. the scandal involving Lalit Modi, a businessman with close links to the ruling BJP and head of the popular Indian Premier League national cricket tournaments. *Hindustan Times* correspondent, All You Should Know About the Lalit Modi, Sushma Swaraj, Raje Controversy, *Hindustan Times*, 18 June 2015. And reports about the complicity of a British MP in the scandal in House of Commons, India (Outstanding Payments to British Companies) § 600, Hansard, 20 October 2015. The UK government was silent about the Indian government's 'human' rights violations and instead announced commercial deals worth £9 billion with India and anticipated 1,900 UK jobs as a result. See https://hansard.parliament.uk/Commons/2015 (accessed 20 February 2015).

CHAPTER 8

1. V.I. Lenin, 'On Slogans' in Pamphlet Published by the Kronstadt Committee of the R.S.D.L.P. (B), in *V.I. Lenin Collected Works*, Vol. 25, pp. 185–92 (Progress Publishers. 1977 [1917]) at 185.

2. See Editorial, The Guardian View on Official Secrets: New Proposals Threaten Democracy, *Guardian*, 12 February 2017; Lisa Kjellsson & Robert Mendick, Journalists Who Obtain Leaked Official Material Could be Sent to Prison Under New Proposals, *Telegraph*, 11 February 2017.

3. Alan Travis, 'Snooper's Charter' Bill Becomes Law, Extending UK State Surveillance, *Guardian*, 29 November 2017.

4. Radha D'Souza, When Unreason Masquerades as Reason: Can Law Regulate Trade and Networked Communication Ethically?, in *Handbook of Communication Ethics*, pp. 475–93 (George Cheny, Steve May and Debashish Munshi eds. International Communication Association Routledge/Lawrence Erlbaum. 2010).

5. See Richard J. Aldrich, OSS, CIA and European Unity: The American Committee on United Europe, 1948–1960, 8 *Diplomacy and Statecraft* (1997); Andrew Mullen, *The British Left's 'Great Debate' on Europe* (Continuum. 2007).

6. See BBC, Trump's Tipped EU Ambassador is 'Malevolent', Say European Leaders, 3 February 2017; Peter Dominiczak, Donald Trump 'Wants EU to Break Up in Wake of Brexit Vote', Outgoing US Ambassador in Brussels Suggests, *Telegraph*, 13 January 2017.

7. See Mohammed Barakatullah (Maulavie) of Bhopal, *The Khilafet* (Luzac & Co. 2nd edn. 1925 [1924]).

8. See Maia Ramnath, *Haj to Utopia: How the Ghadar Movement Charted Global Radicalism and Attempted to Overthrow the British Empire* (University of California Press. 2011). Also Radha D'Souza, Revolt and Reform in South Asia: Ghadar Movement to 9/11 and After, XLIX/8 *Economic & Political Weekly* (Special Articles), 59–73 (2014). For diaspora roles in Pan-African movements see Issa G. Shivji, Pan-Africanism or Imperialism? Unity and Struggle Towards a New Democratic Africa, 8/2 *Social & Legal Studies*, 258–76 (2008).

9. V.I. Lenin, Imperialism the Highest Stage of Capitalism, in *V.I. Lenin Selected Works in Three Volumes*, Vol. 1 (Progress Publishers. 1970 [1917]) at 676–7.

10. See Lenin's report on the Congress in V.I. Lenin, The International Socialist Congress Stuttgart (Proletary), in *Lenin Collected Works*, Vol. 13, pp. 75–81 (Progress Publishers. 1972 [1907]).

11. See for e.g. J. Lovering, Militarism, Capitalism, and the Nation-state: Towards a Realist Synthesis, 5 *Environment and Planning D: Society and Space*, 283–302 (1987); T.M. Porter, *Trust in Numbers: The Pursuit of Objectivity in Science and Public Life* (Princeton University Press. 1995). For the history and philosophy of social sciences see Peter E. Manicas, *A History & Philosophy of the Social Sciences* (Basil Blackwell. 1987).

12. Quoted in William Appleman Williams, *The Tragedy of American Diplomacy*, p. 66 (Delta. 1962).

13. Quoted in id. at 78–9.

14. For an expanded analysis on Lenin and the right of nations to self-determination see Radha D'Souza, Imperialism and Self Determination: Revisiting the Nexus in Lenin, XLVIII/15 *Economic & Political Weekly* (Special Articles), 60–9 (2013).

15. J. Degras, *Documents: The Communist International 1919–1943*, Vol. III (The Royal Institute of International Affairs. 1964).

16. For Mao Tse-tung's analysis on why it was correct that the Third International should be dissolved see Mao Tse-tung, The Comintern Has Long Ceased to Meddle in Our Internal Affairs, in *Selected Works of Mao Tse-tung*, Vol. VI (26 May 1943), available at www.marxists.org/reference/archive/mao/selected-works/volume-6/mswv6_36.htm (accessed 15 January 2017).

17. For a debate between well-known American economists and diplomats John Kenneth Galbraith and Stanislav Menshikov on the similarities between the US and the former USSR see John Kenneth Galbraith & Stanislav Menshikov, *Capitalism, Communism and Coexistence: From a Bitter Past to a Better Prospect* (Houghton Mifflin Company. 1988).

18. V.I. Lenin, What is to be Done? Burning Question of Our Movement, in *V.I. Lenin Selected Works in Three Volumes*, Vol. 1 (Progress Publishers. 1970 [1902]) at 138.

19. V.I. Lenin, Marxism and Revisionism, in *V.I. Lenin Selected Works in Three Volumes*, Vol. 1, pp. 71–8 (Progress Publishers. 1970 [1908]).

20. Ranjan Ghosh, Institutionalised Theory, (In)fusion, Desivad, in *The Oxford Literary Review*, Vol. 28, pp. 25–36 (Edinburgh University Press. 2006) at 25. Also see Radha D'Souza, The Prison Houses of Knowledge: Activist Scholarship and Revolution in the Era of 'Globalisation', 44/1 *McGill Journal of Education*, 1–20 (2009).

21. For the peace process in the Philippines see Alicia Kuin, The NDFP-GPH Peace Process, *The Philippine Reporter*, 24 June 2016, available at http://philippinereporter. com/2016/06/24/the-ndfp-gph-peace-process/ (accessed 15 January 2017). For the peace process in India see Madhuparna Das, Agnivesh Pulls Out of Peace Process, Says UPA Govt Lack Seriousness, *The Indian Express*, 29 August 2010, available at http://archive.indianexpress.com/news/agnivesh-pulls-out-of-peace-process-says-upa-govt-lacks-seriousness/673970/ (accessed 15 January 2017. For the peace process in the Indian state of Andhra Pradesh see the 2007 documentary *The Advocate*, directed by Deepa Dhanraj, produced by Kalpana Kannabiran, Hyderabad, India.

22. Anne Orford, The Subject of Globalization: Economics, Identity and Human Rights, 94 *American Society of International Law Proceedings*, 146–8 (2000) at 147.

23. Ibid.

24. Id. at 148.

25. James Gathii, Human Rights, the World Bank and the Washington Consensus: 1949–1999, 94 *American Society of International Law Proceedings*, 144–6 (2000) at 144.

26. Id. at 146.

27. For how these arguments pan out in social movements see Radha D'Souza, Liberal Theory, Human Rights and Water-justice: Back to Square One?, *Law, Social Justice & Global Development Journal* (LGD), Article 1 (2008).

28. William Hinton, The Importance of Land Reform in the Reconstruction of China, 50/3 *Monthly Review*, 147–60 (1998).

29. See William Hinton, Fanshen: A Documentary of a Revolution in a Chinese Village (Penguin Books. 1972 [1967]).

30. Larry Diamond, Juan J. Linz & Seymour Martin Lipset (eds), *Democracy in Developing Countries: Africa*, Vol. 2 (Adamantine. 1988); Larry Diamond, Juan J. Linz & Seymour Martin Lipset, *Democracy in Developing Countries: Asia*, Vol. 3 (Larry Diamond ed. Lynne Rienner. 1989); Larry Diamond, Juan J. Linz & Seymour Martin Lipset (eds), *Democracy in Developing Countries: Latin America*, Vol. 4 (Lynne Rienner. 1989).

31. Paul Cammack, Review Article: Democracy and Development in Latin America, 3/5 *Journal of International Development*, 537–50 (1991) at 538.

32. See McArthur Foundation website at www.macfound.org/about/ (accessed 15 January 2017).

33. Boaventura de Sousa Santos, *Democratizing Democracy: Beyond the Liberal Canon: Reinventing Social Emancipation*, Vol. 1, p. xv (Boaventura de Sousa Santos ed. Verso. 2005).

34. Id. at vii–viii.

35. Id. at xxx–xxxiii.

36. Readers may be reminded that by the mid 1990s the UN was already working on biodiversity conventions and in 1998 the WB jointly with UNEP and NASA published a study titled *Protecting our Planet, Securing Our Future: Linkages Among Global Environmental Issues and Human Needs* which called for scientific research to highlight the linkages between climate, biodiversity, desertification and forest issues, leading to the Millennium Ecosystem Assessment reporting in 2003. The United Nations Conference on Environment and Development (UNCED), also known as the Rio Earth Summit held in 1992, had called for global recognition of traditional knowledge in addressing environmental problems.

37. For works by de Sousa Santos on the WSF see Boaventura de Sousa Santos, *World Social Forum: A Users' Manual* (Centro de Estudos Sociais. 2004); Boaventura de Sousa Santos, *The Rise of the Global Left: The World Social Forum and Beyond* (Zed Books. 2006).

38. Aspects of India's Economy: The Economics and Politics of the World Social Forum, No. 35, Research Unit for Political Economy (RUPE), Mumbai (2003), available at http://rupe-india.org/35/contents.html (accessed 15 January 2017).
39. Ibid.
40. Ibid.
41. Ibid..
42. For an account of the WSF forum in Mumbai see Radha D'Souza, Carnivals in the Era of 'Gobalisation', Z-Net Commentary, 7 February 2004, available at https://thehandstand.org/archive/march2004/articles/znetforum.htm; see also www.schwarzmarkt.nadir.org/2004/03/649.shtml. For a critique of WSF see Radha D'Souza, The WSF Revisited: Back to Basics?, Colours of Resistance Archive (2004), available at www.coloursofresistance.org/271/the-wsf-revisited-back-to-basics/ (websites accessed 15 January 2017).
43. For reports on Mumbai Resistance 2004 see Lyla Bavadam, A Militant Platform, Frontline (2004); Pao-yu Ching, Critical Views of the World Social Forum – from Mumbai Resistance, 5/2 Inter-Asia Cultural Studies, 331–5 (2004).
44. See for e.g. Henry Veltmeyer & James Petras, Social Movements in Latin America: Neoliberalism and Popular Resistance (Palgrave Macmillan. 2011).
45. For an analysis of one of the most influential early anti-colonial movements in South Asia see D'Souza, Revolt and Reform in South Asia.
46. Gaston V. Rimlinger, Capitalism and Human Rights, 112/4 Daedalus, 51–79 (1983).
47. For more on such questions in our times see D'Souza, When Unreason Masquerades as Reason; Radha D'Souza, Listening to the Elders as Keepers of the Water, in Asking, We Walk: South as New Political Imaginary, pp. 138–47 (Streelekha Publications. Corrine Kumar ed. 2013); Radha D'Souza, What Can Activist Scholars Learn from Rumi, 64/1 Philosophy East and West, 1–24 (2014).
48. Zygmunt Bauman, Wasted Lives: Modernity and its Outcasts (Polity. 2004).

POSTSCRIPT

1. Radha D'Souza, The Rights Conundrum: Poverty of Philosophy Amidst Poverty, in Rights in Context: Law and Justice in Late Modern Society, pp. 55–69 (Reza Banakar ed. Ashgate. 2010).
2. Karl Marx, The Eighteenth Brumaire of Louis Bonaparte 1 (Penguin Books. 1977 [1851–1852]).
3. Incite! Women of Colour Against Violence, the Revolution Will Not Be Funded: Beyond the Non-profit Industrial Complex (South End Press. 2007).
4. Tara Brabazon, The Revolution Will Not Be Downloaded: Dissent in the Digital Age (Chados Publishing. 2008).
5. Sandor Ellix Katz, The Revolution Will Not Be Microwaved: Inside America's Underground Food Movement (Chelsea Green Publishing. 2006).

Index